SYSTEMS CONCEPTS IN ACTION

D1548298

SYSTEMS CONCEPTS
IN ACTION

A Practitioner's Toolkit

BOB WILLIAMS AND
RICHARD HUMMELBRUNNER

STANFORD BUSINESS BOOKS

An Imprint of Stanford University Press
Stanford, California

Stanford University Press
Stanford, California

Special discounts for bulk quantities of Stanford Business Books are available to corporations, professional associations, and other organizations. For details and discount information, contact the special sales department of Stanford University Press. Tel: (650) 736-1782, Fax: (650) 736-1784

Printed in the United States of America

Library of Congress Cataloging-in-Publication Data
Williams, Bob, 1951–
    Systems concepts in action : a practitioner's toolkit / Bob Williams and Richard Hummelbrunner.
        p.   cm.
    Includes bibliographical references and index.
    ISBN 978-0-8047-7062-0 (cloth : alk. paper)—ISBN 978-0-8047-7063-7 (pbk. :   )
  1. System theory.   2. Management science.   I. Hummelbrunner, Richard.   II. Title.
    Q295.W53   2010
    003—dc22   2010030286

Typeset by Westchester Book Group in 10.13 Minion

CONTENTS

ACKNOWLEDGMENTS

Thinking systemically is inherently collaborative. More people were involved in this book than the two names on the cover. What ended up on these pages is our responsibility (including errors and omissions), but there is no doubt that this book has been enhanced greatly by the contribution of others. Those we acknowledge below provided advice, support, case examples, and critical comment. Many generously allowed us to draw extensively on their material and ideas. Our thanks and appreciation to you all.

PEOPLE

Leo Baumfeld

Heather Britt

Phil Capper

Jessica Dart

Rick Davies

Steff Deprez

Bob Dick

Sarah Earl

Cheryl Endres

Yrjö Engeström

Glenda Eoyang

Irene Guijt

Simon Hearn

Royce Holladay

Michael C. Jackson

Paul Z. Jackson

Robert Lukesch

Mary McEthron

Mark McKergow

Konstantin Melidis

Gerald Midgley

Robert Muetzelfeldt

Michael Q. Patton

Kristine Quade

Martin Reynolds   Susanne Tepe
Patricia Rogers   Ricardo Wilson-Grau

PUBLISHERS
We would also like to acknowledge the following publishers who gave us permission to reproduce items from their publications.

AEA/EdgePress

Guilford

IBM

Rand

Rosenberger Fachverlag

Springer

Wiley

Thanks to Stanford University Press for its support for this project, in particular Margo Beth Crouppen, Jessica Walsh, Mariana Raykov, and Ariane De Pree-Kajfez; to our copy editor, Ellen Lohman; to our indexer, Julie Grady; and to our production editor, Barbara Goodhouse at Westchester Book Group.

Finally, our thanks to members and staff of the American Evaluation Association, the W. K. Kellogg Foundation, and the sponsors and attendees of our workshops all over the world. You shared your ideas and gave us opportunities to develop our own. This book would not have happened without your early and often continued support.

INTRODUCTION

WHAT IS THIS BOOK ABOUT?

Within the covers of this book you will find ways of addressing and resolving situations that are wicked, messy, and horribly tangled. Furthermore, the situations often appear impossible to sort out. The approaches and methods in this book will help you understand, analyze, manage, learn, change, and evaluate these complex and complicated situations.

Essentially, the book serves a triple purpose:

- It is a *workbook*: it offers a selection of methods that can be used by the reader, based on the information provided. Free online references and other sources are provided if you are interested in more details.

- It is a *primer*: the introductory chapter gives an overview of systems thinking, its origins, and major parts of the field. And it connects with the methods described throughout the book.

- Last but not least, it is a *learning tool*: the methods are not intended to serve as "recipes" or standard tools, but as a menu of options from which to choose. You are invited to combine these instruments in a creative manner. For instance, at the start of each chapter there is a set of questions that highlight the kinds of issues each method addresses. This will allow you to assemble a mix of methods depending on the situation you are faced with.

WHAT THIS BOOK CONTAINS

This book contains approaches and methods that allow you to think and act systemically. Wherever possible, we have included methods that you can take away and use immediately. That is the workbook aspect of this book. In addition, we provide ample information about the principles that underpin the methods, so you can find out more about them and expand your knowledge.

Each chapter contains a description of the approach or method, where the idea behind it came from, when are the best circumstances to use it, how to avoid traps, and a short case to give you an idea of how the method or approach can be applied.

Most of the approaches and methods are drawn directly from the systems field. However, some are drawn from other fields that often display the core features of the systems field, such as organizational development, evaluation, policy development, strategy, and planning.

When writing this book, we drew on our experience as facilitators of many systems-related workshops and also as authors and editors of two previous volumes:

- *Instrumente systemischen Handelns. Eine Erkundungstour*: a German-language compilation of systems concepts and methods, coauthored by Austrian systems practitioners Leo Baumfeld, Richard Hummelbrunner, and Robert Lukesch.
- *Systems Concepts in Evaluation: An Expert Anthology*: a monograph with case descriptions on the application of systems concepts in evaluation, edited by Bob Williams and Iraj Imam.

SHOULD YOU BE READING THIS BOOK?

The book targets those who are trying to make sense of or need to intervene in messy situations. You may or may not already have a general interest in systems concepts or being systemic, but you do wish to expand your repertoire of action in dealing with situations that are difficult to address from your existing toolbox.

So this book is aimed at the following groups:

- Evaluators called upon to help people assess the value of interventions that are clearly very messy with lots of possible ways of judging worth.

- Consultants and coaches, who want to demonstrate that systems thinking leads to far more sustainable results than simplistic thinking.
- Development or community workers trying to steer projects along complicated paths in difficult environments.
- Policy workers who are trying to explore the consequences of adopting various strategies and tactics.
- People in networks or intermediary organizations, who mediate between the public sector, the private sector and civil society and thus need to conceive effective ways for communication and collaboration.
- Entrepreneurs and managers, who want to secure their business in a sustainable manner by reconciling, for example, clients' needs, employees' interests, and environmental concerns.
- Researchers, especially action researchers, seeking out new tools for inquiry and analysis.
- Teachers trying to teach their students how to think and learn about addressing and resolving "wicked problems."

WHAT DO WE MEAN BY SYSTEMIC?

The question can be answered in many ways. A Web search will bring up hundreds of definitions. From the extensive literature on systems and systems thinking, three features emerge as common threads to all methods and approaches:

An understanding of *interrelationships*

A commitment to multiple *perspectives*

An awareness of *boundaries*

These features happen to match one way of understanding the development of the systems field over the past fifty years or so. Up to the mid 1960s, the focus in the systems field was strongly on interrelationships. Between the late 1960s and the late 1970s, there was increasing recognition of perspectives as a critical issue, that people would perceive the same interrelationships in radically different ways. As the field progressed into the 1980s and beyond, the realization came that holism was somewhat of an ideal. In reality, all situations, all inquiries are bounded in some way. The choice of boundaries really matters, since it determines what is relevant to a systemic inquiry—and what is not. And systems thinkers began to question who makes those decisions of what is "in" and what is "out"; the systems field formally started to address the issue of power.

All of the methods and approaches in this book display these three features—that is what makes them systemic. Some methods emphasize one feature more than others, but all of the features are there somewhere in all of the methods.

HOW THIS BOOK IS STRUCTURED

Faced with questions about the content and structure of this book, we have drawn on many sources and experiences. In terms of content, what should be the criteria for selecting methods? What is the best balance between theory and practice? Should each chapter be a sales pitch for the approach, or something more critically reflective? What form should examples take, and how detailed should case studies be? How many references should there be in a book that is not intended to be academic? How should we select appropriate references? In terms of structure, how should we organize the methods, historically, thematically, or practically?

What Are the Selected Methods?

This book could have easily contained a hundred or more methods, but space was limited. How did we narrow the selection down to nineteen and their variations?

- Practical. As much as possible we wanted methods you can use "out of the box" without too much extra study. While that's not true of every method, it was a guiding principle.

- Tested. These are not a set of methods that we dreamed up and are trying to inflict on the unsuspecting world. They are all well established, developed by leaders in the field. Just as importantly, we have used them in various forms in our work. These methods are certainly road tested.

- Wide-ranging. We wanted the methods to cover the range of systems concepts and traditions, especially the three notions of interrelationships, perspectives, and boundaries.

- Multidisciplinary. We wanted methods applicable to a wide range of fields, including evaluation, social inquiry, action research, organizational development, and social change.

So, looking at the contents list, why is the systems method you know not included? There may be several answers: first, because it did not, in our view, match the criteria outlined above. Or it was too close to another method—you might find it in the section on variations that ends each chapter. Or it was so complex that it would take too much space to explain. And, of course, given the size of the systems field, we may just have not known about it.

You might also think that some methods do not fit your idea of what the systems field is all about. That is probably because the systems field has different traditions with different associated methods. For instance, Europe, North America, and the United Kingdom have distinctly different histories and emphases in respect of systems ideas. This book dips into all of those traditions.

How Is Each Chapter Organized?

Each chapter starts with a list of questions that the method or approach addresses. It is then divided into five sections:

- A brief description of the method, what it can be used for, and where its roots lie in the systems field
- A how-to section that describes the method in detail
- A case example that shows how the method has been used
- Reflections on the method, including where it is best applied, plus its advantages and challenges
- Variations of the method including potential combinations with other methods

Finally, at the end of each chapter, there are some references where you can find out more about the method (e.g., books, Web sites, and online communities). Where possible, we have focused on key references that are easily available.

How the Chapters Are Grouped

The books starts with an introductory chapter that looks at the systemic concepts that underpin the systems methods that follow. Do not be tempted to skip this chapter, as it also contains some meta-frameworks that will be useful for you.

Categorizing classes of systems approaches is fraught with difficulty. Many have tried, and many terse articles have been written about those efforts. It would be tempting to allocate the methods into which of the three features, interrelationships, perspectives, and boundaries that we consider are the core features of any systemic task. But these are features rather than categories.

So we chose to order the methods pragmatically. Which part of an inquiry does a method contribute to most? We identified three distinctive aspects of an inquiry:

- Describing and analyzing situations
- Changing and managing situations
- Learning about situations, which is the metalevel link that allows us to understand changes, as well as to change understanding.

Of course, the methods do not fit neatly into these three categories, any more than any method is entirely about interrelationships, perspectives, or boundaries. On the other hand, this structure is a useful way to express where each method most powerfully fits and will be useful.

We also feel this structure helps promote one very important aspect of the systems approach: the application of multiple methodologies to any given situation. Most applications of systems ideas will have aspects of describing, analyzing, changing, and learning. And these aspects are interconnected. For instance, we can gain new insights by trying to change a situation, and the subsequent analysis of the result leads to learning. This implies, at least to us, that using a multiple-methodology approach (either the principles or the whole method) in a particular inquiry can often be better than using a single-methodology approach (Midgley 2000). An inquiry that combined elements of, say, Critical Systems Heuristics, Cynefin, and Circular Dialogue would be a very strong inquiry indeed.

The next section briefly describes each method and identifies questions we believe each method addresses most powerfully. In some cases just asking these questions is enough, but most of the time it is useful to know the approach as well!

PART ONE: DESCRIBING AND ANALYZING SITUATIONS

Part One focuses on methods that are primarily used to describe situations systemically and analyze the various boundaries, perspectives, and interrelationships that are observed.

Causal Loop Diagrams

The use of causal loop diagrams is a method drawn from System Dynamics that maps how components of a situation relate to each other. This method is used to explore nonlinear interrelationships.

It addresses the following questions:

- What are the key variables in the situation that interests us?

- How do they link to each other?

- How do they affect each other? Does a variable have a reinforcing or dampening effect on the variables to which it is linked?

System Dynamics

System Dynamics is a method that seeks to explore the consequences of nonlinear relationships and delay. It is usually, although not always, used in conjunction with computer simulation.

It addresses the following questions:

- How does the structure of feedback affect the behavior of a situation?

- How does "delay" in that feedback impact the behavior of a situation that is rich in interconnections?

- What controls the way in which resources flow through the situation? How does this affect behavior?

Social Network Analysis

Social Network Analysis is a field of endeavor that maps the nature of relationships between actors. It is extensively used to understand the consequences (especially for information flow) of different strengths and depths of interrelationships.

It addresses the following questions:

- What are the structural characteristics of a network?

- Who are the key actors in a network, why, and for which purpose?

- How can the network structure or information flows be changed?
- How do these changes affect the network's performance?

Outcome Mapping

Outcome Mapping is a method from the evaluation field that explores the way in which interventions contribute to a result and in particular the way in which changes in behavior of certain stakeholders contribute to a result.

It addresses the following questions:

- How does our intervention contribute to an ultimate goal?
- Whose behavior can we influence in terms of that contribution?
- What is a realistic strategy to achieve that behavior change?
- How do these behavior changes affect our role, and which changes do we have to make to be an effective partner?

Process Monitoring of Impacts

Process Monitoring of Impacts is a mapping process that distinguishes between results and actions that contribute to a result. It usually follows the convention action → result → action → result up a hierarchical chain of increasing and broadening impact. It is very good for clarifying the boundary of an intervention and the interrelationships between action, result, assumptions, and context.

It addresses the following questions:

- How can the behavior of diverse actors be steered in a desired direction?
- What are the key processes for achieving the intended results of an intervention?
- What are the consequences for achieving effects if those processes do not take place as foreseen?
- What should be done if such gaps between plan and reality occur?

Strategic Assumption Surfacing and Testing

Surfacing deep but key assumptions is more difficult than it seems. Strategic Assumption Surfacing and Testing is a well-established method that homes in on them using a mixture of multiple stakeholder perspectives, strategic questioning, and dialectic.

It addresses the following questions:

- Who are the stakeholders that can affect the adoption or implementation of a strategy?
- What assumptions is each stakeholder making about other stakeholders in believing that the preferred strategy will succeed?
- Which assumptions of the other stakeholders does each stakeholder find the most troubling?
- How can these differences be resolved in the service of the strategy?

PART TWO: CHANGING AND MANAGING SITUATIONS

All systems methods are inherently focused on applying the insights they generate to improve or sustain situations. However, some are specifically focused on understanding and influencing the dynamics or perceptions of a situation.

Strategic Area Assessment

Strategic Area Assessment is a means of applying innovative solutions to specific situations and contexts. It is primarily used in regional development.

It addresses the following questions:

- What are the main innovation potentials of an area?
- By which combination of potentials can local and regional stakeholders achieve a maximum leverage effect in changing the development patterns of their area?
- How can local and regional stakeholders ensure that the chosen development strategy will be conducive to the sustainable development of the whole region?
- Which strategic priorities may unleash these potentials, and who is taking charge to pursue these common goals?

The CDE Model

The CDE model is a complex adaptive systems method drawn from Human Systems Dynamics. It explores the way in which framing systems properties as containers (C), differences (D), and exchanges (E) can enable us to understand and influence how complex systems work.

It addresses the following questions:

- What are the conditions that shape a self-organizing process?
- What interventions might influence the path and outcomes of a self-organizing process?

Assumption-Based Planning

Assumption-Based Planning is a method developed by the RAND Corporation that focuses attention on the importance of assumptions made about the nature of interrelationships. In many cases it is a more robust and reliable alternative to business planning or strategic planning.

It addresses the following questions:

- What are the key assumptions underpinning the achievement of a plan?
- What can be done to assure that these assumptions are sustained?
- What can be done to make the plan more robust to assumption failure?

Cynefin

Cynefin is a framework drawn from the network analysis, knowledge management, and the complex systems fields. It distinguishes among "simple," "complicated," "complex," and "chaotic" aspects of a situation and suggests how each aspect can be successfully managed. Cynefin is a powerful analytical tool for matching a situation with a response.

It addresses the following questions:

- How are we framing the situation: as simple, complicated, complex, or chaotic?
- What are the implications of this framing for how we manage a situation?
- What are appropriate ways of managing a situation on the basis of this framing?

SOLUTION FOCUS

Solution Focus is a technique that was originally developed in family therapy. Problems are "ignored" by directly exploring solutions based on events occurring in the past or present, which helps to overcome states that previously have been considered problematic.

It addresses the following questions:

- What would it be like if the problem suddenly disappeared?
- Who should be doing (or stop doing) what to reach that ideal situation?
- How can these actions be supported and by whom?
- Which elements of the solution take place already?

Viable System Model

The Viable System model is a long-established method drawn from the cybernetics tradition. It illustrates the information requirements and necessary interrelationships between five generic, interconnected systems present in every purposeful organization. It is powerful for identifying necessary information flows between the systems and the consequences of getting these flows out of balance.

It addresses the following questions:

- What are the operational, coordination, management, strategy, and governance needs of the situation to deliver on its purpose?
- What information is needed at each level of the situation to achieve the purpose?
- How does information flow through the situation?
- Is the right information available at the most appropriate level of a situation's hierarchy of tasks?

PART THREE: LEARNING ABOUT SITUATIONS

There are data, there is information, and there is knowledge. While the transformation of data into information is essentially about context, the translation of information into knowledge is a sense-making process, often deeply personal. Your knowledge is merely data until I have made sense of it. The early days of so-called knowledge management assumed data were knowledge, that your knowledge would automatically become my knowledge in exactly the same shape and form. (It is still a common view, unfortunately.) There are, of course, many forms of sense-making and entire bookshelves dedicated to "learning." The distinction we make about learning is very simple. Learning is the process of taking things that puzzle us and transforming them into deeper understandings of a situation that is of interest to us, and how we can intervene.

The important concept here is that of dialectic: the process of bringing together opposites, contradictions, and different perspectives and holding them together until we can in some way reframe, resolve, or, in Russ Ackoff's famous phrase, "dissolve" the tension. These methods are usually highly participative and encourage multiple viewpoints.

Cultural-Historical Activity Theory

Cultural-Historical Activity Theory (often shortened to Activity Systems) is one of the few systems approaches based on learning theory as well as systems theory. This approach specifically seeks to understand how addressing contradictions within systems promotes innovative solutions.

It addresses the following questions:

- What fundamentally are the motivations underpinning the achievement of a goal?
- What tools, rules, and roles are necessary for that motivation to be translated into goal-directed activities?
- How does the system handle contradictions in tools, rules, roles, and motivations so that the goal is achieved?

Soft Systems Methodology

Soft Systems Methodology brings together alternative ways of viewing situations that can be used to address problem situations.

It addresses the following questions:

- What are the different ways in which a situation can be framed?
- How does each of these ways, on its own, provide a means of comprehending how a situation behaves?
- What are the implications for any changes to the situation?

Dialectical Methods of Inquiry

This chapter describes three methods of inquiry that deliberately seek out differences rather than similarities in order to deepen understanding of a situation. These methods are

Option one-and-a-half

Convergent interviewing

Contradiction analysis

Dialectical Methods of Inquiry address the following questions:

- What are the different ways in which people see or can see a situation?
- What are the exceptions or contradictions to the way in which people see or can see a situation?
- How can exploring and making sense of these differences enhance our understanding of a situation?

Scenario Technique

Scenario Technique is a perspective-driven technique that seeks to avoid problem solving by working backward from potential solutions.

It addresses the following questions:

- What are the key influence factors that determine the future development of the system in question (e.g., enterprise, community)?
- How can the system in question thrive under various possible future conditions, using emerging opportunities but avoiding possible risks at the same time?
- What are the core elements of a robust strategy for the system in question?
- Which are the early signals indicating that certain contingencies will eventuate?
- How can the stakeholders foster the system's resilience by obviating even unexpected disturbances?

Systemic Questioning

Systemic Questioning is an approach for exploring the investigative qualities of language patterns. It was originally developed in family therapy. Beyond obtaining information, questions can also be used to trigger change in perception or generate new information and knowledge.

It addresses the following questions:

- How can you get a multidimensional picture of a situation?
- How can you identify leverage points in your quest for solution-oriented interventions?
- How is it possible to address delicate but relevant content without offending the privacy of those in the dialogue?

Circular Dialogue

Circular Dialogue is a method that forces participants to take a critical stance on a topic by progressively shifting the focus of a discussion. Its primary use is to understand perspectives.

It addresses the following questions:

- How can a situation be seen from different angles or perspectives?
- How do other points of view challenge our way of seeing things?
- What can we learn from opposing viewpoints, and how can they be overcome?
- How can different perspectives lead to a new understanding of the situation?

Critical Systems Heuristics

Critical Systems Heuristics is a tool primarily designed to identify key systems boundaries and explore the consequences of setting those boundaries. It is helpful in understanding that "unanticipated" behaviors are often not unanticipated at all.

It addresses the following questions:

- What and who are being excluded or marginalized, or who is made a victim by the way in which a situation is bounded (i.e., being viewed, framed and/or being operated)?
- How might different and often conflicting boundary judgments on a situation be reconciled? What are the implications of not questioning and debating boundary judgments?

REFERENCES AND FURTHER READING

Baumfeld, Leo, Richard Hummelbrunner, and Robert Lukesch. 2008. *Instrumente systemischen Handelns. Eine Erkundungstour.* Leonberg: Rosenberger Fachverlag.

Midgley, Gerald. 2000. *Systemic intervention: Philosophy, methodology, and practice.* New York: Kluwer Academic/Plenum.

Williams, Bob, and Iraj Imam, eds. 2007. *Systems concepts in evaluation: An expert anthology.* Point Reyes, CA: EdgePress/American Evaluation Association.

ABOUT SYSTEMS, THINKING SYSTEMICALLY, AND BEING SYSTEMIC

ABOUT SYSTEMS

The idea of describing phenomena as systems dates back a long way, according to some as far back as Heraclitus and Aristotle. Although the "modern" systems field dates back to the first half of the twentieth century, it did not really develop fully as a field until the 1940s and 1950s.

We are often asked to define what constitutes a "system." Frustratingly—at least for some—there is no single, concise, and generally agreed-upon definition. However, few would disagree that a system is constituted by

- its elements, that is, all the parts that make up the whole;
- the links between the parts, that is, the processes and interrelationships that hold the parts together in view of the whole;
- its boundary, that is, the limit that determines what is inside and outside a system.

Within that broad constituency, almost any phenomenon can be regarded as a "system." Consequently, rather than wasting precious space debating what does and what does not constitute a system, this book focuses on what makes the systemic approach distinctive: the specific ways it describes and makes sense of complex and complicated situations, that is. thinking and being systemic.

When describing a system as a set of embedded and interrelated parts, you have to bear in mind that each representation of a system is necessarily a simplification. The fundamental question is not whether these representations are "right" or "wrong," but whether the essential aspects of a situation have been captured in relation to a specific purpose or issue.

In other words, thinking systemically is a means of making sense of not only a tree and the forest that contains it, but also the landscape in which the forest is embedded and the soil and the atmosphere that provide important resources for the tree's functioning. And seeing the tree as a small part in global exchange processes.

Let us illustrate this point with an apple. An apple's constituting elements are skin, fruit pulp, stem, core, and seeds. Each of these elements can furthermore be subdivided into many other parts. Each of these elements has a specific purpose, and all the elements are related to each other in a specific manner. The skin protects the flesh from becoming dry and being perforated. The fruit pulp protects core and seeds, which are required for the apple's reproduction. But the pulp has other purposes too—attracting animals so they carry the apple away and bury it, in order to assure good conditions for the seeds' germination. And of course the pulp provides nutrition for foraging animals like us.

But where do you stop in these infinite relationships and purposes? In reality, it is physically and cognitively impossible to describe everything, to conceive of every possible purpose from every possible angle. If you are seeking to influence or intervene in a system, having to take every possible thing into consideration would mean you would never make any decision. You would be frozen like rabbits in car headlights, quite possibly with the same result. Holism, in the strictest sense, is not even an ideal.

Perhaps more than any other area of social inquiry, the systems field provides a wealth of approaches that address the conundrum of keeping the big in mind when you can only handle the small. Together the systems tools, methods, and approaches in this book address the world in all its diversity and unknowingness in ways that are practical, comprehensive, and wise.

However, using these tools purely mechanically misses the point. It is how they are used that makes them systemic. Richard Bawden (2007) distinguishes between thinking systemically and being systemic. We think this is a useful distinction that will help you apply the various approaches in this book to your own situations.

THINKING SYSTEMICALLY

The previous section could be taken to imply that systems are wholly physical entities: fixed, universally acknowledged, largely undisputed, and mostly self-evident. Rather like that apple . . .

However, you will notice already in this book that we sometimes refer to "systems" and sometimes refer to "situations." That is because some argue that systems do not exist in any absolute, preordained sense. Instead, they argue that a system is a human construct—quite literally a mental construction that permits us to comprehend more clearly what is going on. So, if we were to sit down and define what your "health system" looked like, or what your "education system" or maybe even your neighbor's plumbing system looked like, it is highly unlikely we would come up with identical descriptions. This difference is unlikely to be purely a matter of observation or definition. Even if we agreed on what constituted a "knowledge management system," we would almost certainly come up with a different answer about *your* knowledge management system. There are many cognitive, social, cultural, pragmatic, and conceptual reasons for this, but all lead to the same conclusion. Our system is never going to be the same as yours.

So thinking systemically is about making sense of the world rather than merely describing it. It is fundamentally a sense-making process that organizes the messiness of the real world into concepts and components that allow us to understand things a bit better. To return to the apple, while an apple may "look" the same to you and me, we may well make sense of what that apple *is* for a range of reasons that this section will describe.

As we suggested in the preceding chapter, we find that the best means of understanding what is involved in thinking systemically is through three concepts or elements: interrelationships, perspectives, and boundaries.

Interrelationships

Interrelationship is the most familiar systems concept, partly because it is the oldest. The concept of how things are connected and with what consequence stems from the earliest writing about systems. It is also the concept most strongly embedded in popular imagination. When we talk about the filing system or the health system, the image we have in our minds is of a set of objects and processes that are interconnected in some way. The popularity of system dynamics (Chapter 2) with its boxes and arrows further cements the notion that interrelationships are an important systems concept.

Thinking systemically about interrelationships poses five main questions:

- How do we make sense of the nature of the interrelationships within a situation?
- How do we make sense of the structure of these interrelationships?
- How do we make sense of the processes between them?
- How do we make sense of the patterns that emerge from those processes, with what consequences, and for whom?
- Why does this matter? To whom? In what context?

When addressing those questions, we need to consider the following aspects of interrelationships:

- Dynamic aspects, the way the interrelationships affect behavior of a situation over a period of time
- Nonlinear aspects, where the scale of "effect" is apparently unrelated to the scale of the "cause"; often but not always caused by "feedback"
- Sensitivity of interrelationships to context, where the same intervention in different areas has varying results, making it unreliable to translate a "best" practice from one area to another
- Massively entangled interrelationships, distinguishing the behavior of "simple," "complicated," and "complex" interrelationships

Perspectives

Thinking systemically is more than making sense of the way that boxes and arrows fit together or how networks operate. Just deliberating on interconnections does not make an inquiry systemic. Thinking systemically includes *how* you look at the picture. When people observe the result of interrelationships, they will "see," interpret, and make sense of those interrelationships in different ways. To return once again to our apple: if our perspective of an apple is as foodstuff, then its aroma, appearance, or nutritional benefits become relevant. On the other hand, if we use the apple as a projectile, then other interrelationships become relevant such as weight and form. Our judgment of the appropriate size may differ.

Thinking systemically about perspectives poses the following questions:

- What are the different ways in which this situation can be understood?
- How are these different understandings going to affect the way in which people judge the success of an endeavor?
- How will people's different understandings affect their behavior, and thus the behavior of the situation, especially when things go wrong from their perspective? With what result and significance?

Addressing these questions requires us to consider three aspects of perspectives:

First, it forces us to comprehend not only that a situation can be "seen" in different ways but that this will affect how you understand the system or situation. That is not an inherently radical idea; the notion of stakeholders and stakeholder interests has been around for a long time. However, thinking systemically pushes us further. We need to understand that different stakeholder groups may share the same perspective, and most importantly, any one stakeholder will hold several different perspectives, not all of which will be compatible with each other. For instance, we have never held a single unified view on any project we have been involved in, including this book. You could understand our desire to write this book from several perspectives: fame, fortune, seeking to make the world a better place, our own learning, improving the skills of our various professional colleagues, something fun to do in our spare time. If we were to review this book from each of these perspectives, we would almost certainly come up with different judgments of its worth.

There is a link between perspectives and motivation and between motivation and behavior. Think about how you handle someone approaching you in the street for money. Your decision to give her $5 will be the result of a complex set of internal arguments and trade-offs that can change in the time it takes for you to reach into your pocket. One of the authors was recently waiting for a bus in a depressed U.S. city. He was asked for a small amount of money and refused, thinking the person was begging. Once on the bus, he realized that the quirky fare structure meant that nobody had the right change and it was common practice for other passengers to supply the difference. Thus the initial request could be seen as both individual "begging" for individual gain and a collective means of handling the eccentricities of the fare structure. In other words, understanding perceptions is important at a behavioral level. Perceptions are more than how people look at a situation; these perceptions generate behaviors that impact on the way the situation operates. Multiply these individual trade-offs up to a family, group, or organizational level, and it is no wonder that situations do not always behave in the way we expect. Thinking systemically about perspectives will help us make sense of those individual, diverse, and unintended behaviors.

Second, perspectives importantly draw the focus away from the system or situation as it supposedly exists in "real life" and allow us to consider alternatives: what it might be like, could be like, or even should be like. Or how different people imagine how it might be like. When this notion was introduced into the systems field in the late 1960s, it substantially widened the field's scope. Not only could you draw conclusions based on a study of the world *as it is*, but you could also compare alternative perceptions of *what people think it is* with *what actually is*, or with perceptions of *what is* or with *what could be*. The similarities and differences between perceptions of *what is, what people think it is*, and *what people think it could be* create puzzles and contradictions that can achieve deeper learning. Acknowledging perspectives also generates better insights into the actual behavior of programs in real life. That is because people usually behave on the basis of their perceptions of what is or what could be rather than some official line imposed by someone else. Thus thinking systemically about perspectives gives us a window into motivations through which we can explain and predict unanticipated behaviors. It acknowledges the reality that it is people who make things work, not some imagined logic or management edict.

Finally, perspectives helps us deal with interrelationships that are massively entangled. When observing a situation, one person might see it as "simple," another as "complicated," and yet another as "complex" (see Chapter 10). Many disagreements in organizations over what to do about something can be traced back to different perceptions of what is going on. Each person's observation may well be accurate, yet because the way each person sees it is different, each person's way of addressing the situation will be different. In principle, everyone is right—but only within the limits of his or her own perspective. Thus thinking systemically about perspectives shifts the focus from seeking patterns and solving issues on the basis of what happened before or somewhere else, toward seeking puzzles and creating new possibilities from what had been contradictions. Thinking systemically forces us to do what we are not always good at: that is, identifying the assumptions we make when we observe and make sense of a situation. We intuitively put ourselves, our values, our beliefs at the center of the analysis. Instead, thinking systemically forces you into being an observer of your own mind and your own behavior.

Boundaries

As we stated earlier, the popular idea that thinking systemically is about "wholes" has a major snag. We cannot think about everything; setting boundaries around our thinking is not optional. We make situations manageable by setting boundaries.

So what are the constituents of boundaries, and how can we think systemically about them? In the simplest form, a boundary differentiates between what is "in" and what is "out." Thus a boundary determines what is deemed relevant and irrelevant, what is important and what is unimportant, what is worthwhile and what is not, who gets what kind of resources for what purpose and whose interests are marginalized, who benefits and who is disadvantaged. Boundaries are the sites where values get played out and disagreements are highlighted. Boundaries also determine how we approach a situation, what we expect from it, and what methods we might use to manage it.

Power issues are often wrapped up in boundaries. Just as the person with the magic marker controls what goes on the whiteboard, the person whose perspective dominates a project decides the boundaries. While it is fine to map relationships and it may be fine to acknowledge that there will be different perspectives on those relationships, those relationships and perspectives are not neutral; someone somewhere decides which are most important. Boundaries therefore form an important aspect of thinking systemically, posing the following questions:

- How is a situation being framed? In other words, who is drawing what kind of boundary?
- What are the practical and ethical consequences of this framing, and what do those consequences imply for action?

The subfield of critical systems (see Chapter 19) takes these issues very seriously indeed. It highlights three core boundary issues:

- Marginalization. As soon as you draw a boundary, you marginalize what is outside that boundary. The marginalization might be profound, or it might be (to you, anyway) relatively unimportant. But thinking systemically about boundaries will always focus on the process of marginalization.

- Ethical aspects. There are ethical dimensions of setting boundaries, and by setting a boundary in a particular position, you may exacerbate social or other injustices. Thinking systemically provides ways of exploring what those might be, as well as whether and how to address those consequences..

- Practical aspects. For every action, there is a reaction. Excluding a viewpoint, an institution, or a person when drawing a boundary invites a response. That response may not be in your interests; indeed, it may well undermine everything you do. Thinking systemically provides ways of exploring what those reactions might be and how to manage, neutralize, or accommodate them.

BEING SYSTEMIC

In talking to people about systems ideas over the years, we are struck with how many people feel uncomfortable with the consequences of thinking systemically. If describing systems is essentially a way of observing the world and thinking systemically is essentially making sense of the world, then "being systemic" is an orientation toward the world. It is about the way we engage with situations. Although the systems field is a deeply practical field, many find systems ideas disturbing and unsettling. Systems ideas confront our ideas about expertise, purpose, values, and certainty in ways that are often more emotional than cognitive. Some people are comfortable about these challenges and ambiguities, while others are not.

So what kind of orientations allow you to be systemic?

Be Reflective

There are many definitions and understandings of what it means to be reflective. At the core, it means observing yourself as others might. It means being aware of your assumptions, your mental models, and your values. It means seeking out ideas that contradict your own, engaging in those ideas, and making sense out of them. It means being very aware of how your own assumptions and values affect what you see and hear. It means checking constantly to see if the assumptions you are making are valid. It is a life of puzzling things through rather than always leaning back and grabbing what worked elsewhere. Above all, it implies a fundamental understanding of and skill using perspectives and boundaries.

Trust in Self-Organization

Treating every situation as if it were a simple system (i.e., linear, predictable in that the same input will always lead to identical output, managed by fixed roles and routines) is not uncommon. The way most organizations are formally structured and supposedly run is based on that world view, the desire to control. There is nothing inherently wrong in a desire to control. Most of us are very happy that certain aspects of organizations, like payroll, are not allowed to self-organize. But there are benefits from allowing certain situations to self-organize. To allow that to happen, you have to work in a slightly different way. Self-organization does not just happen; you have to set the conditions for self-organization—and then breathe through your nose and allow it to happen.

But what is self-organization? Is it just a directionless ramble, disorder rather than order? Or is it something more manageable?

One of the tools in this book explicitly focuses on these questions (see Chapter 8), but in the meantime, here is an introduction to the notion of self-organization.

The unpredictability yet relative stability of complex adaptive systems results from their specific capacity to self-organize. Complex adaptive systems maintain their structure by continuously renewing their elements in a process of self-creation ("autopoesis"), for which they only dispose of their own operations (operational closure). This is the mechanism that brings forth self-referential behavior, that is, the tendency to focus on internal structures and processes. But systems are not entirely closed off from their context; they are linked to their environment—including other systems. Thus systems and their context mutually influence each other; they continuously adapt and co-evolve.

Therefore, the behavior of complex adaptive systems is determined by both their internal structure and contextual relations. Change can be induced from the outside, but these contextual influences do not result in uniform, predictable output; as these external perturbations are ambivalent, they can be both disturbing and the source of further development. They are modified and rearranged in line with the system's internal state and structure. The resulting behavior can be explained neither by the external influences on the system nor by its internal states alone, but through the interaction of both. So having trust in self-organization is about paying attention for emerging patterns and responding to them.

Assume Evolution

Self-organization assumes development, that is, the gradual transformation of situations through their capacity to produce and reproduce structures that are capable of dealing better with changes in the environment.

The appearance of new structures, patterns, and properties during the process of self-organization is called "emergence." This can take place when a number of interrelated elements or systems form a new and more complex collective behavior. Emergence often does not take place continuously, but can come rather suddenly and represents a new level of a system's evolution. Emergent properties are not the properties of any single element, nor can they easily be predicted or deduced from their behavior; they are the result of their complex interaction.

For instance, the evolution of self-organizing systems can be characterized by a succession of distinctive properties. Reflective systems mirror changes of their environment and determine the impact of external influences. Autopoetic systems recognize which external factors are good for their existence; they are capable of analyzing their environment and constructing models. And re-creative systems are capable of defining their own goals and taking measures for achieving them, thus consciously influencing their environment.

Act in a Responsible Manner

In simple systems, where the relationship between cause and effect is clear and predictable, the notion of "accountability" and blame at the individual level is plausible and valid. For complicated and complex systems, the notion of "I am accountable to" should be replaced by "I feel responsibility for."

Our behavior is based on decisions taken as a result of value-laden judgments, and the values of individuals are in turn influenced by the social groups in which we grew up and were socialized. The values that guide our behavior are controlled by our consciousness, the link between us and the groups to which we are attached. This relation works both ways: we feel guilty when acting against the rules established for a group, and the group transfers the responsibility upon individuals to act in line with (or at least not against) the principles of the group and for its benefit.

Individual accountability makes it possible to blame someone for undesired consequences, even though in many cases it is a gross simplification to single out individual actions from a range of factors. Such well-established, simplistic patterns tempt us to think in linear categories (cause and effect, culprit and victim), even in cases where manifold influences would require more profound and sophisticated approaches. Since our actions become more and more entangled, we need to move on from using only simplistic cause-and-effect thinking. In more complex situations, every interaction can be both cause and effect and does not only work one way.

In contrast with being held accountable, responsibility can be regarded in a "circular" manner, by connecting individual actions between them and with the wider context. On one hand, the transfer of specific tasks and the attribution of consequences for these actions should always acknowledge a wider range of factors or influences, but on the other hand, every individual should assume their own responsibility before blaming others. When seen in this interlinked way, all involved actors in a social system are responsible for a given problem—and for finding solutions (but of course with differences in power, resources, etc.). No one is to be singled out and "blamed" individually; instead, the aim is to become aware of mutual interdependence and respective tasks or capacities.

Be a Part of the World

Being systemic is about balancing on the edge of reality and meaning. Yes, there is an objective reality, but we all gain meaning from it in different ways. Furthermore, reality is bounded; we experience only one specific part of reality. We are often not aware of the blind spots, because "we don't see what we don't see." Interactions in social systems are the results of actions and the meaning attributed to them observed with others, who in turn are observing others. As an observer, you construct a frame of reference, an internal map, consistent with your orientation.

Systemic family therapy was one of the first applications of systems thinking for inducing social change. These therapists made explicit use of the links between the reality constructions, emotional well-being, and capacity for action of their clients. Their approaches dismissed the intention to reveal truth; instead, they took their clients' model of the world as granted and used it to achieve intended change. In doing so, it was not important to thoroughly understand how the intervention worked, as long as the defined goal was reached (e.g., mental well-being, family consensus).

Being part of the world also implies that you as an "observer" are part of the system. The notion of an observer being uninvolved or outside the boundary of what he or she is observing is inconsistent with being systemic. As consultants, teachers, evaluators, and researchers, our very presence makes a difference to the situation we are supposedly observing.

Act Circular

Circularity means that a system's operations are interconnected, and thus the result of one operation leads to other operations within the same system. But as we mentioned earlier, every system is also connected to its respective environment and therefore has to reach beyond such operative closure.

All living (e.g., social) systems possess an inherent paradox: the contradiction between closure (= self-referential, autonomous) and openness (= structurally linked to their context). Living systems can neither be reduced to their internal dynamics nor be completely controlled from the outside. Any attempt to overcome this paradox in a directive manner (e.g., through external force or hierarchic orders) can be ineffective beyond simple systems because such an attempt threatens the system's identity and reinforces its defensive structures. Complicated and complex systems can therefore best be influenced in an indirect manner, and external interventions are most effective when they build on their capacity for self-organization.

We can train for this by mentally stepping inside systems, learning about their structure and processes, and discovering the rules that steer their behavior. Or on more general terms, by assuming various positions or roles and seeing the world from these different perspectives. Being conscious and responsible for our boundary decisions.

In other words, welcome to our book.

REFERENCES AND FURTHER READING

Bawden, Richard. 2007. A systemic evaluation of an agricultural development: A focus on the worldview challenge. In *Systems concepts in evaluation: An expert anthology*, ed. Bob Williams and Iraj Imam. Point Reyes, CA: EdgePress / American Evaluation Association.

Three books provide excellent historical overviews of systems ideas. They are:

Jackson, Michael C. 2003. *Systems thinking: Creative holism for managers.* New York: Wiley.
Midgley, Gerald. 2000. *Systemic intervention: Philosophy, methodology, and practice.* New York: Kluwer Academic/Plenum.
Ramage, Magnus, and Karen Shipp. 2009. *Systems thinkers.* London: Springer.

PART ONE

DESCRIBING AND
ANALYZING SITUATIONS

There is only one thing in life worse than being talked about, and that
is not being talked about.
  Oscar Wilde

1

CAUSAL LOOP DIAGRAMS

What are the key variables in the situation that interests us?

How do they link to each other?

How do they affect each other? Does each variable have a reinforcing or dampening effect on the variables to which it is linked?

WHAT ARE CAUSAL LOOP DIAGRAMS?

Causal loop diagrams (CLDs) provide a language for articulating our understanding of dynamic, interconnected situations. They can be considered sentences that are constructed by linking together key variables and indicating the causal relationship between them. By connecting several CLDs, a coherent story can be told about a particular situation or issue.

CLDs visualize variables and their relationships over time. They permit us not only to analyze current states and relational patterns but also to make assumptions about the dynamic behavior. They allow us to look beyond individual events and to reach a higher—one might say more systemic—level of understanding, by mapping the structure that is responsible for producing recurring patterns of events over time.

CLDs are based on the concept of "feedback," which was originally developed in the 1940s as part of the emerging science of cybernetics. Feedback is the transmission or return of information, and a feedback loop is a closed sequence of causes and effects: variable X is affecting Y and Y in turn affecting

X. Thus, we cannot study the link between X and Y independently of the link between Y and X. Only by studying the whole feedback loop will we be able to develop a meaningful understanding of the behavior patterns at work in such a system.

Feedback loops are the building blocks of CLDs and appear in two types:

- *Reinforcing* or *positive feedback* (see Figure 1.1) refers to a situation where all the variables respond to each other in the same direction: when A goes up, B goes up as well, which leads to a further increase of A. When A goes down, B goes down as well, which leads to a further decrease of A. Change in one direction is compounded with even more change (sometimes referred to as "cumulative causation"), which can produce both growth and decline. A savings account is an example of positive feedback, as the amount of savings and the interest earned are linked in a reinforcing manner: if savings increase, they will lead to higher interest earnings, which again are added to the savings, and so forth. Contrarily, if savings decrease, the interest earned will also go down, which again affects accumulated savings.

- *Negative* or *balancing feedback* (see Figure 1.2) occurs when at least one variable in the system responds to change in another variable in the opposite direction: when A goes up, B goes down. If the relationship between B and A is positive (i.e., if B goes down, then A goes down too), then change in both variables is attenuated. (See Figure 1.2 in the case application.) An everyday example of negative feedback is a temperature control system. When the temperature in the room rises, the heating is lowered and the temperature begins to fall. As the temperature drops, the heating is increased and the temperature rises again. Provided the limits are close to each other, a steady room temperature is maintained.

Feedback can be used for analyzing the dynamics of a given situation, because it can be associated with specific patterns of behavior:

- Reinforcing feedback leads to exponential growth (or decline) and escalation, whereas balancing feedback results in stabilization.

- Reinforcing feedback by itself is unstable, amplifies small effects, and tends to get out of control. But it is usually counteracted by a balancing feedback of some sort (e.g., spending money, which slows down the growth of a savings account). This might result in s-shaped growth, where initial exponential growth is followed by correctional behavior.

- Delay between variables is the cause of oscillatory behavior, where a variable fluctuates around some level and makes predictions rather difficult. If delays are involved, such oscillations can appear in combination with all the other patterns mentioned above.

The behavior of a system over time is generated through the interaction of these feedback loops and delays. CLDs can also be developed, then, through observing patterns of behavior and identifying the systems structures that are known to cause the pattern. But even if this underlying structure can be mapped quite easily, the resulting behavior is usually far from simple; it is often nonlinear, counterintuitive, and hard to predict. CLDs, then, cannot predict patterns of behavior, nor are they reliable as means of explaining behavioral patterns. To this end, CLDs should be transformed into system dynamic diagrams that allow simulation (see Chapter 2).

DETAILED DESCRIPTION OF THE METHOD AND HOW IT FUNCTIONS

Identifying Relevant Elements

Since CLDs are not an end in themselves but facilitate better understanding, first of all, a situation of interest must be identified, be it an issue, a problem, or an event. This should be as specific as possible because it makes the following choices easier. Next, the time horizon that is considered appropriate should be defined; this should be at least long enough to see the dynamics that are relevant for the situation play out.

Next, the elements that are relevant to the situation of interest (e.g., the factors that explain an event, influence a problem, or are important for achieving a goal) are determined. The elements of CLDs are called variables. It must be possible to state their direction of movement (whether they increase or decrease); that is, they must be able to vary over time. But they do not have to be quantifiable or possess an existing measuring scale.

The choice of variable will depend on the situation and the core relationships to be captured. Most likely this cannot be done in a single attempt and will require an iterative approach that includes several tries, successively eliminating those variables that can be left out without significant effects on the whole. It is also useful at this stage to look at the situation from different perspectives and compare and discuss views on what is considered relevant.

This selection will inevitably require drawing a boundary, in order to stay focused and reduce complexity to a level that can be handled via CLDs. It is important to remember that CLDs are not a holistic undertaking aimed at drawing the whole picture but should only include what is critical for the situation of interest. You are trying to diagram only the problem or issue, not the entire system—a common mistake in working with CLDs. The same holds true for the level of detail to be included, which once more will be guided by the situation of interest and the time horizon.

Determining Relationships

The relations between variables are illustrated by connecting them with arrows, which indicate the direction of influence. A symbol at the end of the arrow indicates the type of causality:

- *Positive causal link* (marked by a plus sign [+] or "s" to mean "same") means a positive correlation, where an increase in variable A leads to an increase in variable B, and a decrease in A leads to a decrease in B. It is important to understand that the plus sign at the arrowhead does not necessarily mean that the variables are increasing, only that they are changing in the same direction (i.e., increase or decrease together). (See Figure 1.1.)

- *Negative causal link* (marked by a minus sign [–] or "o" to mean "opposite") is one of negative or inverse correlation, where an increase in variable A leads to a decrease in variable B, and vice versa. (See Figure 1.2.)

Where required, the quality of the relationships can be analyzed still further, for example, in terms of the degree of influence exerted (e.g., strong, medium, weak) or its temporal duration (e.g., short-, medium-, long-term). Other important information is the continuity of an influence over time. Here two factors are of particular importance for understanding dynamic behavior patterns: whether a delay or time lag is to be expected in a link (often denoted by drawing a short line across the causal link) or if effects have a nonlinear sequence (e.g., exponential curves and "threshold" or "tipping-point" effects).

Forming Feedback Loops

The linked variables are further connected with each other to form meaningful and closed loops. This is an important completeness check of the CLD: *all* the variables should be connected and lead to closed circles of influence. Either the variables without an obvious link to others can be left out of the diagram, or—if they are considered relevant for the situation of interest—the connecting links that are still missing must be investigated before including the variable.

What emerges is a causal network that consists of various interconnected feedback loops. This replaces linear cause-and-effect relations, which are inappropriate for complex and complicated situations because in a connected system one cause can lead to several effects (and vice versa), which in turn become the cause for other effects, and so on. Cause and effect cannot be determined in an unequivocal manner but depend on the respective position: what someone considers a cause, others might consider an effect.

The type of a feedback loop is determined by adding up the negative causal links (–) (see Figures 1.1 and 1.2 in the case application later in this chapter):

- Reinforcing loop (marked with + or "R") if the sum yields an even number (including zero)
- Balancing loop (marked with – or "B") if the sum yields an odd number

To determine the type of loop: start with an assumption, for example, "Variable A increases," and follow the loop around. If at the end of the loop you end up with the same result as the initial assumption, it is a reinforcing loop; if the result contradicts the initial assumption, it is a balancing one.

If the behavior over time for the situation of interest is known (at least qualitatively), you can also proceed the other way around to generate feedback loops: identify whether the existing pattern fits one of the reference behavior patterns (e.g., exponential growth, s-shape, oscillations), identify the corresponding type of feedback, and finally determine the variables and their linkages which make up the loop. But this mainly refers to individual loops. When loops are interacting and contain delays, it is very difficult to match particular patterns of behavior to a CLD.

Analysis of Feedback Loops

This can yield further insights about behavior patterns. Important perspectives are the following:

– *Number* of feedback loops. A high number suggests that the system is relatively independent and predominantly depends on internal factors, whereas a low number suggests that it is rather a "flow-through system" dominated by external factors.

– *Length* of the causal links. Lengthy feedback loops involving many elements mean that effects might take place only after a considerable timespan; short feedback loops, on the other hand, could mean fast reactions (unless the links themselves are characterized by considerable delay).

– *Connection* of the variables. The number of input and output relations indicates the function of the variables (e.g., whether they are more active or more passive); it is also possible to define "start variables" and "end variables," or the most important interfaces in causal networks.

CASE APPLICATION OF CLD

CLDs were used during the evaluation of a program that provided funding for consulting services to private enterprises. Low use of the fund was evident from data previously collected, and this was identified as the core issue to be explored. To collect explanatory factors for this situation, several group interviews with stakeholders were held (e.g., beneficiary businesses, consultants providing services, and business institutions acting as delivery points).

Then these factors were arranged and connected to form a CLD in three consecutive steps:

1. Identifying Relevant Elements

First, all of the factors were written on cards and displayed on a pin board. Then two factors were selected as immediate causes for the low use of funds: the number of applications handed in by enterprises and the support delivery by the business institutions involved in the program. The other factors were then grouped around each of these two causal factors, thus resulting in two clusters of factors, each attributed to one "strand": the beneficiary enterprises or the business support institutions. Factors that could not be directly associated to one of these strands were put aside for the moment.

2. Determining Relationships

Next, the factors were connected according to their respective influence, using the explanations provided during the interviews as background information. The arrows indicate the direction of influence, and + and − are used as symbols to mark whether they are positive or negative causal links. For instance, the ease of the institutions' application procedures and the enterprises' information level on the fund were seen as positively influencing the number of applications. An increase in the information level and easier procedures both meant that more enterprises prepared applications. On the other hand, changes in institutions' personnel had negative effects on the delivery of support. If staff changes became more frequent, service delivery was interrupted, quality management standards were lowered, and subsequently the quality of support declined.

In addition, important time-lags were identified which explained the dynamics of certain relations. For instance, there was a considerable delay between the time when enterprises were informed about the funds and when they actually handed in applications, as this depended on a range of other factors (which were not included in the diagram): their capacity to write applications, the market situation, or the availability of their own financial resources, as the fund only provided cofinancing. These delays were shown in the relationships as a double line across the respective arrow. (See Figure 1.3.)

3. Forming Feedback Loops

As a last step, the factors were further connected with each other to form closed loops and to determine their type. For instance, a reinforcing loop was built by connecting the enterprises' information level on the fund and the exchange of information between enterprises: the more enterprises communicated among themselves on the funds, the better they became informed— and vice versa (see Figure 1.1).

A balancing loop was, for instance, established, as the bureaucratic attitude of business institution staff acted as a "corrective" factor, which has an inverse effect on the ease of application procedures: handling applications in

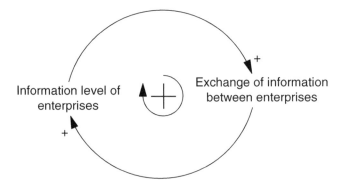

Figure 1.1. Reinforcing Feedback Loop

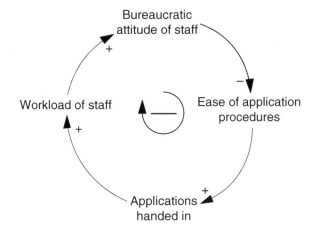

Figure 1.2. Balancing Feedback Loop

a bureaucratic manner makes it more difficult for enterprises to apply for the fund's support, which reduces the number of applications handed in and the workload of staff, which in turn reduces the pressure on staff to act in a bureaucratic manner, thus stabilizing the entire loop (see Figure 1.2).

The various relationships and interconnected feedback loops were then assembled to form the CLD for the entire situation of interest (see Figure 1.3). This causal network provided those responsible for the program with a range of interconnected factors that were responsible for the low use of funds. And it allowed them to identify the leverage points, that is, factors that can be di-

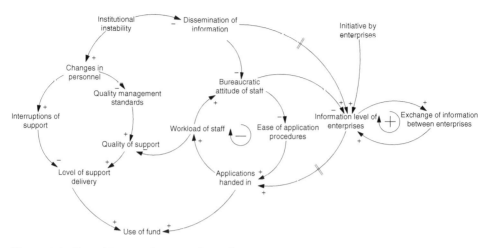

Figure 1.3. Causal Loop Diagram of Fund Use

rectly influenced by them and can have considerable influence on other elements.

REFLECTIONS ON THE USE OF CLDS

CLDs have been widely applied since the 1970s in diverse fields, such as environmental management, urban and regional development, business management, or organizational development. They are especially appropriate for visualizing strongly interconnected situations and for recognizing the underlying structures behind patterns of events.

From an evaluation perspective, the value of CLDs lies in the fact that they can be used to analyze relationships of a situation through the interaction of feedback loops and delays. The method is of greatest value in complicated situations, for example, for analyzing problem situations that are influenced by numerous and related factors, which for this very reason are difficult to structure (verbally). Or it can be used to identify structures underneath observable phenomena ("symptoms"). For instance, when unintended effects of an intervention are linked to its original theory of action (modeled as feedback loops), their generative mechanisms can be revealed and indications given on how to curb or even avoid them. CLDs are a significant advantage over linear models often used to explain theories of action, since they reveal how systems will "push back" against or reinforce interventions to change a situation.

The following practical advice should be observed when drawing CLDs (see Kim 2000):

- Use nouns or noun phrases when choosing a variable's name rather than verbs or action phrases, because the action is represented by the arrows (links), not the variables (e.g., "cost" instead of "increasing cost").
- Be sure that the definition of a variable makes it clear which direction is up (e.g., "tolerance for crime" rather than "attitude toward crime").
- Be sure that causal links imply a direction of causation and not simply a time sequence (not "first A then B" but "if A increases, then B increases").
- If a variable has several consequences, start by lumping them into one (general) term while completing the rest of the loop; later on, unbundle them if considered relevant.
- Think of the possible unintended consequences that might occur in addition to the influences being drawn, and decide whether to add links for representing them.
- Start with a central loop or process, and add loops later to fill in details (e.g., unintended consequences, long-term effects).
- If a link between two variables requires much information to be clear, redefine the variables or insert an intermediate term.
- Balancing feedback implies goal-seeking behavior; thus be sure to include the goal in the loop as well as the gap that is driving the loop toward the goal.

Pros / Advantages

CLDs are a relatively easy visualizing method; they can be generated on paper, on pin walls, or on a computer by using specific software (e.g., Vensim). They give a quick synoptic overview, can be modified rather easily, and facilitate communication on complex issues, so they are appropriate for collaborative settings, people attempting to address and deal with an issue together in teams or groups.

CLDs also provide specific advantages when dealing with complex or messy problem situations. By understanding causal linkages and relationships between variables, one can identify suitable points of leverage or entry that might lead to rather simple solutions and to understanding why a change in a variable might lead to changes in the relationships of the whole situation of interest. This will also reveal that the set of variables bringing forth a problem is not necessarily the same one as the variables that are required for the solution.

CLDs can also be used for constructing a more comprehensive picture of a situation, based on various perspectives. Connecting individual views or explanations can lead to multiple descriptions of the same phenomenon, and being able to see—and value—emerging "both-and patterns" instead of "either-or" relations can create new insights and open the way for new options or solutions.

Cons / Challenges

CLDs have been used successfully to model change processes in organizations, but these are relatively closed settings that lend themselves to simplifying diagrams. For processes on a larger scale, CLDs are less appropriate and might lead to large, unwieldy images.

But choosing a narrow boundary for CLDs can also work the other way; keeping the diagram simple might result in viewpoints that are too narrow. For instance, if more distant variables (stakeholders, effects) are not included, they might be overlooked and the conclusions drawn might have little relevance for real-life situations.

When CLDs are drawn up in a collaborative effort, the very process of consensus building may be misleading if stakeholders hold inherently different interests or unequal powers. Enforcing a consensus may overlook or obscure the existing power dynamics; consensus may be imposed by the most powerful or vocal, which will skew the modeling process.

One of the most common mistakes is to use CLDs for explaining or predicting patterns of behavior. This is possible only in the case of simple loops and becomes very difficult once feedback loops are interacting and delays are introduced. CLDs explain relationships between variables and primarily produce qualitative images of a situation. But they are not adequate to model a system's behavior over time and thus might give a partial and possibly misleading picture of a system's behavior. And they do not lend themselves to quantitative analysis, as this requires mathematical modeling.

To understand and determine patterns of behavior, computer-based methods based on System Dynamics, such as Stock-Flow diagrams, are more appropriate, as they allow simulations (see Chapter 2). CLDs often serve as the starting point for simulation models, although this is controversial and some argue strongly against translating CLDs into Stock-Flow diagrams.

VARIATIONS

Sensitivity Model Prof. Vester and Networked Problem Analysis

In the 1970s, the German biologist Frederic Vester developed a specific form of analyzing complex situations within the framework of his "bio-cybernetics" approach (2007). Drawing on insights from systems theory and cybernetics, he combined feedback loops and matrices to identify the "trigger points" crucial for bringing about change. His Sensitivity Model Prof. Vester enables reducing complex systems to just a few key elements. In this way, the sensitivity of systems to internal and external influences can be analyzed, and promising leverage points for change can be identified.

At the core of this model is the so-called paper computer, an influence matrix that is applied once the elements of a given situation have been defined and linked to form closed feedback loops. These elements are then listed in the columns and rows of a matrix, and subsequently the intensity of influence between all the elements is assessed. As a result of this analysis, four types of elements can be identified:

- *Active* elements, which exert a strong influence on others but are themselves influenced by these others only to a minimal degree
- *Reactive* elements, which exert only a weak influence on others but are themselves heavily influenced by these other elements
- *Critical* elements, which both strongly influence others and are themselves equally strongly influenced by others
- *Buffering* elements, which exert only a weak influence on others and are themselves equally weakly influenced by others

Initially, the Sensitivity Model Prof. Vester was used for analyzing ecological systems and problems. Later it was also used successfully in other areas (e.g., traffic planning and urban and regional planning). Since the 1980s, it has been taken up by the Swiss St. Gallen Management Center and was incorporated in their evolutionary management model. In particular, it served to deal more comprehensively with problems in enterprises and avoid being locked in by individual symptoms. The so-called networked problem-analysis approach is characterized by shifting the focus away from problem solving in the narrower sense toward the recognition and definition of a problem, that is, to grasp its interconnection with a multiplicity of influencing factors and thereby to avoid tackling not the problem itself but only its superficial symptoms.

Systems Archetypes

Systems archetypes are simplified and standardized variations of CLDs (or rather influence diagrams), which were originally developed by Daniel Kim and popularized through Peter Senge's "Fifth Discipline" (1990). They are generic combinations of balancing and reinforcing loops that represent structures that create common behavior patterns.

Kim (1992) originally identified eight systems archetypes, which can be used, for instance, for the following applications:

- Drifting goals: staying focused on vision
- Escalation: competition
- Fixes that fail: problem-solving
- Growth and underinvestment: capital planning
- Limits to success: planning
- Shifting the burden or addiction: breaking organizational gridlock
- Success to the successful: avoiding competency traps
- Tragedy of the commons: resource allocation

More systems archetypes developed later. They supposedly reveal the simplicity underlying complex situations and can be used to describe, predict, and explain behavior. They can also help in finding appropriate leverage and entry points for changing a situation. The main value of systems archetypes appears to be generic learning about system behavior by studying their structure and implications, which can then be applied to various situations. But despite the claim that they are ready-to-use, applicable templates, applying them can be rather difficult, and figuring out which archetype fits the situation at hand can be rather time consuming. There is also a great danger that situations are molded to fit the templates, which in turn might lead to wrong assumptions and conclusions about the situation at hand.

REFERENCES AND FURTHER READING

Flood, Robert L. 1999. *Rethinking the fifth discipline: Learning within the unknowable.* London: Routledge.

Kim, Daniel. 1992. *Systems archetypes I: Diagnosing systemic issues and designing high-leverage interventions.* Waltham, MA: Pegasus Communications.

Kim, Daniel. 2000. *Systems thinking tools: A user's reference guide.* Waltham, MA: Pegasus Communications.

Richardson, George, and Alexander Pugh. 1981. *Introduction to systems dynamic modeling.* Waltham, MA: Pegasus Communications.

Senge, Peter. 1990. *The fifth discipline: The art and practice of the learning organization.* New York: Doubleday.

Vester, Frederic. 2007. *The art of interconnected thinking: Ideas and tools for dealing with complexity.* Munich: MCB-Verlag.

See also the following Web sites:

http://www.thesystemsthinker.com
http://www.clexchange.org/ftp/documents/system-dynamics/SD1997-09ProblemsInCLDsRevi.pdf
http://www.frederic-vester.de/eng/sensitivity-model/

2

SYSTEM DYNAMICS

How does the structure of feedback affect the behavior of a situation?

How does "delay" in that feedback impact on the performance of the situation that is rich in interconnections?

What controls the way in which resources flow through the situation? How does this affect performance?

WHAT IS SYSTEM DYNAMICS?

System Dynamics (SD) is an approach for understanding the dynamic behavior of systems, in particular social systems. These behaviors defy intuitive solutions, and attempting to apply ordinary processes of description and analysis leads to inconsistencies and contradictions. Since these systems are made up of multiple, nonlinear feedback loops (see Chapter 1), the human mind is not able to interpret how they behave. Consequently, a system's actual behavior differs substantially from its expected behavior.

SD was originally developed in the 1950s at MIT by Jay Forrester. His goal was to bring his background in science and engineering to bear on core issues faced by corporations. Thus SD is based on common foundations that underlie engineering and management. Forrester intended to combine the strength of the human mind and the capacity of computers through modeling, that is, compensating for the unreliable part of our understanding of systems by using mathematical rigor.

The concept of SD is based on the idea that systems consist of elements that have, at a specific point in time, a value ("stock"), which can change over time through inflows and outflows. For example, in a bank account, savings are the accumulating (stock) variable, whereas income (e.g., from interest) and spending are the in- and outflows. The dynamic behavior of a system is explained by the relationship between stock and flow variables, which is expressed in a stock-flow diagram. Stock variables accumulate past events; they constitute the "memory" of systems. Delays often arise because an inflow is stored in a stock variable.

Stock and flow variables must be quantified, their relationships as well as their behavior over time defined in mathematical terms or in diagrams. However, these quantities do not have to be "real" numbers and can also be symbolic. Computer models translate all relationships into mathematical equations, which are used to model behavior, simulate system-states, or explore variations. Since the 1980s, easy-to-use software has been available for creating such models.

DETAILED DESCRIPTION OF THE METHOD
AND HOW IT FUNCTIONS

The SD process starts by identifying the situation of interest, be it a problem, puzzle, or issue. A clear initial identification is crucial for the success of an SD investigation. As with causal loop diagrams (CLDs), you should not attempt to model the entire situation within which the system of interest sits, but rather define a clear boundary and remain focused on elements that are relevant to the problem or the issue to be modeled.

The next step is to develop a dynamic hypothesis that explains the core of the situation of interest. Sometimes this is done by first drawing a CLD and then translating it into a stock-flow diagram. By differentiating between variables that accumulate and those that flow, more precision about the structures producing the dynamics is achieved.

However, some doubt the utility of CLDs and prefer to start right away with stock-flow diagrams (Richardson 1986) because CLDs obscure the stock and flow structure and, through their emphasis on feedback structure, lose the crucial role of the accumulation process. Since changes in stocks and flows cannot accurately be represented in CLDs, their utility for capturing dynamic behavior is limited and might even lead to wrong conclusions. Therefore SD modeling should either use CLDs extremely carefully, or use them for explanation after an SD model has been created and studied (Forrester 1993).

The components of a stock-flow diagram and their graphic conventions are as follows (see Figure 2.3 for a simple example of a stock-flow diagram):

- *Stock variables* (sometimes called Accumulator). These are quantities accumulated from the past that exist at a specific point in time, in other words, anything that builds up or dwindles, for example, water in a bathtub, savings in a bank account, and inventory in a warehouse. In a stock-flow diagram, they are represented as a rectangular box.

- Some stocks are quite visible, but others can be intangible but nonetheless very real (e.g., knowledge, greenhouse gas). Those invisible stocks can easily be overlooked. In order to identify them, one can investigate for every flow if—and where—accumulation takes place and what the implications of these accumulations are.

- *Flow variables* (sometimes called Rate). These describe the change of stock variables, so a distinction must be made between inflow and outflow. They can be represented as absolute values (e.g., interest) or in the form of a ratio measured per unit of time (e.g., interest earned per year). They are represented by a double-lined directional arrow and a valve.

- *Boundaries*. A cloud symbolizes the limit of the particular system under consideration, that is, factors that are considered exogenous to the model, as they influence other variables that are not calculated.

- *Auxiliary variables*. These do not have a direct influence on the system but serve to illustrate relations between variables (e.g., "variables of transformation" or "variables of connection," "time lag variables"). They are represented by other symbols or can be drawn as influence diagrams or feedback loops.

When drawing up stock-flow diagrams, it is advisable to start with one or more fundamental relationships between variables. This can be gradually expanded by adding other variables that have an influence on flows, for example, in the form of feedback loops.

Stock and flow variables must be quantified and the relations between variables exactly defined. This means that for every relationship between variables, a mathematical function must be defined which represents linear or nonlinear relations (the latter often can only be estimated).

The last step is to build a simulation model by assembling all the elements defined so far and express all relations as mathematical equations. Checks should be carried out to assure the correctness of the model and that modeling standards are met, for instance:

- Stock values can be changed only by flows.
- Every flow should be connected to a stock.
- Stocks should not be linked directly to stocks.

Once the model has been elaborated, simulations can be run for testing the model's validity (e.g., in relation to real behavior) or exploring the consequences of different amounts of intervention, timing, delay, and feedback. Playing around with the model can provide insights about the probable behavior of the modeled system. For instance, an investigation into three different strategies for tackling diabetes (better housing, better health services, more supportive communities) discovered that sustained reduction in diabetes levels depended on the sequencing of these three strategies. Counterintuitively, the model suggested that better health services should be the last strategy introduced (after building supportive communities, followed by better housing) rather than the first strategy that was the dominant assumption (Milstein 2008).

CASE APPLICATION OF SYSTEM DYNAMICS

SD was used with the evaluation of a micro-loan scheme linked to an HIV/AIDS prevention program in a mining area of a West African nation. The project had multiple goals, one of which was for local sex workers to be more assertive in demanding the use of condoms by allowing the sex workers to develop additional means of income—and thus be less dependent on taking on any client, whatever his demands. The most feasible alternative income was developing a hairdressing sideline. However, that needed start-up money for equipment. Thus a micro-credit scheme was established, financed by a

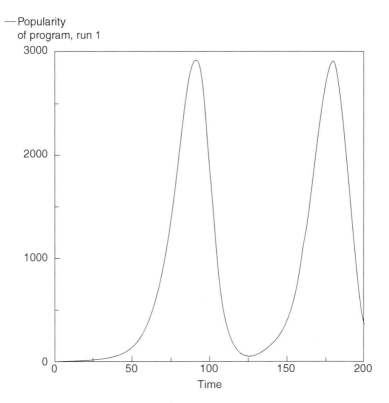

Figure 2.1. Assuming Rating Chart

European aid agency and administered by a local nongovernmental organization (NGO). The case is structured according to the five steps of the classic
SD process.

1. Identify a Problem, Puzzle, Evaluation Question, or Issue

The evaluation of the scheme showed that it swung violently in popularity. As
can be seen from Figure 2.1, sometimes it was hugely popular, and other
times it was not.

The European aid agency insisted that a plausible reason for this variation
should be identified and means of addressing the problem identified. After
considerable discussions with stakeholders, it was concluded that the issue had
much to do with the fact that when loans appeared to be plentiful, the popularity of the scheme was high, and less so when they appeared not to be plentiful.

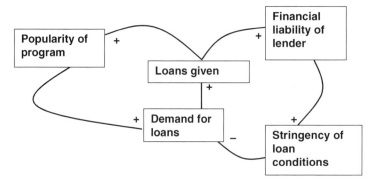

Figure 2.2. Causal Loop Diagram of Micro-Loan Scheme

2. Develop a Dynamic Hypothesis Explaining the Cause of the Problem

On further investigation, two major dynamics contributed to the scheme's popularity. One was the overall availability of the money—the greater the availability, the more popular the scheme. The other dynamic had to do with the stringency the NGO placed on the scheme—the more stringent the conditions, the less popular the scheme. Somewhere in these two dynamics were both the problem and the solution.

3. Build a Model of the System at the Root of the Problem

Stakeholders were gathered together and asked to discuss how these dynamics might be reflected in a CLD. The CLD form was chosen because it was the easiest for people to understand. What evolved during the discussions could be represented in the form of a reinforcing loop and a balancing loop (see Figure 2.2).

So this was what was thought to be at the core of the issue, but it does not explain how the identified pattern of popularity emerged. Simulation is needed to do that, which meant converting the above CLD into a stock-flow diagram (see Figure 2.3).

The following components were identified:

- Three stocks: popularity of the program, number of loans, and the financial liability of the funding agency

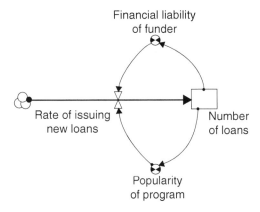

Financial liability
of funder

Rate of issuing
new loans

Number
of loans

Popularity
of program

Figure 2.3. Causal Diagram of Fund Use

- One flow: the rate of issuing new loans
- One boundary: essentially the micro-loan system (which was part of a much wider situation of HIV prevention)

4. Ensure the Model Reflects the Behavior Seen in the Real World, or Explore Similar Models That Have Already Been Tested

This was done by playing around with the model to see what insights it gave about the issue.

The first thing was to find out the pattern of popularity of the scheme that this set of interrelationships would generate (see Figure 2.4).

This is a classic limits-to-growth pattern. The sine curve indicates that there is a natural level at which the stringency of the loans will set a limit to the popularity of the program. This explains the first half of the variation (the "up") and the rise in popularity, but not what is causing the crash. Assumptions were made about this dynamic by showing this graph to several people. Their response was "Yes, but it often took a while for people to know what was going on about the loans." Knowing that communications in the sex worker sector were difficult, maybe the availability of the loans was poorly communicated within the sex worker community, in which case the problem could be solved by better communication.

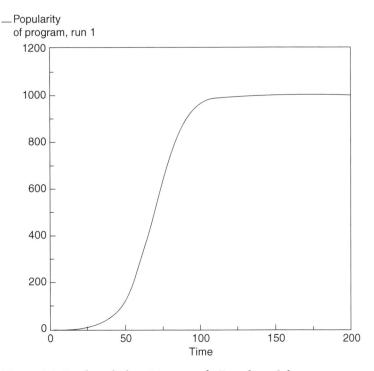

Figure 2.4. Stock and Flow Diagram of Micro-loan Scheme

So to check this hypothesis a delay was put between the availability of the loans and the popularity of the program (see Figure 2.5, run 2).

This delay apparently was not the cause of the problem, as it did not generate the *pattern* of behavior that was actually observed. If communication among the sex workers was a problem, then all that would happen is that the popularity of the scheme would have been slower to take off and reach a peak.

The next thing considered was the communications within the NGO providing the loans. Earlier research suggested that there was absolute chaos within the NGO in administering the loans. Could it be that the NGO's information systems were so poor that there was a delay between lending the money and understanding the liability that the loan had created? So a delay was put between "financial liability of lender" and "stringency of loan conditions" (see Figure 2.6).

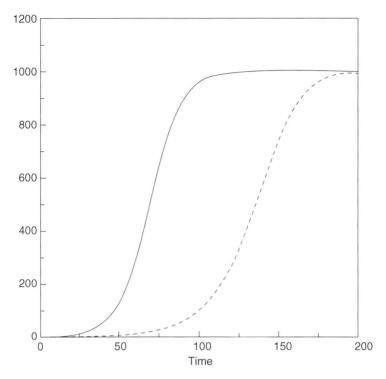

—Popularity of program, run 1

- -Popularity of program, run 2

Figure 2.5. Popularity with a Delay in Knowledge About Loan
Availability

Although this did not exactly reveal the real-life result, at least it showed a
similar *pattern*. Not as extreme, but it provided a clue about what might be
the answer to the question. Unlike the actual result (Figure 2.1), the curve is
decreasing in intensity. Maybe if the delay were reduced even further one
might see a greater improvement. And indeed, reducing the delay in the
simulation led to less intense swings of popularity and furthermore a move,
over time, toward a steady state (see Figure 2.7, Run 2).

5. Conclusions from the Insights

Two things were taken back to the client. First, the pattern that was closest
to real life was the one that was created by a delay in the awareness of loan

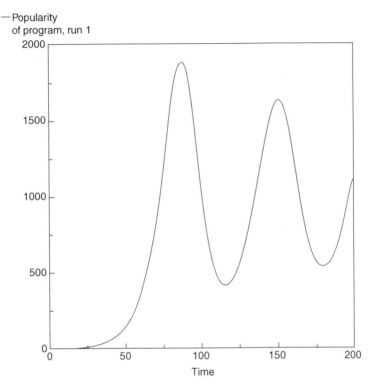

Figure 2.6. Popularity of Micro-loan Scheme with Delay Between "Financial Liability of Lender" and "Stringency of Loan Conditions"

liability. So improving the performance of the NGO is likely to be more effective than improving the communications within the sex worker community. But it also suggests something else, that the system might appear to be a bit disorganized at the start but will improve, even if nothing extra is done. In other words, do not panic if things look a little problematic at the beginning.

Of course, this is just a simulation, an attempt to explain the pattern seen in real life. This model cannot predict or determine how much the NGO has to be sorted out or in what way. But this model suggested that the solution did not lie in improving communication among the sex workers—and that a steady state may take a while to emerge. Both valuable lessons.

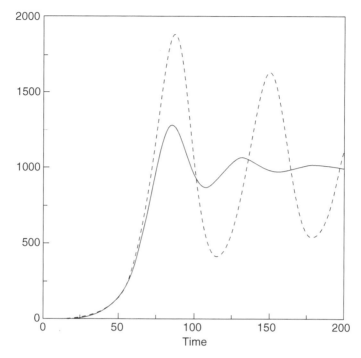

—Popularity of program, run 1

- -Popularity of program, run 2

Figure 2.7. Popularity of the Scheme with Different Delays Between "Financial Liability of Lender" and "Stringency of Loan Conditions"

REFLECTIONS ON THE USE OF SD

SD offers valuable insights into the dynamic behavior of complex systems and has been widely applied with substantial success. It has moved beyond its original field of application, management and industrial processes, to many other domains and at much larger scales (e.g., Dennis and Donella Meadows's models for global human-environment interaction). SD is now being used throughout the public and private sectors for policy analysis and design.

SD models capture the structural forces at work and provide a stable basis for understanding that will work even in times of turbulent change. In this respect they differ from forecasting models, which provide information about the future by looking at the past but provide little insight into what actually produces predicted behavior. They are also different from nonstructural models (e.g., regression models) that identify correlations or explain variance but, like forecasting models, are inadequate for gaining insight into how a system actually operates.

SD can be useful for various evaluation purposes. It allows the evaluation of a program's design prior to its start, by clarifying the underlying mental model and generating scenarios of how the program's behavior may change over time. It enables testing the hypothesis of causality or the impact of policy options on outcomes and devising alternative routes to improve a program's effectiveness. After a program is implemented, it can be used to understand why it is (not) behaving as planned and evaluate the likely effect of alternative policies on the system's behavior.

Pros / Advantages

The SD approach is of greatest value in complicated programs. Computer simulations are necessary to make the most effective use of the method, because we simply cannot predict the likely outcomes of nonlinear interaction of multiple system components over time.

Forrester (1993) emphasizes that an SD model should give people a more effective understanding about a system that has previously exhibited puzzling or controversial behavior. Influential SD projects are those that change the way people think about a system; to do this, the models must relate to and improve mental models.

Insights from SD models can be very valuable for evaluators and policy makers alike, for instance, for understanding that elements of a system interact through feedback loops, that causes often are not linked directly in time with effects, and that delays can cause unanticipated behavior. The ability to capture nonlinear dynamics, identify unanticipated consequence of system behavior, and rapidly test policy options and resource allocations can make SD an important tool for many evaluation studies.

Cons / Challenges

People often expect SD models to predict how things will happen. However, modelers distinguish between models that provide insights and those that provide predictions. Prediction models are often so complicated (e.g., weather forecasting, economic forecasting) that insights are rarely gained. In contrast, models that provide insights are often simpler—focusing more on revealing patterns of behavior than predictions of behavior. SD models generally fit into the latter category.

SD requires some expertise in modeling and mathematical thinking. However, this is nowadays less important, since the available software (e.g., ithink, Simile, STELLA, Vensim) consists of drag-and-drop graphical programs that do not require working with a programming language or writing equations. But while the software is easy to use, it will still take its users some studying and much practice to become adept at developing effective SD models, because converting a real-life situation into a simulation model is more an art—requiring experience or intuition—than a scientific endeavor.

A frequent danger with SD models is to regard them as representations of reality rather than as aids for the development of deeper understanding. The modeling process and the insights generated tend to be experts' work, and risk neglecting the involvement of other stakeholders. SD models can tempt viewing human beings primarily as objects to be manipulated as parts of larger systems instead of individuals with their own goals and behavior. This is a particular risk if SD models are used in change processes, because proposing recommendations without properly involving those who would be affected by or have to implement that change is often unacceptable for stakeholders and might lead to resistance or ignorance.

Excluding stakeholders was quite frequent in the early days of SD. Later on, care was taken to value the insights of stakeholders and bring them into activities of planning and decision making. Nowadays it is much more frequent to see SD models being used as a device for aiding communication between stakeholders on complex issues and not necessarily as a reflection of reality. The expertise required lies rather in facilitation than in modeling.

VARIATIONS
Agent-Based Modeling
Agent-based models explore the dynamics of a situation in a radically different way to stock and flow–based models. Rather than being based on generic variables (e.g., interest rates, population), agent-based models seek to model

the cumulative effect of individual agents complying with sets of simple be-
havorial rules (see Chapter 8). An agent is any entity whose behavior is autonomous yet complying with implicit or explicit behavioral rules. Agent-based
modeling is based on the principles that underpin notions of complex adaptive systems.

Agent-based modeling can be beneficial when applied to human systems,
as it simulates a system composed of "behavioral" entities. It is particularly
useful when agents exhibit complex behavior and the interaction between
agents is complex as well. And it is flexible because it allows adding more
agents and varying the agents' characteristics or their rules of interaction. It
also permits changing the levels (from individuals to subgroups or large entities); thus it is useful in situations where the appropriate level of analysis is
not known ahead of time and requires some tinkering to find out.

Agent-based models are predominantly used to analyze emergent phenomena, because the modeling takes place bottom-up, starting with the behavior of individual entities and their interaction. They are used to model
flows, for example, traffic jams or the dynamics of traffic systems, since traffic
can be understood as a consequence of simple rule behaviors. Other applications are the simulation of markets (stock markets, labor markets, voters), the
behavior of organizations, and diffusion processes, for example, technologies
or innovation.

As with all modeling methods, the application must serve a specific purpose, and the model must be built at the right level and with the relevant
amount of detail. Since agent-based models often model human agents, it can
be difficult to quantify or calibrate the soft factors that are used to determine
their behavior. And since agent-based models deal with systems at the level of
their constituting units, the computational requirements can be enormous
when it comes to modeling large systems.

REFERENCES AND FURTHER READING

Forrester, Jay W. 1993. Systems dynamics and the lessons of 35 years. In *A Systems-based
approach to policymaking*, ed. Kenyon B. De Greene. Boston: Kluwer Academic
Publishers.
Massachusetts Institute of Technology. Sloan Systems Dynamics Group. http://sdg
.scripts.mit.edu/. Includes the "Road Maps," that is, introductory courses on SD.
http://sysdyn.clexchange.org/road-maps/rm-toc.html.

Meadows, Dennis L., Donella H. Meadows, and Randers Jorgen. 1993. *Beyond the limits: Confronting global collapse, envisioning a sustainable future.* White River Junction, VT: Chelsea Green Publishing.

Milstein, Bobby. 2008. *Hygeia's constellation: Navigating health futures in a dynamic and democratic world.* Atlanta, GA: Syndemics Prevention Network, Centers for Disease Control and Prevention. Available at http://www.cdc.gov/syndemics/monograph/index.htm.

Richardson, George P. 1986. Problems with causal-loop diagrams. *System Dynamics Review* 2 (2): 158–170.

Sterman, John D. 2000. *Business dynamics: Systems thinking and modeling for a complex world.* Boston: Irwin / McGraw-Hill.

System Dynamics Society. Provides basic information and references to studies on the use of SD and Stock and Flow Diagrams. http://www.systemdynamics.org/.The SD mega link list is available at http://wwwu.uni-klu.ac.at/gossimit/linklist.php.

A useful description of agent-based modeling can be found at http://www.pnas.org/content/99/suppl.3/7280.full.

3

SOCIAL NETWORK ANALYSIS

What are the structural characteristics of a network?

Who are the key actors in a network, why, and for what purpose?

How can the network structure or information flows be changed?

How do these changes affect the network's performance?

WHAT IS SOCIAL NETWORK ANALYSIS?

Social Network Analysis (SNA) is a set of techniques for analyzing social systems. It can be used to understand networks and their participants, that is, to grasp and describe the organization of the network as a whole as well as the position of individual actors. It offers a variety of techniques for measuring, visualizing, and simulating relationships and allows analyzing these relationships in visual as well as mathematical terms.

SNA has its origins in sociological theories that explain social phenomena as interactions of individuals. These theories were being used at the start of the twentieth century to investigate the behavior of (small) groups and later on were applied to analyze kinship relations and communities. In the 1970s, SNA experienced a revival. The "sociogram" (developed by Jacob Moreno) served to visualize the communicative behavior of groups. Through linking with graph theory and the use of computer-supported mathematical methods, SNA now allows analyzing the behavior of larger groups and expressing this visually.

In recent years, SNA has spread beyond its original fields of application (sociology, ethnology, and social psychology). It is nowadays used above all in communication science, product marketing, and political consulting. It is also applied in economic development (e.g., diffusion of innovation) or in geography (especially urban and regional development).

The latter are fields where the success of interventions increasingly depends on "social capital," that is, the form and quality of collaboration between actors having access to or being responsible for resources needed to bring about desired change. A more thorough understanding of interrelationships, then, allows identifying factors that are critical for explaining present or past performance as well as for devising desirable changes.

SNA essentially provides a set of representational techniques for the analysis of social ties. SNA assumes that social ties matter because they influence behavior or transmit information and goods. However, the approach is not linked to a specific theory of how these networks function. Compared to other forms of analyzing social phenomena, SNA emphasizes the importance of the structure of relationships between people, not just their attributes as individuals (e.g., age, education, or status).

DETAILED DESCRIPTION OF THE METHOD
AND HOW IT FUNCTIONS

A social network is a number of actors connected by some kind of relationship. Actors can be individuals, groups, or organizations. Relationships can take on many meanings, depending on the topic and type of network under study (e.g., communication ties, business cooperations, informal relations, membership ties). Networks can also include actors' relationships with other kinds of entities, such as events they attend or activities in which they are involved. In terms of data collection, in egocentric networks, data are gathered from one actor (ego) about that actor's relationships with others, and in whole networks, data are gathered from all those in the network.

SNA systematically analyzes network data and describes the social order contained therein. The basic unit of analysis is the individual with the individual's economic, social, or cultural relationships. Society is not seen as an aggregate of individuals and their attributes, but as a structure of interpersonal ties. Thus, the focus is on both the relationships of actors and their attributes. The aim is to explain the actions of individuals with reference to these social structures.

With SNA, a network can be represented and analyzed using three types of interrelated tools, which can be used either alone or in combination: collecting data on relationships (matrix); visualizing relationships (maps); and assessing the network structure (measures).

Collecting Data on Relationships: Matrix

Information about specific relationships in a network is gathered and represented in a relational matrix (similar to the influence matrix mentioned in Chapter 16). Each cell in the matrix shows the number of times a specific relationship takes place. Besides showing whether a relationship exists or not, cells in a matrix can also be used to describe other aspects of the relationships, for instance, the type and value of relationships, the frequency of interaction, or the sequence of the relationships. In smaller networks, the cells can even contain text entries for describing details of a relationship.

For example, the matrix in Figure 3.1 shows the relationships between a set of nongovernmental organizations (NGOs) in Ghana. The matrix was established through an analysis of progress reports, and each cell contains the number of times a relationship was mentioned in an NGO report. The convention with such matrices is that the cell entries always show the relationships that exist from the row actor to the column actor. Thus in this case each row shows the relations with others as reported by this actor. A matrix like this presents information from both parties about their particular relationship. If information is not reciprocated (see ABANTU and WILDAF), this may suggest the relationship assessment was incorrect, or it might suggest a status difference, with one actor being more keen to report a relationship.

In the above case, the actors on the left side (in the rows) of a matrix are of the same kind as those listed across the top (in the columns). This is called a one-mode network. But matrices can also be used to represent two-mode networks, where the row and column entities are different kinds. For example, the rows may list actors and the columns may list the different projects that they are involved in.

The downside with matrices is that the larger they get, the harder they are to handle and analyze in participatory settings. Also, the structure of rela-

	ABANTU	ARK	ASDR	CDD	CEPA	FIDA	FOSDA	IDEG	IEA	ISODEC	ISSER	NGND	TUC	TWN	WANEP	WILDAF
ABANTU	0	1	0	0	1	0	4	0	4	1	0	0	0	0	0	3
ARK	0	0	0	0	0	1	1	0	1	0	0	0	0	0	0	1
ASDR	0	0	0	0	0	0	0	0	0	0	0	0	0	0	0	0
CDD	0	0	0	0	0	0	0	0	0	0	1	0	0	0	0	5
CEPA	1	0	0	0	0	0	0	0	0	0	1	0	0	0	0	0
FIDA	0	1	0	0	0	0	0	0	0	0	0	0	0	0	0	1
FOSDA	0	0	0	0	0	0	0	0	0	0	0	0	0	0	0	0
IDEG	1	0	0	0	0	0	0	0	0	0	1	0	0	0	1	1
IEA	1	0	0	0	0	0	0	0	0	0	0	0	0	0	0	0
ISODEC	0	0	0	0	0	0	0	0	1	0	0	0	0	0	0	2
ISSER	0	0	0	0	0	0	0	0	0	0	0	0	0	0	0	0
NGND	0	0	0	0	0	0	0	0	0	0	0	0	0	0	0	0
TUC	0	0	0	0	0	0	0	0	1	2	0	0	0	1	0	0
TWN	1	0	0	0	0	0	0	0	2	2	0	0	0	0	0	0
WANEP	0	0	0	0	0	0	0	0	0	0	0	0	0	0	0	2
WILDAF	0	1	0	2	1	0	0	0	1	0	0	0	0	0	0	1

Figure 3.1. Relational Matrix of NGOs in Ghana
SOURCE: Rick Davies, "The Use of Social Network Analysis Tools in the Evaluation of Social Change Communications" (2009).

tionships is not immediately visible when looking at a large set of data in matrix format, although there are techniques that can be used for identifying relational patterns with large sets of data (block models). To overcome these weaknesses, the same data can be used to produce network maps.

Visualizing Relationships: Maps

With the aid of specialized software (e.g., Pajek, NetDraw, Visone, Netminer), it is possible to transform the matrix into a map of relationships. The software calculates a diagram and visualizes network data. The conversion of relational data to network-graphs can provide an easily accessible image with recognizable patterns, previously hidden, that permit new insights. By addressing our visual sense, network maps are able to convey complex information and make it possible, even for newcomers, to recognize patterns at first glance.

Maps visualize networks by means of nodes and lines connecting them. The nodes are the elements of a network. Either they can be of the same kind

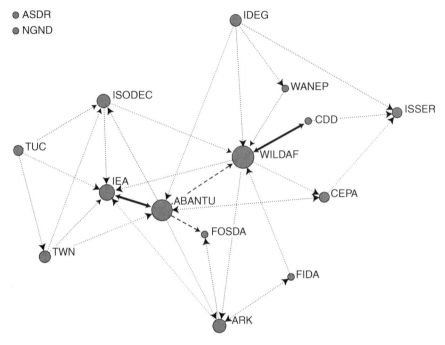

Figure 3.2. Network Map of NGOs in Ghana
Source: Rick Davies, "The Use of Social Network Analysis Tools in the Evaluation of Social Change Communications" (2009).

(e.g., all nodes represent individuals), or—in the case of two-mode networks—two different sets of nodes can be used (e.g., individuals and projects). The lines show the relations between the nodes. They are called edges if they illustrate relations that are reciprocal (e.g., e-mails sent in both directions). Lines are called arcs if they represent relations that are not reciprocal (e.g., e-mails sent only one way).

Maps can convey much more information on actors' attributes and the quality of their relationships than is possible in a matrix. Color, size, and shape of nodes can be used to code actors' attributes and similarly the size and line type to code the relations between actors (see Figure 3.2).

This network map was produced with the data contained in the relational matrix (Figure 3.1). It highlights the structure of the relationships: who is central (WILDAF), who is peripheral (FIDA), who has many working relationships

with others (big circles), and who has few (small circles). You can see reciprocated (black lines) and unreciprocated (dashed and dotted lines) relationships. There is a clique of NGOs on the left where all the NGOs are linked to
each other. In the top left corner there are some isolated NGOs (ASDR,
NGND) that are not connected to the network.

Such a relationship map shows the centrality of actors, the density of the
network, and the existence of subgroups of unconnected entities. It also shows
the (potential) channels for the exchange of information, knowledge, and resources. The map also offers the opportunity to check one's own knowledge,
to exchange different interpretations, and to discuss with network members
questions about the efficiency and stability of the network or its capacity for
innovation.

Assessing the Network Structure: Measures

In addition to visualizing relationships in maps, it is also possible to analyze them in a quantitative manner, expressing the significance of each
node and line in figures. By analyzing the structural characteristics and their
internal as well as external connections, different networks can be compared
(even without graphic representation) with respect to their structure and
performance.

SNA provides various structural measures and concepts to describe the
characteristics of a network, both at the level of individual actors and at the
level of the entire network. Out of the many different terms that can be used,
the essential parameters for networks are the following:

On an individual level:

• Centrality measures:

– *Degree centrality* refers to the number of direct links an actor has with
others. It is a measure of activity.

– *Closeness centrality* takes indirect relationships into account and calculates the average distance between an actor and the rest of the network. It gives an idea of an actor's accessibility and relative autonomy.

– *Betweenness centrality* measures the degree of control that a particular actor can exert over others.

- Brokerage positions:
  - *Cut points* control the flow of information from one part to another part of the network. They are bottlenecks.
  - *Mediators* can exert this function either between groups (e.g., representatives, gatekeepers) or within groups (e.g., coordinators, brokers)

On a network level:

- *Density*, the proportion of actual (as compared to potential) relationships, tells how tightly interconnected a network is.
- *Average degree* allows for a comparison of network cohesion and density; a higher degree of actors yields a denser network because actors have more ties with each other.
- *Fragmentarity* indicates whether there are components, that is, smaller networks not linked to each other.
- *Connectivity* identifies subgroups within the network (clusters or cliques).
- *Centralization* provides a clear boundary between the center and periphery. In a centralized network, information spreads easily, but the central actors are required for transmission.

These structural features require careful interpretation that cannot not be left to SNA experts alone. Because the meaning of these features is context specific and depends on who is being asked, the involvement of stakeholders and in particular the actors of the network under investigation must be sought. Network maps and structural measures need to be interpreted from various perspectives and considered alongside the attributes of actors, their theories of (social) action, and their concerns on the existence and content of relationships.

Detailed, participatory, analysis allows, for example, identification of strengths and weaknesses in communication, stable and less stable parts of the network, the distribution of power, or the position of individual actors. By means of special simulation models, it is also possible to test assumptions made about the behavior of a network and to forecast effects, or the prospects for success, of actions and interventions.

CASE APPLICATION OF SNA

This example is taken from an analysis of Austrian involvement in European Union (EU) cooperation programs. These programs promote collaboration among actors across Europe in order to exchange experience or generate new knowledge. Each program promotes specific topics and selects projects independently from each other. This leads to the situation that in each EU state cooperation patterns emerge, which are focused around projects and bounded by the programs. For instance, some actors might be working on similar topics but are not aware of this because information is commonly not shared across projects or programs.

Austrian national authorities took the initiative to influence these emerging cooperation patterns so they can function more effectively as networks for the exchange of information and knowledge at the national level. SNA was used in this case to obtain an overview and to inform strategic choices.

The first step was to construct a network map of existing cooperations in three of these programs. The information was taken from existing databases and was first gathered in a relational matrix (not reproduced here). Since it was important to know exactly which actors are involved in which projects, a two-mode network was chosen. The anonymized map in Figure 3.3 shows the involvement of Austrian institutions (circles) as partners in cooperation projects (triangles) in a specific thematic area (in this case, spatial development). The size of the elements expresses their degree-centrality, that is, the number of actors involved in a project or the number of projects each actor is involved in.

This map shows the key structural features at individual and network levels and how the emergence of subgroups pivots around involvement in the various projects. For instance, the network has three subgroups not connected with each other. The two subgroups on the upper right were geographically focused; each of them contained only actors from the same province of Austria, whereas the actors in the large, remaining subgroup are located across all of Austria's nine provinces—which of course makes it more difficult for the actors to know each other and exchange information.

Since the aim in this case was to improve information flows, it was of particular interest to identify actors who are in a pivot position for such a task:

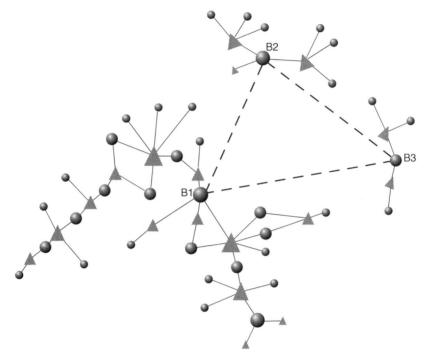

Figure 3.3. Network Map of Austrian Institutions in EU Transnational Cooperation Programs

- Actors B1, B2, and B3 were identified as brokers of their respective sub-groups. Through their involvement in many projects, they have the best access to information and can be considered as "network hubs."
- B1 and to a lesser degree B2 and B3 are in this case also cut points, which control the flow of information between parts of their subgroups. They are also bottlenecks of information—if they leave the network (or function poorly), the entire subgroup falls apart.

A more detailed structural analysis was possible through the various measures, thus identifying the properties of specific actors (e.g., betweenness and closeness centrality). By taking into account additional attributes, for example, the type of institution (e.g., public administration, NGOs, private business) or the geographic location (national or provincial level), other structural measures were determined, for instance, who is best placed to act as representative of a ministry, a specific provincial government, or an NGO group.

This structural analysis helped improve information flows. For instance, by connecting B1, B2, and B3 (indicated through the dotted lines on the map), new information flows were established, which allowed the entire network to be connected. In addition to improving the information flow within the network, these brokers can also communicate more effectively with the network (instead of communicating with all the actors), for instance, by involving them (as representatives of their subgroup) in strategic decisions concerning the entire network or for exchanging with other networks (at the national or European level).

SNA can be further applied as a tool for knowledge management. Since in these projects a range of outputs were produced (and documented) in a decentralized manner, it is also relevant to know which actors were collaborating for producing which outputs (e.g., a study, a plan, a manual). To this end, a two-node network map was developed that connected actors and project outputs. Since this map showed which information on a particular output can be obtained from which actor(s), it can be used for improving information flows. But it can also facilitate a more focused exchange or collaboration: because now the pivot is not projects but outputs, links can be encouraged between actors working on similar (or complementary) outputs. This information can be used to manage knowledge in a decentralized manner. The outputs do not need to be transferred, that is, documented or stored centrally, but can remain where they are. Instead, the information about where to find which output must be made available to all.

In this case application, SNA permitted a good overview of the emerging networks of collaboration and provided new information and insights for all actors. By identifying who were the best-suited actors for specific functions, it allowed improved network performance based on sound analysis. Of course, the SNA findings had to be shared and validated with these actors before making these decisions to check whether the information collected beforehand was correct, to interpret the data from the actors' perspectives, and finally to involve the key actors in the actual decision making in order to obtain their approval and commitment.

REFLECTIONS ON THE USE OF SNA

SNA provides a conceptual framework and a series of procedures for describing and analyzing social structures. It facilitates an overview of relationships and makes it possible to plan them. The visualization of networks makes implicit knowledge visible and thereby also communicable; different perceptions can be compared and brought together.

SNA is suitable for systematic and empirically well-grounded analysis of all types of networks. However, when being used in evaluations, participatory assessment and reflection of network analyses or visualizations is in the end decisive for the utility of the instrument.

Pros / Advantages

The method is both stimulating and easy to grasp; it is methodologically clear and can be put into practice rather easily. Simple and (in most cases) free software is now available, which has greatly simplified the process of drawing up relationship maps and has made SNA very popular in recent years. Network plots can be produced swiftly and constitute a good basis for further reflection and discussion.

Using SNA offers several advantages:

- First of all, the SNA techniques are applicable for all kinds of networks, from friendship networks in schools to complex policy networks, including private business, intermediate bodies, and political actors.

- The techniques are scalable in various ways. Thanks to the computer power now available, they can be applied with networks of nearly any number of entities. They can be used for relationships between entities of different sizes and levels. Because entities can be aggregated and converted into a single one for use at other levels (and vice versa), it is possible to connect network representations involving different levels of scale and conceive maps and matrices as modular building blocks.

- Primary data can be collected using standard methods like surveys, interviews, or workshops, but in many cases, relational data for network analysis are already available (e.g., import-export figures, project databases, attendance lists, etc.) and just have to be processed with SNA software.

- Visualization may change the self-perception of the actors. SNA makes it possible to identify the resources that circulate among various social actors by looking at the relational patterns between them. And it allows us to understand the relationships between network actors that can either facilitate or impede knowledge creation, information transfer, and joint action.

- Results and plots from network analyses are a resource for reflection with network actors. They are an inspiring basis for further discussion because they provide a bird's eye view on the relational environment of network actors.

Cons / Challenges

However, there are also limits that need to be considered. Since all network measures, indicators, and plots require data, the quality of analysis depends very much on the initial data about a network. Therefore great attention must be paid to the collection and treatment of initial data—and to people's commitment to provide accurate data. Just a few missing or erroneous relations can significantly change the structure of the network and lead to wrong interpretations.

Important boundary questions must be resolved when carrying out an SNA. On the one hand, those related with the selection of actors and relationships should guided by their relevance for the concrete issue and the possibility to gather data with proportionate efforts. As with any simplification, what is left out of a network map can be as important as what is included, and often only a look at the overall picture will reveal the importance of others not yet included. On the other hand, the available software offers a wealth of analytical possibilities, and choices must be made to keep SNA simple and obtain useful visualizations or meaningful network measures.

Even though basic structural characteristics visualized via network graphs can be easily perceived, their interpretation needs some caution. Stakeholders, in particular the network actors, should be involved, but also some expert knowledge will be needed, for instance, in identifying appropriate questions to ask about relationships. Finally, the quality and performance of a network can be assessed only through simultaneous examination of structural characteristics and the purpose of the network. For example, research networks are subject to different criteria of excellence than production networks.

VARIATIONS

SNA as an Alternative to Logic Models

Because SNA lends itself well to capturing complex relationships, it can also be used as an alternative to prevailing linear stage models for representing theories of change. Programs involving various actors and operating at different levels of scale can be conceptualized as networks, in terms that are easy to understand and possible to verify.

The UK-based evaluation and monitoring consultant Rick Davies outlines three potential applications for SNA-based models of change (see his Web site, which is listed in the References and Further Reading section at the end of this chapter, for corresponding material):

- SNA can be used to move from Logical to *Social Frameworks*. A network perspective replaces the stages in time of most logic models (that describe the sequence of events from activities to achievement of goals) by a sequence of actors, connected by their relationships (e.g., intended beneficiaries, partner organization, project staff). This can be seen as a potential impact pathway along which influence, money, and material objects can pass in both directions. Responsibility for achieving results is distributed along the whole chain of actors, and the respective changes expected from each actor can be described. But this pathway takes place within a wider network of actors, and the map shows the range of possible relations between actors. This can serve to identify alternative pathways for achieving desired changes, which can then be used for defining viable options and guiding subsequent monitoring and evaluation efforts.

- SNA can also be used to move beyond overly simple logic models (which display a single causal chain from activities to achievement of goals), for example, by connecting events that take place at different levels. For instance, *complex causal relationships* can be represented by linking output (indicators) and results (respectively objectives) and by assembling the expected contributions of each output. This is best done in a participatory manner, by using matrices projected on screens in workshops, and progressively filled in by participants, line by line, and revised as discussion of each relationship proceeds. If the matrix becomes too difficult to handle, it could be simplified by focusing only on the most important linkages (those above a specific threshold value) and transforming the information into a network diagram. In this way, SNA tools can be used alongside logic models and applied for aspects that cannot be captured easily by the latter.

• SNA can be applied in situations where multiple organizations work together without a joint plan or theory of change. Here network structures can be considered as *emergent outcomes*, resulting from the decision making of individual actors. For example, individual organizations often make their own decisions about which issue coalitions to support, but these individual decisions can result in an aggregate structure that may not be optimal for the network as a whole. The process of mapping those networks, and feeding back the results to the network members, has the potential to facilitate decentralized planning and evaluation processes without impinging on each actor's autonomy.

These examples point at ways in which SNA tools can be used for developing new methods of participatory and decentralized planning or evaluation in situations that involve a diversity of objectives and actors. By aggregating the views of individual actors, identifying their consequences, and resolving gaps through reiteration, strategies can be built from the bottom up. Such a process can also provide useful information to all about overall objectives as well as guidance to individual actors about whom they need to work with and about what.

Cynefin

The Cynefin framework (see Chapter 10) draws heavily on network theory. Indeed, the distinctions between simple, complicated, complex, and chaotic situations can be described entirely in network analysis terms:

Simple: high centrality, low density

Complicated: high centrality, high density

Complex: low centrality, high density

Chaotic: low centrality, low density

NOTE

Our thanks to Rick Davies for permission to use some of his material and to reproduce Figures 3.1 and 3.2 from his paper "The Use of Social Network Analysis Tools in the Evaluation of Social Change Communications" (2009). And to the SNA expert of ÖAR Regionalberatung, Konstantin Melidis, who provided valuable information as well as material for the case example, including Figure 3.3.

REFERENCES AND FURTHER READING

Davies, Rick. http://mande.co.uk/special-issues/network-models/.

Durland, Maryann M., and Kimberly A. Fredericks, eds. 2005. Special issue: Social Network Analysis in program evaluation. *New Directions for Evaluation* 107 (Jossey Bass & American Evaluation Association).

Hanneman, Robert A., and Mark Riddle. 2005. *Introduction to social network methods.* Riverside: University of California.

Institute for Social Network Analysis of the Economy. www.isnae.org/index.html.

International Network for Social Network Analysis. www.insna.org.

The following Web sites are available for download of software and documentation (manuals, instructions for use, etc.):

http://pajek.imfm.si/doku.php?id=download
http://visone.info/
http://www.analytictech.com/products.htm (for UCINET and NetDraw)

4

OUTCOME MAPPING

How does our intervention contribute to an ultimate goal?

Whose behavior can we influence in terms of that contribution?

What is a realistic strategy to achieve that behavior change?

How do these behavior changes affect our role, and which changes do we have to make to be an effective partner?

WHAT IS OUTCOME MAPPING?

Outcome Mapping (OM) is an approach to planning, monitoring, and evaluating social change initiatives. It is a set of tools and guidelines that steer project or program teams through an iterative process to identify their desired change and to work collaboratively to bring it about. Its originality lies in the shift away from assessing the impact of a program—and toward changes in the behaviors, relationships, actions, or activities of the people, groups, and organizations with whom a program is working directly and seeking to influence—and of the program being influenced by these interactions.

OM was developed in 2001 by the International Development Research Centre (IDRC) in Canada with research partners in Asia, Africa, and Latin America as a response to the weaknesses and criticism of other monitoring frameworks, in particular in areas involving complex change processes. In these contexts, results-based management frameworks, or management by objectives, have been shown to be counterproductive, hindering projects and programs by too narrowly focusing planning, monitoring, and evaluation activities. This hinders innovative approaches, learning, and flexibility—a strong marker for failure in complex situations.

OM is an approach for modeling what a program intends to do but differs from other logic models (e.g., Program Logic, Log Frame) in several ways. Foremost, it recognizes the importance of perspectives, that is, that actors operate within different logic and responsibility systems. It is not based on a linear cause-and-effect framework but assumes that multiple (often nonlinear) causes lead to change. And it departs from the notion of attributing that change to specific interventions but assumes that only contributions are made—and tracks these contributions by looking at the logical links between interventions and behavioral change.

The focus of OM is on one specific type of outcome: changes in the behavior of those individuals, groups, and organizations with which a program works directly and anticipates opportunities for mutual influence. These outcomes should at least be logically linked to a program's activities (but not necessarily directly caused by them). While recognizing that challenges beyond the scope of the program exist, OM limits performance assessment to a program's direct sphere of influence. It monitors and evaluates whether a program has contributed to intended behavior changes and programs—and does so in ways that can be sustained in the future. It is one of the most boundary-conscious monitoring and evaluation (M&E) approaches.

In operational terms, OM defines three distinct but highly interrelated sets of activities and changes and provides tools to monitor them: changes in partners, program strategies, and organizational practices. By linking the program's organizational assessment with monitoring the changes of its partners, OM assumes that a program needs to grow and develop in order to make a significant contribution. Programs are encouraged to be viewed and managed as dynamic organizations, improving their ability to work with their partners by reviewing and adjusting their own goals and methods.

OM assumes that change is controlled by the partners of an initiative and that external agents (such as funders and overseas aid agencies) can only facilitate the process by providing access to new resources, ideas, or opportunities for a certain period of time. A focus on partners' behavior emphasizes the need to effectively devolve power and be responsible to endogenous actors as a condition for success.

Although data are gathered on the program's actions and on changes in its partners, OM does not attempt to imply a causal relationship between the two. The program can make a logical argument regarding its contributions to change, but the program cannot claim sole credit. By combining the data on external outcomes with data on internal performance, a program will be able to tell learning stories illustrating how it has improved its work in order to encourage the transformation of its partners. And it can document the extent to which the partners have moved in the desired directions.

DETAILED DESCRIPTION OF THE METHOD AND HOW IT FUNCTIONS

Four guiding principles underpin the OM framework:

- Actor-centered development and behavior change. OM recognizes that people and organizations drive change processes. The problem to be tackled, the aims of the project, and the indicators of success are defined in terms of changes in the behavior of these actors.

- Continuous learning and flexibility. OM emphasizes that the most effective planning, monitoring, and evaluation activities are cyclical, iterative, and reflexive. They aim to foster learning about the actors, contexts, and challenges involved in influencing social change.

- Participation and accountability. By involving stakeholders and partners in the planning and monitoring process and emphasizing reflection on relationships and responsibilities, participation incorporates valuable perspectives and fosters two-way accountability and responsibility.

- Nonlinearity and contribution. With OM, processes of transformation and change are owned collectively; they are the result not of a causal chain beginning with "inputs" and controlled by funders but of a complex web of interactions between different actors, forces, and trends.

There are three stages and twelve steps to OM. They take the program from reaching consensus about the macro-level changes it would like to support to developing a monitoring framework and an evaluation plan. These twelve steps are also the elements of an OM design workshop.

The first stage, *intentional design*, helps a program establish consensus on the macro-level changes it will help to bring about and plan the strategies it will use. This assures that a program frames its activities based on the changes it intends to help bring about and that its actions are purposefully chosen to maximize the effectiveness of its contributions. Defining the elements of the intentional design stage is easiest if the members of the program already have a shared understanding of the ultimate purpose of their work. Based on experience, the OM community has recently added a step "0," which includes all processes and actions that take place from the conception of a project to the preparation for intentional design.

The logic of the program is articulated by following the first seven steps:

1. A vision statement describes why the program exists and provides an inspirational focus.

2. A mission statement describes how the program intends to support the vision. It states the areas in which the program will work (but does not list all the activities in which it will engage).

3. The boundary partners (those with whom the program will work directly) are identified so that they can contribute to the vision.

4. The outcome challenge statements identify the results that the program would like to see its boundary partners achieve.

5. Progress markers are identified for each of the outcome challenges and boundary partners and represent the information to be gathered for monitoring achievements toward the desired outcome.

6. The strategy maps for each outcome challenge identify the strategies used by the program to contribute to the achievement of an outcome.

7. The organizational practices describe how the program's contributions to the vision will be framed by focusing on what it will do.

The second stage, *outcome and performance monitoring*, helps a program clarify its monitoring and evaluation priorities. Outcome and performance monitoring provides a framework for ongoing monitoring of the program's actions in support of its boundary partners' progress toward the achievement of outcomes, the strategies the program has employed to foster those changes, and the program's organizational practices. Based on predefined monitoring priorities, data collection sheets are developed to track outcomes, strategies, and/or organizational practices. However, the value of these data collection instruments depends on their integration into the program's ongoing management and reporting processes and on the commitment of program members to collect data regularly and reflect on their work honestly. Since OM cannot interpret the data collected, they are intended as self-assessment tools to be used by the program team in regular monitoring meetings.

OM assesses a program holistically by monitoring three parallel processes: changes in the development setting, strategies and activities, and functioning as an organizational unit. OM is based on the premise that a program needs to know not only about results but also about the processes by which they were attained and about the program's own internal effectiveness. It is through the combination of information and knowledge in these three areas that a program can build a better understanding of what it is achieving and how it can improve its levels of success.

The framework for ongoing monitoring consists of the next four steps, which are interrelated:

8. Monitoring priorities are set by defining what to monitor on an ongoing basis and what to evaluate in depth in the future. OM identifies three types of information to be monitored, but the information to be gathered is deliberately limited in order to keep the effort manageable and sustainable. The program may choose to implement a "light" monitoring system, in which teams meet regularly for reviews, or a "heavy" monitoring system, in which data are documented more extensively.

9. An outcome journal is established for each boundary partner, which includes the graduated progress markers, a description of the level of change, and identification of who among the boundary partners exhibited the change. Information explaining the reasons and circumstances for the change, evidence of the change, unanticipated change, and lessons for the program is also recorded in order to keep a running track of the context for future analysis or evaluation. Progress markers articulate the results that a program helps to achieve, but data collected on the markers needs to be contextualized and explained in order to be useful. These markers are not unchangeable but should be revised if considered appropriate.

10. A strategy journal records data on the strategies being employed to encourage change in the boundary partners. The generic format includes
the resources allocated (inputs), the activities undertaken, a judgment
on the effectiveness of those activities, the outputs, and any required
follow-up. To use the strategy journal as a learning and management
tool, the program should also reflect on the scope for improvement,
thus building its own capacity to be effective and relevant.

11. A performance journal records how the program is operating as an
organization to fulfill its mission. It includes information on the organizational practices being employed by the program to remain relevant, sustainable, and connected to its environment. Data on these
organizational practices can be gathered through quantitative indicators, qualitative examples, or a combination of the two. This journal
should also be used as a learning tool and can be fed into future work
plans.

In these three journals, a program will have a systematized set of data
about its operations and the results being achieved by its boundary partners.
Ideally, the program should be able to make a logical connection between
its strategies and practices and its boundary partners' achievement of
outcomes—but the relationship is not causal. Some people have been experimenting with causal pathways and the concept of causal mechanisms in their
attempts to adapt OM to suit their needs. Analyzing and interpreting the internal and external monitoring data requires the program to reflect on the
environment in which it and its partners are operating and contextualize its
achievements and failures.

The third stage, *evaluation planning*, helps the program identify evaluation priorities and develop an evaluation plan to assess a strategy, issue, or
relationship in greater depth. Whereas through monitoring, a program can
gather information that is broad in coverage, by conducting an evaluation,
specific aspects can be studied and assessed in depth. Evaluations should be
utilization focused, and to this end, use of evaluation findings needs to be
planned early on. The primary users should be identified, and the primary
users' involvement in the entire process should be assured. This stage consists
of only one step, which is also the final one of the OM process.

12. An evaluation plan provides a short description of the main elements of the evaluation to be conducted by the program. This plan should outline the evaluation issue, the questions, the information sources, the evaluation methods, the evaluation team, the dates for the evaluation, and the approximate cost. It will guide the evaluation design or the elaboration of terms of reference.

CASE APPLICATION OF OM

This example illustrates the use of OM by VECO, an Indonesian nongovernmental organization (NGO), for elaborating a country program to promote agricultural development. The focus is to improve the livelihoods of organized family farmers by developing the entire chain of sustainable agriculture and food production. In the past they have used the Log Frame approach to guide their work, but for their new country program they opted for a more learning-oriented framework.

OM was introduced gradually to VECO, starting with a strategic planning workshop that initiated the intentional design. Based on these strategic boundaries, the OM process was started, which included a series of activities such as OM training, two OM workshops for staff, a donor meeting, and an OM workshop with partner organizations. The result was a program proposal document based on OM for the VECO Indonesia program for 2008–13.

The main focus of this application was to develop a new monitoring and evaluation system based on the principles of OM and a learning-oriented M&E practice. A one-year participatory action research process together with program and management staff and partners' representatives guided the development of a Planning, Learning, and Accountability system (PLAs). As part of this PLAs, VECO Indonesia designed the key organizational spaces within a monitoring and learning process (e.g., home weeks, partner meetings, midyear reflection, and knowledge cafés), developed the appropriate reporting systems (e.g., field office reports and outcome journals), and initiated the establishment of useful information and knowledge management systems (e.g., a database and a "living document" for progress monitoring).

The development of the program framework involved customizing the methodology to fit the specific context and to comply with internal and external requirements. In the case of VECO Indonesia, the most important factor was the donor requirement to use a Log Frame–based format for the program proposal and reporting. However, as VECO made the strategic choice to develop a more learning-oriented program management approach, it was decided to continue developing an OM-based program framework. This required a complicated process to integrate the Log Frame with OM to satisfy both of these needs. A number of tensions between the two approaches made this a particularly difficult task, for example, the different underlying paradigms and logic between the two models, the differences in language with hardly any resonance in the meaning of the terms used, and the differences in focus. Whereas the Log Frame focuses on changes at the beneficiaries' level, specific objectives, and intermediate results, OM is interested in changes at the boundary partners' level and focuses on actors and respective behavioral changes.

But VECO managed to develop a new model on which to build its program that served both of these purposes (see Figure 4.1). In line with the vision and mission, VECO organized its program around three specific objectives that indicate the desired ultimate changes within the scope of the program. The first focuses on sustainable agricultural chain development (SACD), the second focuses on lobbying and negotiation for SACD, and the third focuses on consumer awareness of sustainable agriculture products. A set of indicators for each objective was developed to monitor the progress and results for each of the respective objectives. Each objective had its own set of boundary partners. For example, related to the first objective, VECO Indonesia identified its boundary partners as local service NGOs, farmer or producer organizations, and private actors along the food production chain. For each of the boundary partners, a respective set of outcome challenges, progress markers, and strategy maps was developed to guide the program. Where a specific boundary partner featured in more than one objective, multiple outcome challenges were drawn up for that boundary partner linked to each of the objectives.

One aspect of OM that VECO decided to tweak was the organizational practices step. Rather than going through the step as described earlier, VECO decided to create a fourth objective on organizational learning. It is a unique objective in the sense that it describes a change at the level of VECO Indonesia and therefore has no boundary partners. To improve its own perfor-

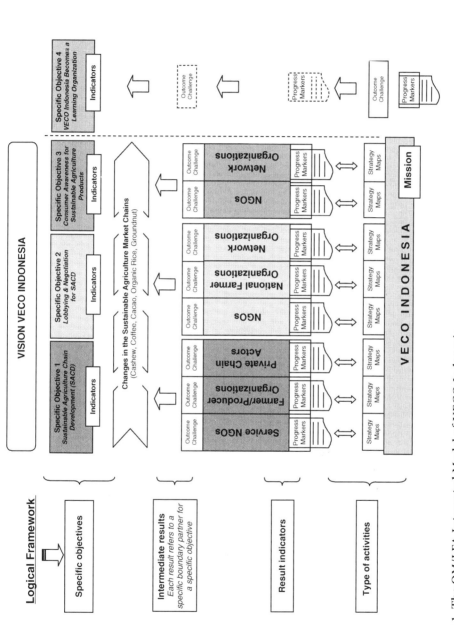

Figure 4.1. The OM/LFA Integrated Model of VECO Indonesia

SOURCE: Stief Deprez, "Development of a Planning, Learning and Accountability System for a Sustainable Agriculture Development Programme in Eastern Indonesia: Outcome Mapping in Action," paper presented at the EASY-ECO Conference, March 2008, Vienna.

mance, VECO Indonesia developed an outcome challenge for itself, along with progress markers.

A number of lessons emerged about adapting OM under these conditions:

- Customizing the methodology to fit the specific context and complying with internal and external requirements has been crucial for VECO.
- VECO developed its own way of fitting OM in alongside a Log Frame to satisfy the need to report to donors and the desire to build learning into its programs. While there are some inherent tensions this application shows that these two tools can be used in conjunction with each other to a certain extent.
- Supporting the local intermediary actors had become an important focus of the program, and OM helped orient the learning process toward VECO's interactions with them instead of toward measuring the impact on the end beneficiaries.
- OM's focus on actors allowed them to be more strategic about crucial areas, for example, whom to influence in order to achieve change, whom to work with as strategic partners, and how to involve them. OM helped the team prioritize among actors and to clarify roles and responsibilities.
- VECO staff felt that looking at behavior change gave them a better chance to understand their direct influence. This helped them become more systematic about the task of capacity building, and a clearer specification of what is expected and what changes are aimed at.

OM was chosen as the guiding framework to design the new VECO Indonesia program. However, because of OM's particular logic and setup, it initially facilitated critical self-reflection on the previous and existing program objectives, approach, structure, and assumptions on which the program was based. This in itself was already a valuable process and clearly shows the potential of OM to be used as an assessment tool in addition to program design. Program members also found OM to be of great value in prompting debate, for example, on the purpose and relevance of impact assessment.

The reflection, analysis, and decisions about the new role of VECO Indonesia as a supporter of specific partner organizations have led to changes in the organization and future program. By identifying a wider scope of strategies for capacity development of partner organizations—based on the strategy maps tool provided by OM—some strategies became more prominent in the program design, such as facilitating multistakeholder processes, facilitating market chain assessments, generating and documenting evidence and lessons learned, tailor-made capacity building, provision of market information, and networking.

During the last decade, VECO Indonesia supported mainly local NGOs in Indonesia toward improved livelihoods for organized family farmers. Because of the new directions of the program, VECO realized that new types of partner organizations should enter the partner mix. OM turned out to be very helpful through its concept of boundary partners as crucial actors in the program framework and resulted in the selection of new partners and an improved partner mix for VECO.

REFLECTIONS ON THE USE OF OM

OM unites process and outcome evaluation. Therefore it is well suited to the complex functioning and long-term aspects of programs where outcomes are intermeshed and cannot be easily or usefully segregated from each other. In OM, planning, monitoring, and evaluation are not discrete events but are designed to be cyclical, with one feeding into the other. Planning is done based on the best knowledge available, and monitoring and evaluation are used as reflective tools to assess change and choose appropriate actions.

OM is not necessarily the appropriate methodology for all programs, as it may require a change in perspective and approach that is not possible. The program needs to be able to focus on outcomes—defined as changes in the behaviors, relationships, activities, or actions of the people, groups, and organizations with whom it works directly. OM also involves a commitment to change on the part of the program and requires that the program consider itself part of the change process.

OM is best used at the beginning of a program once the main focus of the program, strategic directions, or primary program areas have been decided. It helps sort out who is likely to be affected, in what ways, and through what program activities. It then permits a program to design a monitoring and evaluation system to help document and manage outcomes. Applying OM does not necessarily require having to go through all twelve steps, and users may take whatever parts of the method they need for their particular purpose and context. Although there is a logic to OM as a whole, it has proven itself sufficiently robust to be useful when taken apart as well.

Provided that partners can be identified whose behaviors should be influenced, OM can be used at two levels:

- At the project level, it is particularly effective in planning, monitoring, and evaluating large projects. It is best used from the start of a project but can also be used as an assessment tool (for external or self-assessment) either during or at the end of a project. If used after a project is under way, it will usually require a reformulation of vision, mission, boundary partners, and outcome challenge statements, as few project statements can be translated directly into behavioral terms without consultation among the key participants.

- At the program level (involving several projects), it often requires that the program organize its activities in terms of its subprogramming areas. If a program is too general, it is difficult to identify who will change and how they will change, thereby reducing the likelihood of success. A program must be sufficiently specific to be able to identify who or what will influence the key groups.

Adopting OM for appropriate projects can help increase the effectiveness of interventions. OM can assist a project or program in adopting an actor-centered, learning approach to development problems, helping projects work toward agency commitments such as mutual accountability and ownership. There is also evidence that OM will help agencies and organizations meet commitments to managing for results.

Pros / Advantages

When working in partnership, OM helps to clarify the roles of different stakeholders—beneficiaries, partners, strategic allies, or implementers—letting them explore the most relevant (and sustainable) set of activities on which to focus. OM is suited to ensuring that projects and programs work through local partners and institutions rather than through parallel structures. OM fosters greater ownership and commitment and enables more sustainable change by unifying the visions and coordinating the work of multiple actors.

OM is particularly useful for interventions where capacity building is (or should be) an important aspect. It can help produce meaningful monitoring data for these complex processes, which involve knowledge processes and where technical concerns can obscure the crucial human dimensions of program challenges. By presenting the overarching objective as a series of progressive behavior changes of the actors involved, program staff can track progress toward the goal and learn as they work.

OM is well suited to areas involving complex change processes, where there are a number of interconnected issues, where progress relies on the interactions of many different actors, and where causality and future changes are hard to forecast. By integrating learning and reflection and highlighting the need for projects to be flexible and adapt to lessons learned as they go along, the framework puts in place processes to help address such large challenges.

OM was developed in response to the increasing need for greater learning and reflection within international development programs—a need that was not met through existing monitoring approaches. It encourages the building of the space that project teams and partners need to reflect on their progress. Whether this can actually be accomplished, however, will depend mainly on the nature and quality of the monitoring and learning process, as OM requires a high M&E capacity from program managers and field staff.

Cons / Challenges

In its purest form, rather like Social Network Analysis (see Chapter 3), the data collection demands can be very high. And if data collection cannot be integrated with existing activities or work routines, gathering and recording information can become quite cumbersome. This is a challenge particularly in situations where interventions receive funding from various sources and with different requirements for monitoring and accountability or in situations where the capacities for monitoring activities are quite limited and additional tasks are difficult to accommodate.

By focusing explicitly on boundary partners, OM neglects the relevance of more distant partners within a change process. And since the focus is on individual actors, the wider structure of actors and the aspects of networking and interrelationships are not taken adequately into account. Yet these features are often found at play with complex change processes.

OM consists of a comprehensive package that includes a precise sequence of steps, uses specific typologies (e.g., for strategies and organizational practices), and requires understanding a terminology that is specific to the model (e.g., boundary partners). It is therefore difficult and time consuming for newcomers to familiarize themselves with the methodology or to unpack the whole set and use only certain elements.

VARIATIONS

The Web site of the OM Learning Community contains a range of descriptions of OM applications. Among them are some that are quite "out of the ordinary" in their approach or context, such as those described in the following sections.

The RAPID Outcome Mapping Approach and RAPID Outcome Assessment

These two methods were developed by the Research and Policy in Development program (RAPID) of the Overseas Development Institute (ODI) in London. They both draw heavily on OM but also incorporate elements from other methodologies, notably episode studies (i.e., tracking back from policy changes to identify key actors and factors) and case study analysis.

The RAPID Outcome Mapping Approach (ROMa) was conceived for promoting evidence-based development policy and is intended for policy entrepreneurs wishing to maximize the impact of research on policy. It consists of eight steps. First, a clear, overarching policy objective needs to be defined. Second, the policy context is mapped. Third, the key influential stakeholders are identified. Fourth, once the target audience of key influential stakeholders is decided, a theory of change is developed; that is, the changes needed among them if they are to support the desired policy outcome are identified. Fifth, after identifying the necessary behavior changes, a strategy is developed. Sixth, steps are defined to ensure that the team has the competencies required to implement the strategy. The final steps are seventh, to establish an action plan and eighth, to develop a monitoring and learning system.

The aim of RAPID Outcome Assessment (ROA) is to assess and map the contribution of a project to policy or the policy environment. It has three main stages. The first is a preparation stage, during which a basic understanding of the situation is developed. This stage involves document review and conversations with key stakeholders to obtain a draft picture of the situation and the intended changes. The second stage is a workshop, during which the key policy change processes are identified by the stakeholders, which includes mapping the behavioral changes in key actors, external influences, and key changes in the project and determining crucial linkages between these elements. The final stage is a follow-up process, which allows refining the stories of change by gathering in-depth information from key actors to validate the workshop results.

Gendered OM (OMg)

Gendered OM (OMg) was developed by a local development network based in Pakistan and integrates concepts of gender as well as Information and Communication Technologies (ICTs) with OM. It presents a comprehensive methodology for infusing a gender focus within the project design, coupled with a utilization-focused perspective to project evaluation. As a unique feature, it includes gender analysis at the outset of the project's development and hence integrates the gender perspective into all phases of the project, including design, implementation, and evaluation.

The OMg framework assists in articulating how changes in people's behavior (especially that of women) will contribute to more large-scale development changes. The framework helps to create a deeper understanding of the challenges and opportunities that women are confronted with to help develop strategies and interventions that can improve female participation in a project as well as increase a project's benefits for women. The process of OMg is organized into four phases: intentional design, M&E planning, monitoring, and evaluation.

People-Centered Evaluation (PCE)

OM is an approach whose principles and application can be recognized in other methods of evaluation and social inquiry. For instance, the idea of "boundary partners" is incorporated into People-Centered Evaluation (PCE), which was developed by Jessica Dart and her colleagues at Clear Horizon Consulting in Australia. PCE draws from a range of evaluation approaches such as Contribution Analysis, Realistic Evaluation and Outcomes Hierarchy, as well as certain aspects of Social Network Analysis (see Chapter 3). Like OM, PCE is highly participative and starts from the premise that it is important to understand whom the program can realistically influence and what outcomes or practice changes are expected from those people.

A visual logic model is created with intermediate outcomes that are derived through network mapping to help decide who needs to be influenced to achieve the desired outcomes. Another important feature of PCE, influenced by Realistic Evaluation, is the construction of three or four different logics of an intervention rather than a single logic. PCE acknowledges that interventions work for many reasons depending on the context and the perspectives of those participating in an intervention. The models are used by project staff to develop sensible measures to track, report on, and learn about their progress.

NOTE

Our thanks to Sarah Earl from the Canadian International Development Research Centre (IDRC) for her support in preparing this chapter and providing us with additional information from the OM community; to Simon Hearn for information on the OM variations developed at RAPID and permission to draw heavily on the paper by H. Jones and S. Hearn (2008), "Case Study on VECO Indonesia," for the case example; and finally to Steff Deprez of VECO Indonesia for providing us with the figure drawn from his paper (2008), "Development of a Planning, Learning and Accountability System for a Sustainable Agriculture Development Programme in Eastern Indonesia: Outcome Mapping in Action," presented at the EASY-ECO Conference, March 2008, Vienna.

REFERENCES AND FURTHER READING

Dart, Jess, and Phil McGarry. 2006. People centred evaluation. Paper presented at the Australasian Evaluation Society Conference, Darwin. http://www.aes.asn.au/conferences/2006/papers/099%20People-Focused%20Evaluation.pdf.

Earl, Sarah, Fred Carden, and Terry Smutylo. 2001. *OM: Building learning and reflection into development programs.* Ottawa: International Development Research Centre.

Hearn, S., H. Schaeffer, and J. Ongevalle. 2009. *Making OM work.* Vol. 2, *Innovations in participatory planning, monitoring and evaluation.* Ottawa: International Development Research Centre.

Outcome Mapping Learning Community. http://www.outcomemapping.ca/. Contains a resource library, OM applications, discussion forums, and the community newsletter.

Overseas Development Institute. http://www.odi.org.uk/resources/. Contains briefing papers and other information on ROMa and ROA.

5

PROCESS MONITORING

OF IMPACTS

How can the behavior of diverse actors be steered in a desired direction?

What are the key processes for achieving the intended results of an intervention?

What are the consequences for achieving effects if those processes do not take place as foreseen?

What should be done if such gaps between plan and reality occur?

WHAT IS PROCESS MONITORING OF IMPACTS?

Process Monitoring of Impacts is a method for steering interventions (projects or programs). "Steering" means influencing the behavior of involved actors so they follow a desired course, either by staying focused on achieving specified objectives or, in the case of changing contextual conditions, modifying implementation strategies. It is essentially about identifying processes considered relevant for the achievement of results or impacts and then monitoring whether these processes are valid and actually take place.

It was developed by Richard Hummelbrunner in 2005 as an alternative to monitoring practice in European Union (EU) Structural Fund programs. These programs are characterized by multiple objectives and involve several implementing agents. They normally consist of a set of support measures with specific objectives and budgets that are implemented through a large number of projects, within a given time frame and predefined funding conditions.

They have extensive monitoring systems, which contain a set of predefined indicators. However, experience shows that the use of indicators has only limited value for "steering," because indicator data are either obtained too late to be useful (e.g., for results or impacts) or provide little information for improving an intervention, as they only capture a narrow part of the implementation reality.

Regional policy interventions are seen as the interaction of interdependent and self-organizing social systems—they are complex adaptive systems (see Chapter 8). Social systems are complex adaptive systems because they can react differently to the same input (intervention), depending on their internal state. Their behavior is nonlinear and cannot be explained from inputs or their internal states but results from the interaction of both. Under such conditions, the effects of an intervention can be neither predetermined nor reduced to original intentions, and it is difficult, if not impossible, to establish clear relations of cause and effect. It is equally difficult to establish meaningful result indicators and set target levels at the planning stage.

Steering via results or impact indicators is therefore neither feasible nor appropriate. Their achievement is a doubtful measure for the effectiveness of a program, because the influence of program actors is relatively small and many other factors are at play. Thus, what program actors can (and should) be made accountable for is not the actual achievement of results or impacts but their own contribution and performance. This will primarily involve the tasks for which they are responsible—and whether they are carried out in a manner that effectively influences the behavior of other relevant actors (e.g., project owners) in the desired directions.

A monitoring system able to provide meaningful steering information for program actors shifts the emphasis toward those factors that can be directly influenced by them. The key factors are those most decisive for achieving results: the quality of implementing activities, organizational procedures, and changes in the behavior of partners and of target groups. In short, a monitoring system must look at the processes that are expected to lead to results or impacts—and not just at indicators as their final measure.

Process Monitoring of Impacts is a blend of two approaches originally conceived in international development aid, Impact-Oriented Monitoring[1] and Outcome Mapping (see Chapter 4). They were adapted to suit the needs and requirements of EU Structural Fund programs, which have a results-based management framework. In essence, Process Monitoring of Impacts is a theory-based approach that makes use of logic models, transforms them into "circular" ones, and deals with them in a systemic manner.

DETAILED DESCRIPTION OF THE METHOD
AND HOW IT FUNCTIONS

Process Monitoring of Impacts builds on the basic assumption that inputs as well as outputs have to be used by someone in order to produce desired effects. Thus focus is placed on those uses (by project owners, target groups, implementing partners, etc.) considered decisive to achieve effects. These uses are logically linked to a program's activities (but not necessarily directly caused by them) and can be influenced by program actors. The main task is to identify these uses as intended connections between the different effects (output, results, and impacts) and to check during implementation whether these links remain valid and actually take place.

The method differs from other results-based monitoring frameworks by looking at the relationship between interventions and effects in a less linear manner. Instead of claiming causal relations and attributing effects to a specific intervention, it monitors whether interventions contribute to intended effects and what actions should be taken during implementation to improve effectiveness. This perspective is similar to Outcome Mapping (see Chapter 4) but with a different focus on the type of outcome being used for monitoring purposes. Because the objectives of Structural Fund programs are achieved through a large number of supported projects, their performance is considered decisive. And since intended use is considered the key linkage between the various effects, it is used as a core outcome for monitoring relevant behavior patterns.

Process Monitoring of Impacts consists of four main steps:

1. Identify and Structure Intended Effects

All of the effects expected from an intervention (project or program) have to be identified and structured in a coherent manner. Structural Fund programs have a hierarchy of objectives. These can be used as a starting point, but the classification of effects should also take the intended degree of use

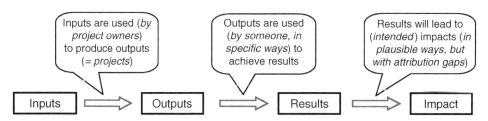

Figure 5.1. Basic Set of Process Assumptions

of inputs/outputs into account by applying the following definitions (see Figure 5.1):

- *Outputs*: the consequence of direct use of inputs by project owners and closely influenced by activities and implementation mechanisms of an intervention (e.g., procedures and criteria for project selection). In general, the outputs of a program are projects.

- *Results*: the consequence of direct use of outputs, which are logically linked with the intervention and thus can also be directly influenced by project owners (although other factors can be important as well). A result is closely related to the program's specific objectives and contributes to their achievement.

- *Impacts*: the consequence of indirect use of outputs or results, which cannot be directly linked with the intervention (attribution gap, influence by external factors) but should at least be plausible. Impacts are normally derived from a program's ultimate or higher-level objectives.

The effects are then visualized in the form of program logic models, which consist of at least three boxes to accommodate the above three effects. Activities and resources are not included in these models but are introduced at a later stage (see step 3 below) as part of the program mechanisms and program inputs.

The classification of three effects reflects their time sequence and the degree of influence that program actors have on them. It is therefore useful for the purpose of steering a program and relates well to the "mental map" of program actors. But this terminology cannot be generalized and might be irrelevant for other stakeholders (e.g., project owners) or when looking at interrelated effects from various perspectives: what some consider a cause can be seen by others as an effect, someone's output (or result) might be an input for someone else, and so on.

In conditions that are not as predetermined by a results-based management framework (as in the case of Structural Funds), other forms for structuring effects might be used. Different conceptual frameworks might be applied, for instance, Outcome Hierarchy, which is suited for designing outcome models to be shared by people from diverse backgrounds (see the following section on variations of PMI). Even the notion of temporal sequencing can be dismissed altogether, by moving from a chain model to systems of effects, for which network tools can be used (see Chapter 3).

2. Define or Agree on Assumptions for the Achievement of Effects

Inputs, outputs, and results are underpinned by assumptions (how? by whom?), which are expected to lead to the subsequent intended effects. These assumptions are often contained in existing material (e.g., program documents) but also reflect the views of relevant stakeholders or experience previously gained (e.g., evaluation, research). They should be formulated as processes, for example, activities, changes, behavior, or communication patterns of the respective actors (e.g., project owners, other beneficiaries).

Basically, assumptions underpin outputs, results, and impact, and they should be inserted in the respective slots of the logic model. This inclusion of (process) assumptions is a fundamental difference to many other logic models, which only foresee assumption at an aggregate level (the intervention) and do not specify the effects that they relate to.

To keep the monitoring task manageable, the number of assumptions should be kept as low as possible (Chapter 6, "Strategic Assumptions Surfacing and Testing," and Chapter 9, "Assumption-Based Planning," contain methods for prioritizing assumptions). Only core processes indispensable for achieving the subsequent effect, should be described. It is not necessary to formulate process assumptions for all three stages. This will essentially depend on the purpose and phase for which the method is used:

- In the early stages of an intervention, focus will be placed on the use of inputs in order to identify obstacles to producing desired outputs and

take steps to improve the situation (e.g., through modification of procedures, promotional efforts, and technical assistance for applicants).

- During implementation, the focus will shift toward the use of outputs
  and the corresponding achievement of results.

- At the end of or after an intervention, assumptions on the use of results
  will be most important, as they allow assessing which factors contribute to the achievement of impacts.

3. Define Areas of Observation to Monitor Processes

The process assumptions must be monitored to verify whether they are actually realized during implementation (see also Chapter 9). For this purpose
they are transformed into a set of questions for observation. This might also
require the definition of milestones (who is expected to act or change until
when or during which period?) or quantified indicators, which express levels
or thresholds reached by the preceding processes (what has been achieved—in
quantitative terms—through the behavior, activities, or changes of specific
actors?).

PMI takes a systemic perspective. The intervention is structured as a system (i.e., elements and their relations) and includes the relevant context. In
the case of Structural Fund programs, the core elements are objectives, inputs, and expected effects (i.e., outputs, results, and impacts). Program mechanisms (e.g., decision making on inputs, procedures for selecting outputs)
have an influence on the relations between these elements (and thus on the
respective process assumptions). In addition, the program's operational context influences implementation in manifold ways (e.g., socioeconomic development, legal or administrative framework, interests of implementing partners and project owners). (See Figure 5.2.) Thus Structural Fund programs
are structured as "circular" logic models, which are then used for defining
the relevant areas of observation.

The structure of this model resembles the Realistic Evaluation approach
(Pawson and Tilley 1997), which explains outcomes by the action of particular mechanisms in particular contexts (what works for whom under which
conditions). But whereas in realistic evaluations "Context-Mechanisms-
Outcome" configurations are predefined and tested, in PMI they are used as

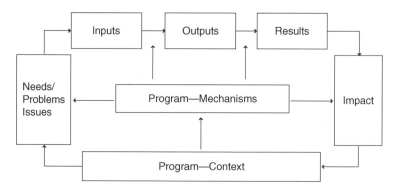

Figure 5.2. Circular Logic Model for Programs

explanatory variables for differences between actual and desired states of effects. It is important to note that in this circular model the linkages express a recursive logic: when impacts modify the context, this has potential influence on program mechanisms, which in turn can affect the transformation of further inputs into outputs, and so forth.

This notion of recursiveness is also shared with some other variations of logic models. For instance, in an Outcomes Hierarchy model, each level is associated with several interrelated items, among them factors within and outside the control of a program or assumptions. A similar comprehensive view of programs is also found with the ProLL (Program Logic and Linkage) model, which has been developed by Aru Rassapan and is used with development programs in Asia and Africa.

If these other approaches and models are implemented in a participatory manner and with the same concern for capturing the perspectives of key actors, they could also be used for defining the areas of observation.

4. Assemble and Interpret Data

In complex adaptive systems, differences from original states are inherent for assuring their stability and to adapt to changing conditions (see Chapter 8 on the CDE framework). For instance, changes in the short term are often necessary for the achievement of long-term objectives. Therefore deviations from intended routes should not a priori be regarded as negative phenomena, but dealt with in a more differentiated manner: Analyzing differences from original plans for outputs or results can help assess the appropriateness of a program in view of the given operational context. And it can provide valuable indications about the internal dynamics and self-organizing forces that are at work and thus improve the understanding of a program and its context.

Differences between plan and implementation can be important sources of information for learning and improving implementation because they help to identify weaknesses, point at possible alternatives, or lead to new solutions. The same holds true for exceptions, discontinuities, unexpected results, and side effects. Therefore, the assembly of information should not be limited to observing intended routes, but should look at the entire range of processes triggered and outcome produced, irrespective of whether they are in line with original intentions. They can provide useful clues, for example, for relevant internal or external changes, newly emerging challenges, and innovative or "informal" ways of handling situations. At this stage, other methods suited for learning can be applied as well, for example, CHAT (see Chapter 13) or dialectical approaches (see Chapter 15).

In the same way, differences among stakeholders should be treated as a resource rather than an obstacle. Differences cannot be resolved by giving preference to one particular view or by synthesizing them through external judgment (e.g., by an evaluator), because ultimately everyone is right—but only within the boundaries of their "mental maps," which describe how we think the world works. Therefore differences should be made explicit and visible for others in a joint dialogue, aimed at reconstructing reality by viewing the situation from multiple perspectives. A more complete picture of reality can emerge by linking individual mental maps and working toward the emergence of collective mental maps. By learning to see things through the eyes of others, actors will become aware of their own limitations and more receptive to other perspectives. Other methods that are particularly useful in dealing with different perspectives can be applied here as well, for instance, circular dialogues (see Chapter 18) or Soft Systems Methodology (see Chapter 14).

Data interpretation will be guided by the "circular" logic model outlined above. Systematically distinguishing between internal factors (mechanisms) and external factors (context) can identify where and how program actors should modify their mechanisms in order to improve the achievement of effects. It can also suggest whether and to what extent program elements (inputs, outputs, or even objectives) need to be modified to achieve the effects in changing contexts. Assessing the likeliness of impact paths based on program mechanisms and context factors will lead to modifications of original logic models and the corresponding theory of action.

CASE APPLICATION OF PROCESS MONITORING OF IMPACTS

This example illustrates the use with the EU Structural Fund program of an Austrian province. In this case, steps 1 and 2 had already been carried out during the preparation phase of the program:

1. The effects were structured based on the hierarchy foreseen in the program document and reflecting the logic sequence envisaged by key actors (funding authorities). For each of the (10) support measures a separate logic model was drawn up. The model structure followed the time sequence of intended effects: outputs were placed to the left, results and impacts located toward the right-hand side of the diagram (see the preceding section, Detailed Description of the Method and How It Functions, for definitions of these terms).

2. In collaboration with program actors, assumptions were identified about the links between the various effects and incorporated in the models. Since the purpose was to guide observation during implementation, emphasis was placed on monitoring the achievement of results. Therefore, detailed assumptions were formulated only for the crucial preceding processes (use of outputs), whereas assumptions for the other dimensions (use of inputs and results) were indicated more generally via arrows connecting the various elements. In addition, a typology of outputs was established, which reflected the intention of program actors about projects they aimed to support (in order to ultimately achieve expected effects). The process assumptions were specified for each type of output. These two features are often not found in logic models but are crucial for identifying and monitoring impact-creating mechanisms that emerge from the behavior patterns of a high number of projects.

The application described here took place at a stage when the program was in full implementation and several hundred projects had already been approved.

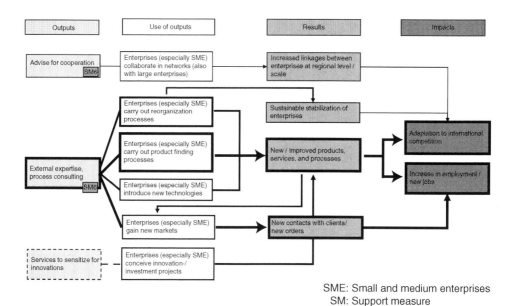

Figure 5.3. Logic Model with Weighting According to Financial Volume
(Public Funds)

It involved steps 3 and 4 of the method and was carried out by the same
experts who were already involved in the preparation phase.

At first, the Managing Authority (responsible for the entire program) outlined the areas of observation by designating five process monitoring measures . These were areas where findings were going to be particularly useful,
because either progress was difficult to track or implementation had already
run into problems. The respective logic models were then validated with
program actors responsible for their implementation.

Next, a preliminary assessment was undertaken of the likely achievement
of effects on the basis of support allocated so far. To this end, the projects
were classified in line with the typology of outputs established beforehand,
and the logic models were weighted according to two dimensions: the number of projects supported and the public funds invested for their support.
Figure 5.3 shows the weighted logic model for one of the support measures
under study (scheme for "soft" measures to strengthen innovation in enterprises). In this diagram, the thickness of the lines and boxes indicates the

weighting, and the corresponding figures are contained in an Excel file, but they can also be imported into the diagram. This diagram allowed the following preliminary conclusions to be drawn:

- So far, most of the funding had been used to support projects that fell under the output type "External expertise, process consulting." The dominant use of this output is that "enterprises carry out product-finding processes"; other uses can also be observed but are less prominent.

- Because of the logic connection, the result "new/improved products, services and processes" is easily achievable through the projects supported so far, whereas the other three results either cannot be achieved at all ("increased linkages between enterprises at regional level/scale") or can be achieved only at a modest scale, because there are only a few projects that are logically connected to these results.

- As a consequence, both of the expected impacts are achievable, but this essentially depends on one single impact path. Therefore impacts will probably be obtained only at a modest scale and are subject to risk. The potential of reinforcing links foreseen in the intervention logic is hardly exploited.

- A new project type was introduced during implementation by the respective funding authority, as indicated by the dotted line: "services to sensitize for innovations" with the intention to stimulate innovation-/investment projects by enterprises. This should contribute to achieving the (already dominant) result "new/improved products, services and processes."

Based on this preliminary assessment, interviews were carried out with a sample of supported projects, in order to capture the implementation reality and validate the intervention logic from the perspective of project owners. These interviews focused on the process assumptions (transformed into questions) as well as the linkages identified in the logic model. The interviews assessed whether these assumptions and linkages remained valid or should be modified in the light of experience. In addition, project owners were asked about specific problems encountered (e.g., delays) or unintended effects. When differences between plan and implementation were identified, the causes were explored, distinguishing among factors that were located inside the project, were related to program activities, or were due to context conditions.

Based on these findings, changes in the intervention theory and the corresponding logic models were suggested by the experts, along with ideas or proposals that came up during the interviews. These recommendations were discussed with the respective program actors, who then decided upon actions to improve the prospects for achieving the desired effects.

The entire evaluation process lasted four months. It was not intended as a one-off activity but repeated later on during implementation, carried out by the same experts.

REFLECTIONS ON THE USE OF PROCESS MONITORING OF IMPACTS

Since its original development, the method has been applied at the various stages of project and program levels: at the planning phase of interventions to structure their theory of action, with ex-ante evaluations to assess the likeliness of achieving expected results and impacts and with ex-post evaluations for capturing in retrospect the core impact-creating processes. Last but not least, it is currently applied in its original sense, as a steering tool, by several Structural Fund programs in Austria.

In this latter case, the specific features of the method provided useful information to program actors for their steering decisions: the validated and weighted connections between the types of projects and intended effects clearly showed the gaps and deficiencies of existing support actions and where those needed to change. The verification, or modification, of process assumptions (on the use of outputs) indicated whether activities or behavior patterns of project owners needed to be influenced (and if so, why and in which direction). In the case of gaps between actual and desired states, the "circular" logic model helped to identify where and how program actors should modify their mechanisms in order to improve the achievement of effects.

Pros / Advantages

Based on the experience gained so far, PMI is particularly suited for interventions with long-term impact chains, where results are produced at the end of the implementation period or even later. Although during implementation it is often not feasible to monitor the achievement of results, let alone impacts, it is at least possible to outline the likeliness of the use of outputs. And because it is based on the observation of processes, it is appropriate to monitor "soft" and "open-ended" interventions (e.g., promoting innovation, improving competitiveness), which are difficult to capture through quantified indicators.

Compared to current monitoring practice in Structural Fund programs, Process Monitoring of Impacts responds to the needs of impact-led management by providing timely information on *impact-creating processes*. It is not necessary to wait until a chosen indicator is met for assessing the achievement of results. Instead, understanding and observing the underlying processes provide early indication of whether an intervention is on the right track or risks missing desired results.

Process Monitoring of Impacts allows steering interventions to be implemented through a large number of projects and independent actors. The process assumptions function as joint rules for maintaining course toward intended effects. In addition, there are several advantages for specific stakeholder groups:

- Program actors obtain orientation for impact-led project assessment and selection as well as an evidence base for joint learning as the program evolves.

- Project owners gain more flexibility during implementation, because the focus on monitoring is not on original plans but the actual achievement of objectives. And they can benefit from streamlined applications and simplified or standardized reporting.

- Evaluators obtain guidance for identifying evaluation questions and for analyzing project-level information.

Cons / Challenges

A major challenge of this (and any other) monitoring approach is to reduce the workload for information gathering. Time and resources can be kept low by integrating this work as much as possible with activities that take place anyway. Data assembly can be facilitated if templates for applications or reports are structured in line with the intervention logic and process assumptions are integrated in the entire management cycle.

The other core challenge is avoiding the lock-in effect that is inherent with logic models, that is, treat them not as blueprints for implementation but as a temporary "mental map." Therefore, it is important to remain alert for unexpected or unintended effects and to consider deviations from intended routes as an opportunity for learning and improvement. But this requires actively inquiring about them, especially when engaging with project owners, who are the primary source for this information.

VARIATIONS
Outcomes Hierarchy

An alternative approach to conceptualizing the causal chains involved in projects, programs, and policies is to represent them as an outcomes hierarchy. An outcomes hierarchy is a specific type of intervention logic that includes only outcomes. It is a vertically structured set of intermediate outcomes that lead to a final outcome. Outcomes hierarchies are visualized in two dimensions and allow for interlinkages between intermediate outcomes across levels.

Outcomes hierarchies can be used for strategic planning, as they help to ensure that all those involved have a shared understanding of the outcome structure, and for determining which indicators to measure in a particular domain, as they enable a rational selection of indicators based on measuring whether or not intermediate outcomes are being achieved. This assists in monitoring progress toward the achievement of a final outcome, particularly in cases where it is difficult, expensive, or even impossible to measure final outcomes. Assumptions and content issues between levels can be identified.

The outcomes hierarchy approach has been used for more than forty years. In 1967 Edward Suchman advocated identifying and checking a "chain of objectives," in 1972 Carol Weiss applied this notion in her early book on evaluation. During the 1980s and 1990s the use of outcome hierarchies was popularized by Bryan Lenne and Sue Funnell and formed the basis of the approach to program monitoring and evaluation used across Australian state and federal governments and in New Zealand.

Outcomes Theory

More recently, Paul Duignan in New Zealand developed a conceptual framework for the functioning and optimal design of "outcomes systems," which can be used as an alternative approach for structuring effects in step 1 of PMI. Outcomes systems are the range of related systems that attempt to specify or measure outcomes (also known as results, goals, objectives, targets, etc.); attribute changes in such outcomes to parties (individuals, projects, programs, organizations, coalitions, joint ventures, governments, etc.); contract or delegate the achievement of outcomes; and hold parties to account (reward or punish them) for changes in outcomes.

Outcomes theory provides a set of definitions and principles for analyzing and improving such systems. It can be used to examine outcomes systems from a conceptual point of view and to understand and identify their similarities and differences for the purposes of critiquing and improving such systems. Duignan has also developed an applied version of outcomes theory (called Easy Outcomes) and a software for building outcomes models.

Outcomes theory intends to improve outcomes system architecture, that is, related systems that deal in one way or another with outcomes, by providing a clear common technical language, thus helping to avoid unnecessary duplication and identify gaps to be filled. Outcomes theory also specifies the structural features and the key principles of well-constructed outcomes systems (Outcomes Systems Checklist). This helps people without significant background in outcomes thinking to construct sound and sustainable outcomes systems.

Similar to Process Monitoring of Impacts, outcomes theory links three elements for providing "evidence-related information" on interventions (outcomes model, indicators, and evaluation). It also integrates indicators into the outcomes model and derives evaluation questions from there. Outcomes theory assists in designing outcomes systems, which can be particularly helpful with interventions that, contrary to EU Structural Funds, do not yet foresee a specific structure.

NOTES
Our thanks to Konstantin Melidis, ÖAR Regionalberatung, who has been involved
in the development of this method from the very beginning and has provided Figure 5.3

on the case application, and to Patricia Rogers for her contribution to the Outcomes Hierarchy section.

    1. Notably used in German Development Aid, e.g., by GTZ (Gesellschaft für Technische Zusammenarbeit).

REFERENCES AND FURTHER READING

Duignan, Paul. 2009. Introduction to outcomes theory. Outcomes Theory Knowledge Base Article No. 218. Available at http://outcomesmodels.org.

Funnell, Sue. (1997) Program logic: An adaptable tool for designing and evaluating programs. *Evaluation News and Comment*, vol. 6, issue 1. Canberra, Australasian Evaluation Society.

Gesellschaft für Technische Zusammenarbeit (GTZ). 2004. *Guidelines for impact monitoring and Assessment*, Eschborn. Available at http://www.gtz.de/en/doku mente/en.

Hummelbrunner, Richard. 2007. *Process Monitoring of Impacts: Applied study for the European Territorial Cooperation Programs*. Vienna: INTERACT. Available at http://www.interact-eu.net/interact_studies/63.

Pawson, Ray, and Nick Tilley. 1997. *Realistic evaluation*. London: Sage.

Suchman, Edward A. (1967). *Evaluation research*. New York: Russell Sage Foundation.

TAFE New South Wales: Outcome Hierarchy Framework. http://www.icvet.tafensw.edu .au/resources/documents/plmatrix.pdf.

Weiss, Carol H. 1972. *Evaluation research: Methods for assessing program effectiveness*. Englewood Cliffs, NJ: Prentice-Hall.

6

STRATEGIC ASSUMPTION

SURFACING AND TESTING

Who are the stakeholders who can affect the adoption or implementation of a strategy?

What assumptions is each stakeholder making about other stakeholders in believing that the preferred strategy will succeed?

Which assumptions of the other stakeholders does each stakeholder find the most troubling?

How can these differences be resolved in the service of the strategy?

SAST PRINCIPLES

Strategic Assumption Surfacing and Testing (SAST) is an approach to problem solving that relies, like many systems methods in this book, on dialectic rather than discussion or discourse for insights. It was developed by Richard Mason and Ian Mitroff but owes a heavy debt to C. West Churchman for its core ideas (Mason and Mitroff 1981).

SAST is designed to be used in situations where problems are highly interrelated and often conceal deep divisions between those addressing the problems. Like Bob Dick's Option one-and-a-half and the Contradiction Analysis method (Chapter 15), it forces people to identify and explore issues that normally remain ignored or hidden. It reflects Churchman's conviction that you need to involve the desired system's enemies, since their worldviews not only need to be addressed to ensure sustainability but also need to be respected as containing relevant concerns. Having done that, SAST seeks to find ways that people can resolve, reframe, and, to use Russ Ackoff's term, "dissolve" problems rather than "solve" problems.

Where SAST differs from methods such as Soft Systems (Chapter 14), Critical Systems Heuristics (Chapter 19), CHAT (Chapter 13), and the other methods mentioned is in the focus on assumptions. Like Assumption-Based Planning (Chapter 9), SAST tries to dig under the surface and locate the assumptions that are being made when addressing an issue.

According to Michael C. Jackson (1989), the method is underpinned by four key principles:

- It is deliberately adversarial, based on the belief that the best judgments about complex situations can be made on the basis of opposing perspectives.

- It is integrative, because an issue can be addressed successfully only by synthesizing these different perspectives.

- It is participative, because the issue can be addressed only with the active support and involvement of all those affected by the issue.

- It is "managerial mind supporting," because in addressing the issue, managers need to be able to understand all the various viewpoints, even those they initially disagree with. It forces them to "walk in other people's shoes," even if they pinch a little.

Jackson also makes the point that at first glance the juxtaposition of "adversarial" and "integrative" seems odd—but like Option one-and-a-half, there is an underlying belief that only by giving permission for and actively seeking disagreement can enough information be generated to resolve an issue with any degree of sustainability.

There are several variations of the SAST approach. The account of the following methodology and case example closely follows the description in *Creative Problem Solving: Total Systems Interventions* by Robert Flood and Michael Jackson (1991).

DETAILED DESCRIPTION OF THE METHOD
Stages
The methodology can be regarded as having four major stages: (a) group formation, (b) assumption surfacing, (c) dialectical debate, and (d) synthesis.

Group Formation

The aim of this stage is to structure groups so that the productive operation of the later stages of the methodology is facilitated. As many individuals as possible who have a potential bearing on the definition of the "problem" and its proposed solution should be brought together. It is important that as many possible perceptions of the "problem" as can be found be included. These individuals are then divided into small groups on the basis of one or more of the following criteria:

- Advocates of particular strategies
- Vested interest
- Personality type
- Managers from different functional areas
- Managers from different organizational levels
- Time orientation (short- or long-term perspective)

In choosing the criteria to be used, the aim should be to maximize *similarity* of perspective *within* groups (to get coherent group activity) and to maximize *different* perspectives *between* groups. Each group's perspective should be clearly challenged by at least one other group.

Assumption Surfacing

Each group develops a preferred strategy or solution. Next the group uncovers and analyzes the key assumptions upon which its preferred strategy or solution rests. Three techniques are particularly important in assisting this process. In the first, *stakeholder analysis*, each group identifies the key individuals, parties, or groups on which the success or failure of their preferred strategy would depend were it adopted. These are the people who have a stake in the strategy. The process can be helped by asking questions like the following:

- Who is affected by the strategy?
- Who has an interest in it?
- Who can affect its adoption, execution, or implementation?
- Who cares about it?

For instance, the list of relevant stakeholders drawn up when this technique was being used in an evaluation exercise with an agency that coordinates organizations that provide social welfare services included the following:

- Funding agencies
- Local city and county authorities
- Local politicians
- Existing not-for-profit organizations
- People in need
- Other local people
- Trade unions
- Various state and county agencies
- Volunteers
- Agency staff
- Agency board members

The main criterion used for constructing this list was the extent to which the groups would be affected by the success or failure of this agency's strategy. Using the list to ask questions about how each of these stakeholders would see success for the agency, it was possible to build up an extremely rich picture of the potential expectations held of it.

The second technique is *assumption specification*. Each group then lists what assumptions it is making about each identified stakeholder that lead it to believe that the group's preferred strategy will succeed. Each group lists all the assumptions derived from asking this question of all the stakeholders. These are the assumptions upon which the success of each group's preferred strategy or solution depends.

The third technique is *assumption rating*. This involves each group in ranking each of the assumptions it is making with respect to two criteria.

- How important is this assumption in terms of its influence on the success or failure of the strategy?
- How certain are we that the assumption is justified?

The results are recorded on a chart such as that shown in Figure 6.1.

Because of their lack of importance, those assumptions falling in the extreme left of Figure 6.1 are of little significance for effective planning or

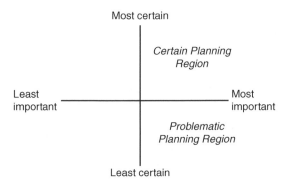

Figure 6.1. Assumption Rating Chart

"problem solving." Those falling in the top right (certain planning region) are important, but it is those in the lower right-hand quadrant (problematic planning region) that are the most critical. Because of their importance and uncertainty they deserve close attention.

Dialectical debate proceeds best if only the most significant assumptions are considered. Each group now, therefore, lists the most significant assumptions on which its preferred strategy depends. These are usually the assumptions on the bottom right quadrant.

Dialectical Debate

The groups are brought back together and each group makes the best possible case for its favored strategy, while clearly identifying the most significant assumptions it is making. Questions of information are allowed from other groups only while these presentations are being made. It is important that each group come to understand the key assumptions upon which the strategies of all other groups rest.

Open, dialectical debate is then permitted between the groups. Each group should have its list of key assumptions on display. The debate may be guided by asking questions such as the following:

- How are the assumptions of the groups different?
- Which stakeholders feature most strongly in giving rise to the significant assumptions made by each group?

- Are the same assumptions rated differently as to "least important" / "most important," "least certain" / "most certain" by the groups?

And especially this:

- What assumptions of the other groups does each group find the most troubling?

After the debate has proceeded for a while, each group adjusts its assumptions. This process of assumption modification continues for as long as progress is being made.

Synthesis

The aim of the synthesis stage is to achieve a compromise on assumptions from which a new higher level of strategy or solution can be derived. Assumptions continue to be negotiated and modifications to key assumptions made. A list of agreed assumptions should if possible be drawn up. If this list is sufficiently long, then the implied strategy can be worked out. This new strategy should hopefully bridge the gap between the old strategies and go beyond them as well. The assumptions on which it is based can be evaluated as it is put into effect. If no synthesis can be achieved (as in the following case study), points of disagreement are noted and the question of what research might be done to resolve those differences is discussed. Meanwhile, any strategy put into effect can be more fully evaluated because of the new awareness of assumptions.

CASE APPLICATION OF SAST: WINTERTON
COOPERATIVE DEVELOPMENT AGENCY

This concerns a project that was undertaken for a cooperative development agency (CDA), the Winterton CDA in the United Kingdom (Flood and Jackson 1991). CDAs served particular regions and aimed to foster, encourage, develop, and promote industrial and commercial activity through the formation of cooperative enterprises—enterprises owned by the people who work in them and which are also, usually, managed collectively. The project was to look at the general operation of the CDA to see how it could more efficiently serve the area in which it operated and how it might market its services in order to achieve its objectives.

Soft Systems Methodology (see Chapter 14) was initially used to tease out the various threads of the CDA's operation and purposes. However, during this process an exceptionally important area of disagreement developed about the desirability and feasibility of one possible future strategy. The debate centered on the following "root definition" of a possible system:

> a system seeking to recruit individuals to form workers' co-operatives in particular fields where business opportunities exist.

The debate centered around a "top-down" approach to carrying out cooperative development work versus a "bottom-up" approach. The top-down approach involved identifying business opportunities and then recruiting individuals into cooperatives to exploit those opportunities. This kind of approach is usually viewed with great distrust in cooperative circles. The preferred approach is bottom-up, essentially encouraging and assisting groups already thinking about starting cooperatives in particular fields. Within Winterton CDA, the idea of trying a top-down strategy had some support, although there was also vehement opposition from other development workers.

It was important to address this disagreement as quickly as possible because it was clearly of such significance for future planning in the CDA. A quick run-through of the SAST methodology was suggested. The description of its use, which follows, is in terms of the four stages of the methodology.

Group formation was easily accomplished. The development workers naturally fell into two groups, one consisting of those with some sympathy for the top-down approach and the other consisting of those opposed. The opposed group was asked to make the best case it could against top-down. It was felt that this, rather than asking them directly to make the case for bottom-up, would lead to the most fruitful debate.

The separated groups were then asked to go through the assumption surfacing phase, by using the stakeholder analysis, assumption specification, and assumption rating techniques. The groups came up with different lists of stakeholders, obviously influenced by initial perceptions about which individuals or groups might or might not support a case for the top-down strategy. Stakeholders listed are shown in Table 6.1.

Table 6.1. Winterton CDA Stakeholders Relevant to Each Viewpoint

Group 1 (for top-down)	Group 2 (against top-down)
The development workers	The development workers
The unemployed	Potential clients
Local authorities	The ideologically motivated
Business improvement schemes	Local authorities
Established cooperatives	Department of Trade and Industry
Funding bodies	Existing cooperatives
Other CDAs	People already in work
Marketing agencies	
Trade unions	
General public	
Other businesses	

SOURCE: Robert L. Flood and Michael C. Jackson, *Creative Problem Solving: Total Systems Intervention* (New York: John Wiley and Sons, 1991).

Table 6.2. The Top Five Assumptions Concerning the Stakeholders Recorded in Table 6.1

Group 1 (for top-down)	Group 2 (against top-down)
Provides another way to set up workers' cooperatives (potential clients)	Mixed feelings of the development workers toward the strategy (development workers)
Increases the CDA's credibility in job creation (funding bodies)	Lack of group cohesion among the cooperators (potential clients)
Ensures continuous support to the CDA (funding bodies)	Lack of willingness to cooperate among the cooperators (potential clients)
Carries out the expectations of the funding bodies (funding bodies)	Getting people who are not motivated (the unemployed)
Strengthens the cooperative sector (established cooperatives)	Less development workers' time on helping existing cooperatives (established cooperatives)

SOURCE: Robert L. Flood and Michael C. Jackson, *Creative Problem Solving: Total Systems Intervention* (New York: John Wiley and Sons, 1991).

The combined, long list of stakeholders facilitated the emergence of numerous assumptions for or against the top-down strategy as each group, during assumption specification, asked itself what it was assuming about each stakeholder in believing its arguments to be correct. These were rated on their importance and certainty by the groups. Table 6.2 contains lists of those assumptions rated most significant by the two groups (i.e., those appearing in the right-hand quadrants of Figure 6.1). The particular stakeholder generating each assumption is noted in parentheses.

The groups were then brought back together to engage in *dialectical debate*. During the presentations, it became clear that the groups were emphasizing assumptions derived from consideration of different stakeholders as the main props for their arguments.

Group 1 (for top-down) arguments drew heavily on the following stakeholders for their assumptions:

- Funding bodies: increase in credibility, ensures continuous support, carries out expectations
- Unemployed: provides employment, gives unemployed a solution in a package

Group 2 (against top-down) arguments concentrated on assumptions generated by the following stakeholders:

- The development workers themselves: mixed feelings, lack of knowledge about business opportunities, lack of experience in the area
- Potential clients: lack of group cohesion, lack of willingness to cooperate, lack of commitment to business idea
- Established cooperatives: less development worker time for them, suspicion

This analysis helped clarify for the participants the nature and the basis of the arguments for and against top-down and contributed to a highly effective and productive debate.

When argument was centered on particular issues, other interesting results emerged. The two groups interpreted the reaction of the stakeholders' funding bodies from entirely different perspectives. Group 1 insisted that the top-down approach would assist the CDA's credibility in job creation, fulfill the expectations of the funders, and so ensure continued support. Group 2 believed that top-down might be seen as a waste of development workers' time on a risky venture and that this dangerous experiment could lose the CDA credibility with the funders if it failed. On the issue of whether top-down promoted industrial democracy, Group 1 argued that more people in workers' cooperatives would inevitably bring this effect; Group 2 argued that the very idea of top-down took choice away from the individuals concerned; Group 1, back again, argued that many of these were unemployed and had few choices anyway, so work in a cooperative could only increase these.

Group 2 (against top-down) were worried that the project would be fatally damaged by the divisions among the development workers themselves and the possible lack of commitment from those brought together in a top-down scheme. Group 1 (for top-down) were most concerned that if no top-down work took place, a genuine opportunity to set up more cooperatives might be forgone along with missed opportunities to improve the lot of the unemployed and to gain credibility with funders.

Despite attempts at *assumption negotiation and modification*, it proved impossible to arrive at any overall synthesis during the final stage of the methodological process. Consensus was, however, reached on particular matters such as the need to seek out sources of information about business opportunities, to research other top-down experiences, and on the desirability of some experiments with a modified top-down approach (which were, indeed, carried out).

The intervention in the Winterton CDA was, therefore, most useful in assisting creativity, in generating a very rich and full discussion, and in helping to clarify where differences of opinion lay. Although *overall* synthesis proved impossible to achieve, the chance of genuine consensus around *specific* issues was improved, and this brought benefits. This is not unusual in dialectical methods (see Chapter 15), and in no way should this be seen as a failure of the method. The inclusion of the items mentioned above in an action plan would not have been possible without the changes in perception brought about through the use of SAST.

REFLECTIONS ON THE USE OF SAST
Pros / Advantages
According to Jackson (1989), Mason claims that dialectical approaches like those captured in the SAST methodology have advantages over the alternative "expert" and "devil's advocate" methods of planning.

In the expert approach, some planner or planning department simply produces an "objective" plan, based upon the "best" evidence, for managerial consumption. The planners' assumptions remain hidden and the opportunity is lost to produce plans premised upon other points of view.

In the devil's advocate approach, managers and planners produce a planning document, which is then subject to criticism by top management. The criticism may uncover some assumptions. However, this approach often encourages top management to be hypercritical, with the added problem that, if they are too opposed, the suggested plan disintegrates with no alternative to replace it. In these circumstances, planners may be tempted to produce "safe" plans to protect themselves from severe criticism. Again, with the devil's advocate approach, the chance is lost to develop alternative plans constructed on different worldviews. A dialectical approach, such as SAST, is seen as overcoming all the weaknesses of the other two methods.

When is SAST most useful? Jackson (1989) considers SAST to be at its best when the situation being explored is systemically relatively simple (or complicated) rather than complex and where there are no fundamental differences between participants—in other words, somewhere in the midrange of wicked problems.

Cons / Challenges

There are several criticisms of SAST (Cosier 1981). The main criticism is of the underlying assumption that dialectical forms of inquiry bring benefits that are greater than more dialogic and expert-led forms of inquiry. Another criticism is pragmatic. It is a very complicated way of getting at assumptions; any expert should be able to identify assumptions without going through all SAST's demanding procedures. Cosier also points out that there is an implicit assumption in SAST that the original strategy is defective in some way. What if it is not?

Organizational culture can also throw spanners into the SAST works. Much management theory shies away from dialectic. Consequently many managers (and the cultures within which they operate) simply do not have the knowledge and experience to support extended debate and argument. Such circumstances, as Jackson points out, skews SAST toward a kind of multigroup brainstorming. Similarly, in coercive environments, SAST can be manipulated to benefit the powerful. Also, in such conditions there would be strong forces preventing assumptions to be willingly and openly exposed.

NOTE

The account of the methodology and case study closely follows the description in Robert L. Flood and Michael C. Jackson, *Creative Problem Solving: Total Systems Intervention* (1991). Our thanks to Michael Jackson and John Wiley and Sons for permission to use the material.

REFERENCES AND FURTHER READING

Cosier, Richard A. 1981. Dialectical inquiry in strategic planning: A case of premature acceptance? *Academy of Management Review* 6: 643–648.

Flood, Robert L., and Michael C. Jackson. 1991. *Creative problem solving: Total systems intervention.* New York: Wiley.

Jackson, Michael C. 1989. Assumptional analysis: An elucidation and appraisal for systems practitioners. *Systems Practice* 2: 11–28.

Jackson, Michael C. 2000. *Systems approaches to management.* Kluwer Academic/ Plenum.

Mason, Richard O., and Ian I. Mitroff. 1981. *Challenging strategic planning assumptions.* New York: Wiley.

PART TWO

CHANGING AND
MANAGING SITUATIONS

Every noble act starts with an impossibility.
    Thomas Carlyle

7

STRATEGIC AREA ASSESSMENT

What are the main innovation potentials of the region?

By which combination of potentials can local and regional stakeholders achieve a maximum leverage effect in changing the development patterns of their area?

How can local and regional stakeholders ensure that the chosen development strategy will be conducive to the sustainable development of the whole territory?

Which strategic priorities may unleash these potentials, and who is taking charge to pursue these common goals?

WHAT IS STRATEGIC AREA ASSESSMENT?

Strategic Area Assessment (SAA) is an instrument for local and regional development. It combines the evaluation of the potential peculiar to a specific local area with identifying the most promising development strategies that leverage innovation. The procedure gathers a broad range of stakeholders, drawing on their specific knowledge, and intensifies their readiness to follow new paths. The main tool used for SAA is called the *innovation compass*. Robert Lukesch developed it inspired by his involvement in an expert team accompanying the implementation of the European Community Initiative for rural development and in a research project for assessing sustainability in regional development (Schleicher-Tappeser et al. 1999).

Since its first appearance in 1999, the innovation compass has been further developed and revised by the author and other users (Lukesch 2009).

The tool helps generate relatively quickly a holistic picture of the development potentials of an area. An area or region can be considered as a complex adaptive system (see Chapter 8) whose prosperity and development are the subject of public concern and often a multitude of support programs. This support is often intended to foster local and regional development by building on potential inside the area and from input from outside. The SAA doesn't just identify and list strengths and weaknesses like a classical Strengths/Weaknesses/Opportunities/Threats (SWOT) analysis, but is based on a systemic understanding of regions and a set of interrelated components. The results of an SAA can be visualized as a cobweb diagram, which identifies the relevant leverage points for innovation.

Strategic Area Assessment can be embedded in a research process, a SWOT analysis, or a participatory strategy building process. The latter is the most recommended way to use this tool, culminating in an SAA conference. The following description relates to this approach.

DETAILED DESCRIPTION OF THE METHOD AND ITS FUNCTIONING
Concept and Structure of the Innovation Compass

The innovation compass is made up of nine components, forming an enneagram (see Figure 7.1).

The nine components are clustered in three triangles, each triangle referring to three different categories. The components and categories were mainly derived from experience, empirical research, and case stories of innovative actions across the whole diversity of European rural areas. They were rearranged until the present configuration somewhat "clicked into place" and turned out to be specifically appropriate when applied in consultancy and evaluation.

The following definitions are used for the three categories and the nine related components:

- *Capital* signifies the natural, economic, and sociocultural endowment of an area.

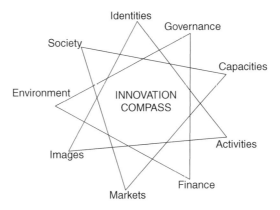

Figure 7.1. Innovation Compass

– *Environment* comprises the nature-borne physical resources as well as human structures such as cultural landscape, built heritage, and settlements.

– *Finance* refers to immaterial and material assets directly expressed as or convertible into monetary value, such as financial capital available to regional stakeholders and entities, immovable property, equipment, place-dependent goodwill, or funding opportunities.

– *Governance* designates the steering structures and processes, the culture and operational modes by which regional authorities, institutions, and local communities accomplish public tasks, how they are linked to larger entities or other territories (regions, nation-states, multilevel governance arrangements), and how they interact with private and civil society actors for managing support to regional development.

Changes in long-term capital usually occur slowly, except for catastrophic shocks.

• *Flows* refer to physical and immaterial resources and potential.

  – *Society* is made up of people, understood from an individual as well as from a collective point of view. People "flow vertically" along the time axis (from birth to death, between generations) and "horizontally" in space (through in- or outmigration and intraregional movements).

- *Markets* signify the actual flow and potential of exchanges of the labor force, financial capital, technology, goods, and services.

- *Capacities* are bound to people (e.g. qualifications), tradable as services (e.g., know-how), or embodied in producer goods (e.g., technology).

Changes in flows underlie shorter cycles than those in capitals, mostly following the ups and downs of macroeconomic and political conditions. Flow components more easily substitute each other than capital components: for example, people (society), goods or services (markets), or licenses (capacities) can be exported to bring money into the region. In the long term, the states of flow components determine the states of the capital components. In other words, flow components ensure the quality and resilience of capital components.

- *Levers* are catalysts influencing the flow components and hence, indirectly, the capital components. Expressed the other way around, capital components shape the context (potential and limits) of lever components.

  - *Identities* designate behavior and communication patterns, cultural identity and "ways to be," the "felt reality" which is often referred to as typical for an area.

  - *Images* are the espoused written or visual representations of reality, present perceptions or future projections of the area, its people, and its destiny, including shared visions and development strategies.

  - *Activities* refer to any endeavor (be it for profit making, self-fulfillment, or social aims) influencing the development of the area and of its subsystems (settlements, enterprises, organizations, communities, families), undertaken by individual people or collective actors from inside or outside the area.

The levers are entry points for change, even rapid change, and their change takes effect on the flow and capital components. To roll up one's sleeves (*Activities*) is one way to change the conditions. Development may take a new turn through a strategy shift in regional policy or a new public *Image* of the area, or if territorial boundaries are redrawn, leading to the emergence of new *Identities*.

The components *Identities* and *Images* are plural terms considering the multiplicity and complexity of ways of life and perceptions that always prevail in a given territory.

The specific shape of the enneagram shows that the components belonging to different categories follow each other periodically. Moreover, there is a distinctive pattern in the respective position of the components. Components on the left side of the innovation compass represent the heritage from the *past*. They are also less likely to be influenced by purposeful action, at least in the short term. The right side of the innovation compass reveals *present* or *future* aspects, which means that they are more easily influenced by rational planning. The upper hemisphere represents *intrinsic* aspects, the lower part *extrinsic* ones.

SAA assumes that it is possible to draw appropriate strategic conclusions on the basis of a diagnosis of an area by using the innovation compass. This assumption is linked to the specific position of the nine components in the enneagram.

Each component is divided into five subcomponents, which means that there are forty-five subcomponents in total (see Figure 7.2).

The SAA tool provides three questions per subcomponent, which amounts to a total of 135 key questions to be worked on and answered by the users, be they local stakeholders, regional development experts, or researchers (Lukesch 2009). For rapid appraisals, the number of questions can be reduced substantially.

How to Organize a Strategic Area Assessment

The SAA is embedded in a process of developing a local or regional strategy. The entire process may last from two to eighteen months. An SAA conference is a key event that occurs between the analysis and implementation phase of a local or regional development program.

In essence the SAA conference is a gathering of local or regional stakeholders under the motto "Diversity beats competence." The quality of the outcome is less determined by bringing together the apparent "gurus" and most brilliant thinkers or even the most powerful people in the area but much more by the diversity and broadness of representatives, from farmers to

Figure 7.2. Innovation Compass: Components and Subcomponents

engineers, mayors, retired persons, and youngsters to sportspeople, artists, entrepreneurs, and public officials. Good facilitation is a key to excellent outcomes. This means

- good knowledge of the instrument and sufficient knowledge of the area in order to be able to connect the cobweb profile to its specificities; and

- mastering "classical moderation tools" (such as integrating all participants, being impartial in case of divergences, communicating respectfully, keeping motivation high, paying attention to time, concisely resuming interim results, highlighting constructive contributions).

There are five steps in an SAA conference. Step 1 starts some time before the conference, and step 5 points beyond its closure. The five steps are as follows:

Step 1: Preparing the SAA conference.

Step 2: Processing the key questions.

Step 3: Making the cobweb diagram.

Step 4: The critical point: drawing conclusions.

Step 5: Pitching the path ahead.

CASE APPLICATION OF STRATEGIC AREA ASSESSMENT

The case relates to an area located in the mountainous region of East Tyrol, Austria. It is predominantly rural and comprises around 50,000 inhabitants who live in small towns and villages. The area is quite remote and has no direct access to a major transit route.

A number of municipalities and other stakeholders (social partners, environmental and cultural initiatives, entrepreneurs, people from the education sector, youth associations, local development initiatives, and others) decided to form a partnership and apply for financial support from the European rural development program LEADER. Funding is granted to local initiatives (so-called Local Action Groups) for area-based strategies and actions. The approach relies on participatory and networking practices in the context of local self-organization. Two major criteria need to be met in order to get funding for a seven-year implementation period:

– To present an appropriate area-based and multisectoral development strategy, via a facilitated participatory process

– To build a consolidated, accountable public-private partnership promoting the development strategy

Prior to the SAA conference, the main proponents of the partnership, with the technical assistance of an inter-communal development agency, organized stakeholder meetings. In addition, the development agency had gathered a host of information, thus providing a rough statistical overview and a SWOT analysis from external experts' point of view.

Step 1: Preparing the SAA Conference

The proponents drew up a list of people from different realms of public, economic, and civic life in the area. This list of about 120 people was well balanced in terms of place, gender, age, profession, political and religious background, profit and nonprofit, public and private activities, active and retired persons, people with specific needs, and other representations. Around ninety people showed up at the conference.

Step 2: Working Through the Key Questions

After a short presentation of the SAA concept and the procedure, the conference participants were subdivided into nine working groups (each one comprising approximately ten people). Each group was assigned, at random, two components of the enneagram to work on. They were asked to nominate a spokesperson who at the same time acted as timekeeper during the rating process.

Each group addressed the thirty key questions relating to their two components (i.e., 3 questions × 5 subcomponents × 2 components). Each question was posed in a way that allowed the answer to be rated along a scale of 1 to 10 (e.g., How attractive is the area for highly qualified workers and managers? Unattractive = 1; Very attractive = 10). The highest score (10) was based either on the area's intrinsic development potential as imagined by the participants, or by comparing the situation with an extrinsic benchmark from another region. The participants were asked to give an appreciation not only of the present situation, but also for the situation ten years ago. For instance, a rating of 9 at present and of 5 ten years ago would have pointed toward a considerable improvement in the recent past. Where consensus was not possible within a group, the scores were averaged and the nature of the disagreement noted on colored cards. The same was done when brilliant ideas or memorable quotes emerged from the group discussions. The average score for each subcomponent was calculated and then these scores averaged for each component. As each of the nine groups had to work on two components, each component was rated by two groups independently. This "double rating" served as a coherence check: if component and subcomponent rates of two groups showed gross differences, the divergent perceptions would have to be examined in more depth. This was not the case, as the results turned out to be astonishingly similar. The spokespersons recorded the rating results back to the plenary. The final cobweb diagram was then drawn up by the facilitator, using the rating results of the nine groups after calculating the definite average for each component.

Step 3: Making Up the Cobweb Diagram

The resulting profile (Figure 7.3) was then displayed on a large sheet of paper. One enneagram showed the appraisal for the present state, and one

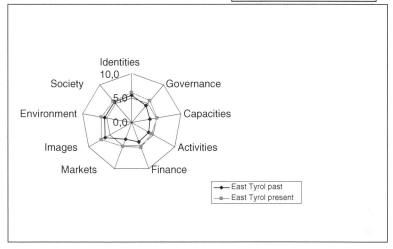

	past	present
Images	6,2	7,1
Environment	5,6	6,2
Society	5,4	5,7
Identities	5,5	6,1
Governance	4,4	5,8
Capacities	3,8	5,2
Activities	4,0	4,5
Finance	4,2	5,4
Markets	3,7	5,2

Figure 7.3. Cobweb Diagram

showed the appraisal for the situation ten years ago. The facilitators also collected the colored cards from the group discussions (with "hot issues," divergent opinions, ideas, and memorable quotes) and clustered them on adjacent pin boards.

Step 4: The Critical Point: Drawing Conclusions

This plenary session marks the turning point from the assessment part to hammering out strategic priorities for innovation. First the cobweb profiles (for the present and for the past) were displayed (see Figure 7.3). Then the debate started for identifying the thematic areas that promised to leverage the development of the areas as a whole. There is no "scientific" approach to judging leverage at this point; it is based on intuition, experience, and conversation.

The SAA offers six rules of thumb for drawing conclusions:

1. *Resource orientation*: the selected strategy should always build on the highest-rated components. In our example, the highest-rated components are *Images, Environment,* and *Identities* (quite typical for an Austrian mountain tourism region).

2. *Completeness*: A well-formed strategy should build on at least one component from each of the three categories (i.e., Capital, Flow, Levers). In our example, *Environment* represents the highest-rated Capital component, *Society* the highest-rated Flow component, and *Images* the highest-rated Lever component.

3. *Symmetry*: The selected strategy should build on components well distributed over the enneagram; in other words, they should not be one-sided. In our example, the highest-rated triplet (*Environment, Society,* and *Images*) is "left-sided." The triplets *Governance, Capacities,* and *Images,* as well as *Environment, Markets,* and *Identities,* are more evenly distributed.

4. *Entrainment*: A component flanked by two components that both feature consistently higher or lower ratings underlies a strong entrainment effect. In our example, the components *Capacities* and *Finance* are expected to exert positive influence on *Activities.*

5. *Equalization (the "triangle effect")*: If two components of the same category feature a similar rating level, the third component of the same category is likely to converge. In our example, the Levers *Identities* and *Images,* both featuring high ratings, would exert positive influence on *Activities.*

6. *Sustainability*: In the long term, the chosen strategies should aim at stabilizing the three Capital components at the highest possible level in order to ensure lasting results.

In this example, three priorities were selected as a result of the discussion in this plenary session:

- Tourism and leisure based on nature adventure and sports (*Environment, Markets, Identities, Images*).
- Economic development through the coordinated promotion of education and vocational training (*Governance, Capacities, Activities*).
- Combining and marketing of typical, ecological regional products (*Environment, Markets, Activities*).

Step 5: Pitching the Path Ahead

After having identified the priorities, participants signed up to new working groups for each priority. They agreed on operational goals and concrete steps for elaborating the detailed strategy in the wake of the SAA conference. The working groups nominated thematic speakers and fixed the dates for further meetings.

After the conference, the local development agency continued supporting the local action group in finalizing their application for cofunding. Eventually, the submission was successful and the group was granted a seven-year budget for its local development plan.

REFLECTIONS ON STRATEGIC AREA ASSESSMENT

SAA is an instrument for local and regional development with the SAA conference as its key event and the innovation compass as its main tool. It is a powerful, time-saving method drawing on what could be called "collective intuition," nurtured by a dynamic mixture between (individual) intuitive knowledge and lively deliberation in small groups as well as in the plenary.

Pros / Advantages

The main advantages of the SAA can be characterized as follows:

- *The tool is "light."* It can be used without much theoretical background but requires group work for unfolding its benefits. The more participants from diverse backgrounds are involved, the better the results will mirror the "collective mental maps" of local and regional people. The number of actors and the required time can be adapted to the purpose.

- *The tool helps save time.* The high redundancy, that is, multiple appearances of some aspects in various questions, produces robust and useful results. It is possible to go through the questions linked to each component quite quickly; some questions can be omitted if they do not make much sense in the respective context.

- *The tool is flexible, though within limits.* The questions are more relevant if they are adapted to the respective context beforehand, for instance, by a small preparative work group. The tool has been applied on a large variety of areas, ranging from 20,000 to 2 million inhabitants, or from 1,000 to 10,000 km².

Cons / Challenges

The preparation, organization, and facilitation of an SAA conference require high attention. The following items should be accordingly taken into consideration to assure a good SAA process.

- According to experience, the minimum number of participants for a valid SAA conference is about thirty people. If the number of participants rises above fifty, there needs be at least two facilitators to ensure quality.
- The group working on the key questions should be diverse and comprise more than five people.
- The time requirement for an SAA conference varies with the number of participants. If there are fewer than fifty participants, one day should be enough, but beyond that the conference should be scheduled for at least one and a half days, and up to two days if the number of participants rises over 150.
- The most critical element is the plenary discussion after presenting the cobweb profiles. In a large plenary (over fifty participants), the discussion can be protracted by unfocused contributions. To avoid that risk, step 4 (drawing conclusions) should be subdivided into three parts:
  - During the first part, the aggregated results and the cobweb profiles are presented in the plenary, with a short debate just for clarifying issues. The participants should be made familiar with the "rules of thumb" for interpretation.
  - During the second part, the plenary should split into smaller groups that discuss the results and bring up different perceptions of the strategic priorities to be selected.
  - In the third part, back in the plenary, the group work results should be condensed into the (two to four) priorities.
- The rules of thumb should be applied pragmatically while discussing the cobweb profile and focus on usefulness. Some terms used in the

questionnaire might seem abstract to the concrete reality of the place. They should therefore be explained if necessary.

- The interpretative discussion in the plenary should not last longer than one and a half hours. The longer it lasts, the more likely that creative tension fades away. The facilitator summarizes the discussion, focusing on a few strategic priorities through the combination of components (triplets or quadruplets).

VARIATIONS

The innovation compass is an open resource tool that can be freely downloaded, used, and further developed by interested people. Variations of SAA exist in central Europe and in Latin American countries, derived from different versions since 1999.

The functional principles of the innovation compass may be transferred to other social systems (e.g., organizations), but this has not been sufficiently tested so far.

NOTE
Our thanks to Robert Lukesch, senior associate of ÖAR Regionalberatung, for permission to draw on his writings and to extract extensively from his paper "Strategic Area Assessment" (2009), which also contains the figures used in this chapter and the 135 questions!

REFERENCES AND FURTHER READING
AEIDL. 1997. *Innovation and rural development*. Rural Observatory Dossier Nr. 2/1997. Published on behalf of the Directorate General Agriculture of the European Commission. Brussels: AEIDL.

AEIDL. 1999. *Territorial competitiveness*. Rural Innovation Dossier 6/1. Published on behalf of the Directorate General Agriculture of the European Commission. Brussels: AEIDL.

Lukesch, Robert. 2009. Strategic area assessment. This paper is available for free download on the Web site of ÖAR Regionalberatung. It contains the most recent (English) version of the innovation compass, including detailed descriptions and a standard template for all 135 key questions. http://www.oear.at/e<->downloads.html. Click on Innovation Compass V5.

Schleicher-Tappeser, Ruggero, Robert Lukesch, Filippo Strati, Gerry Sweeney, and Alain Thierstein. 1999. *Instruments for sustainable regional development*. Final Report of the Research Project INSURED (1996–98), funded from the 4th Research and Development Framework Programme of the European Commission.

8

THE CDE MODEL

What are the conditions that shape a self-organizing process?

What interventions might influence the path and outcomes of a self-organizing process?

COMPLEX ADAPTIVE SYSTEMS AND HUMAN SYSTEMS DYNAMICS

The distinction between complex systems and simple systems has many parents. In modern times, the earliest systems thinkers addressing these issues were probably Norbert Weiner and Warren McColloch, followed by Ilya Prigogine, Per Bak, and Stuart Kauffman. Later came the specific idea of complex adaptive systems (CAS). Complex adaptive systems comprise semi-autonomous agents that interact to form system-wide patterns that are not obvious or predictable from studying the properties of that system. While patterns of behavior will evolve and be recognized, they cannot be predicted by knowing the starting conditions. Complex adaptive systems are said to display self-organization, because there is no central command structure.

Complexity principles are increasingly being applied in management, social research, and evaluation.

Human Systems Dynamics (HSD) was developed in the late 1990s by organizational consultant and systems thinker Glenda Eoyang. While it draws heavily on CAS concepts, it draws on other systems and social theories to broaden its base and encompass common social research approaches to inquiry. One of the unique features of HSD is a means of understanding self-organization through the notion of dimensions that influence the speed, direction, and coherence of self-organizing processes in human systems. These dimensions are containers, differences, and exchanges; together they form the basis of the CDE model. The three systems dimensions used in this book (boundaries, perspectives, and interrelationships) owe a debt to the CDE model.

CONTAINERS, DIFFERENCES, EXCHANGES: THE CDE MODEL

We often complain about constraint. Yet, high levels of agreement and certainty within a system result from constraints that reduce the system's degrees of freedom. We all can, and do, establish constraints by using procedures, rules, and other expectations to attempt to control behavior and interactions. There's nothing inherently wrong with those rules and procedures. I like to be assured that the house I own was built to withstand the 120km/hr wind blowing around my office as I type this chapter. Building regulations—constraints—played a part in that guarantee.

Sometimes, however, we need the system to be less constrained so that it can adapt to an unpredictable environment. When we want a situation to self-organize in that manner, we cannot by definition control every interaction, nor can we predict the result, either at the individual or at the system level.

That does not mean that we have no role in shaping those responses, guiding them toward a desired result. Glenda Eoyang, through her research in organizations, identified three elements that influence how self-organization takes place in a complex adaptive system: containers, differences, and exchanges (CDE) (Eoyang 2007).

In the CDE model, the relative balance of containers, differences, and exchanges determines where a situation lies on the continuum from organized through self-organizing to disorganized. Skillfully used, the model provides insights that enable you to use those elements to influence system change.

DETAILED DESCRIPTION OF THE METHOD

Considering human systems as complex adaptive systems can help us understand in retrospect the patterns that emerged and the developmental path that may have shaped those patterns. Such insight is not sufficient, however, to shape intentional action that affects the dynamics of human systems. In order to influence emergent patterns, we need to know and adjust the conditions that determine the speed, path, and outcomes of self-organizing systems. The CDE Model defines three conditions for self-organizing in human systems.

Containers (C)

A container (C) bounds the system and determines the subset of agents that will interact to form collective patterns that are of interest to us. Any self-organizing system is distinguished from its environment in some way. The physical boundary that distinguishes the system from its surroundings functions as a container during the process of self-organizing.

In an enterprise, we can observe a variety of factors that function as containers. Each management level is a boundary of sorts and generates patterns of systemic behavior over time. Individuals in an organization hold their own histories and identities, making each of them a relatively contained, self-organizing structure. A new initiative can function as a relatively independent, emergent system.

Any human system includes an unknowable number of containers. They may include professional groups, cultural or racial identity groups, groups with shared history, those with seniority, pay grades or scales, and so on. Luckily, dealing with all possible containers is unnecessary; you focus on the most relevant emergent patterns and the containers within which those patterns emerge.

Significant Differences (D)

Difference is the engine that drives self-organizing behavior. Without difference within a container, nothing will happen—entropy rules. Thus difference is a necessary condition for self-organizing to occur. If all of the agents of the system are identical, the difference in the system is too small and no interaction will take place, and no new system-wide patterns will emerge. If the difference in the system is too great, then the system will not be able to sustain connection among the agents, and it will split, or bifurcate.

Differences can be about geography, gender, age, organizational responsibilities, schedules, professional orientations and standards, motivations, political viewpoints, culture—indeed, any difference that matters, that has some significant impact on patterns of behavior. Every container (management levels, individuals, work groups, change initiatives, and so on) includes its own set of significant differences (Eoyang 2007).

Not all configurations of difference in a system generate coherent self-organizing processes. If the difference is too great along one dimension (e.g., age), then the system may bifurcate—split into two—because the container is not sufficiently resilient to hold the system together across it (adolescents vs. adults). If difference cuts across too many dimensions (e.g., age, gender, politics), then the system dissipates energy trying to handle too many potentials simultaneously.

Transforming Exchanges (E)

Significant differences alone, however, are not sufficient for coherent self-organizing processes to occur. If the agents are inert and are not able to connect with each other across the differences, then the potential energy represented by the difference will not be actualized (Eoyang 2001). Any transfer of information, energy, or material between two agents can function as an exchange and bind the parts of the system together into the whole. This interdependence, which is critical to their ability to self-organize into system-wide patterns, is called a transforming exchange (E).

The transforming exchange is a necessary condition for self-organizing processes to occur. If the agents are not connected in a meaningful and transforming way, then the potential of the differences is not actualized—nobody notices—and the container gives way to other competing containers for self-organizing processes.

Language is the most obvious means of transforming exchange between individuals, but many other transfers can serve the purpose as well. Flow of funds, nonverbal signals, and electrical or thermal connections are other examples of exchanges that can be transforming. In human systems, many different exchanges are taking place simultaneously, and each may contribute toward one or another pattern that emerges as the self-organizing process moves through time. Exchanges in a system vary in strength and in number.

For the purposes of self-organization, many relatively weak exchanges can be more productive than a few very strong ones. In some cases, too many exchanges generate confusion, which can be viewed as noise in the system. The rates, paths, and products of self-organizing processes depend on both the number and the strength of the transforming exchanges.

Transforming exchanges alone, however, are not sufficient for coherent self-organizing processes to progress. If the container is too constraining or not constraining enough, the exchanges are random and patterns do not persist. If the differences are below or above the optimal thresholds (determined by the system state at a given time), then the transforming exchanges become redundant, and no new options for transformation present themselves (Eoyang 2001).

Interaction Among C, D, and E

The three conditions are necessary to self-organizing because any system that exists in reality has all three. What would happen if you had a collection of agents that did not exchange any information, material, or energy? Regardless of the boundary around them or their individual characteristics, they would not generate system-wide patterns. What would happen if you had a collection of agents that exchanged information, material, or energy inside a boundary, but all the agents were identical? No new system-wide patterns would emerge. What if you had agents with different characteristics that exchanged information, but there was no condition that held them together over time? No system-wide patterns would develop. In the absence of any one of the conditions, the self-organizing process would not generate new system-wide patterns, so all three of the conditions must be necessary to the self-organizing process (Eoyang 2001).

For example, a team might work within the containers of membership, purpose, and deadline. The team's significant differences might include departmental association, levels of expertise, or professional vocabularies. The transforming exchanges for the team might include e-mails, minutes, and a final report.

While each of the conditions shapes the self-organizing process, each is also shaped by the process as it progresses. As patterns emerge, they exaggerate or weaken the existing containers, differences, or exchanges. These new conditions then affect the future iterations of the self-organizing process. In this way, the self-organizing process changes over time in a dynamical way.

The labels are not fixed and are affected by scale. For instance, a difference at one level in an organization may function as a container at a lower level of organization. For example, differences among teams can influence the dynamics of a department. At the same time, each team functions as a container in which the individual team members' interactions shape the emerging patterns within the team. Conversely, a container at one level may function as a difference at a higher scale. A container is a particular difference that distinguishes one self-organizing system from another.

Transforming exchanges form the mechanism in some circumstances for magnet-like or affinity-like containers. For example, a network of e-mail communications within a team supports transforming exchange, and it can also provide the mechanism by which the team members are held together as a whole system. Being "on the list" or "off the list" may describe the functional container for the team as it emerges.

Along a single dimension (e.g., salary), a transforming exchange will affect the system differently than exchanges between different dimensions. Difference in magnitude along a single dimension usually responds to simple and consistent exchanges between agents. For example, a difference in salary is negotiated through transactions related to compensation only. On the other hand, differences across several dimensions (e.g., professional standing, departmental association, gender, culture, and communication style) all affect the team's dynamics. These usually require more complex and multiple exchange mechanisms.

Because the conditions all affect the self-organizing process of the whole and also affect each other, each of the conditions can compensate in the process of self-organizing for the others. For example, a large container with a low agent density may still be able to self-organize relatively quickly if the transforming exchanges are strong enough and/or if the significant differences are small. On the other hand, a large number of differences and weak exchanges may delay self-organizing processes, regardless of the size of the container. Generally, the size of the container and the differences threshold are inversely proportional to the strength and number of exchanges.

Using the CDE Model

The CDE model is useful because it allows us to observe and influence how future patterns are formed. For example, let's say we choose to integrate two organizational departments in the belief that this will lead to faster decisions, because there will be more resources to draw on. Increasing the size of the organizational container (e.g., widening the role of a department) tends to weaken the exchanges and increase the number of differences in the pattern. In the larger container of an expanded department, old relationships are disturbed and new connections are formed. Because the new exchanges are more numerous and cross a wider range of concerns and interests, individual and systemic behavior are less constrained over time, and emergent patterns are slower to form and less coherent. So our hope that a larger department will be quicker to respond to issues may not be realized.

However, though the CDE model can provide insight into relationships, emergent patterns, and options for action, it cannot be used to predict or control systemic outcomes. The reason is simple. The system is much more complex than any specific CDE description can capture. A systemic description focuses on a small number of containers, differences, and exchanges that appear most relevant to the patterns of interest. In reality, however, conditions considered irrelevant to a particular description can (and frequently do) disrupt anticipated systemic behavior. For instance, toward the end of the following case application, the county board and the county administrator became interested in the assessment project. They were disappointed that community input had not been included in the evaluation process, though the community was not a container that had been considered in the project specifications or ensuing design. This shift in interest from the institution to the community affected how findings were implemented and how subsequent projects were designed in ways that could not have been predicted or controlled (Eoyang 2007).

CASE APPLICATION OF CDE MODEL:
COPE COUNTY REDESIGN

Since the mid-1980s, integration has been the "holy grail" for the delivery of public human and social services in the United States. Many policy makers believed that integrating these services would not only reduce client frustration but also lower costs and improve outcomes because clients could receive a package of services that responded to their unique needs and challenges. In spite of a clear belief in and commitment to integrated services and extensive efforts by states and counties, nonprofits, and business interests during the 1980s and 1990s, few integration programs have been successful. Programs that have succeeded in a limited scope or time frame have proven not to be scalable or sustainable. The experience in Cope County mirrored this national pattern.

Cope County is a large, urban county in the midwestern United States. In January of 2004, six human and social service departments of the county merged into a single Social Services Department (SSD). The purpose of the redesign was to integrate services to improve client outcomes. The newly formed department included 3,000 employees and took responsibility for a comprehensive list of human service functions, including children, adult, and family services; community health; economic assistance; training and employment assistance; and veterans services. Management and governance structures were redefined and a consolidated budget was developed. Almost a year later, in the fall of 2004, senior management decided to assess the progress of the redesign effort. The assessment was to focus on three questions:

- How is the organizational change progressing?
- What recommendations can be made for improving the progress?
- How can we assure that the change supports employees in meeting the needs of clients and communities?

Assessment Design

Because the C, D, and E are causally connected to each other, assessment questions about one of them can reveal information about the state of others. The assessment of the organizational change of Cope County considered five primary containers: management levels, individual employees, service delivery processes, change initiatives, and the department as a whole. Seeing the patterns in terms of the CDE allowed the consultants to identify ways in which the patterns of organizational change had developed and also could be more effective and efficient in the future.

The evaluation posed five questions (one for each container) about either the differences or exchanges that formed patterns within the overall organizational change. The sequencing of the activities was somewhat arbitrary. They could have been completed in any sequence.

Q1 Vertical Alignment (management levels container)
How well are management levels (C) aligned in the factors they consider in decision making (E)?
This focused on exchanges within the container of levels of management. The purpose was to provide insights into the similarities and differences among managers at each level in the organization and between management levels. These connections—between and among levels of power within an organization—provide the capacity to support individuals and processes as an organization undergoes change. Seventy-nine people from four management levels participated in five focus groups to consider the factors that affected the decisions they made.

Q2 Networks of Meaning (individual employees container)
What are individual employees (C) saying about their experiences (D) of the shift to one department?
This articulated the differences among individuals and revealed insights into their methods and modes of exchange. Each employee of the new department was invited to voice insights and concerns by submitting open-ended response to two questions: "What's working in the shift to one department?" and "What's not working in the shift to one department?" These questions focused attention on two critical differences: working/not working and before/after. Of 3,000 employees, 736 submitted responses; most of those were received by anonymous e-mail. Patterns of response were identified by a variety of qualitative methods.

Q3 Horizontal Alignment (service delivery container)
How do the different service delivery processes (C) of the department connect (E) with each other to provide service?
Exchanges between and among work groups as containers were explored to identify the different levels of integration and how integration activities had

changed over the previous year. This elicited information about how different work groups across the department were interacting with each other on a daily basis. Such interactions were the core of integration of services, and the data collected provided a portrait of integration that could be used to identify options for action and to evaluate integration as it progressed. One hundred sixty-two staff members participated in a total of ten focus groups. Data were collected in graphic form as each participant indicated input and output connections for their own work processes and identified interactions that had changed and whether the effect of those changes had been positive, negative, or as yet undetermined.

Q4 Common Language of Change (change initiatives container)
How do projects and initiatives developed for the change process (C)
define their work (D) to implement specific changes?

This focused on the differences between and among change projects across the department and stimulated new exchanges between and among individuals and projects across the department. Change agents from across the department shared their insights, provided an understanding of the types and amounts of change activity currently under way, learned a shared model for the process of emergent change, and celebrated their accomplishments. Rather than arbitrarily defining "change leaders" or centrally selecting persons to be included, managers and supervisors recommended persons who had been involved in or led a change-related project over the previous year. Everyone who was recommended was invited to an event. One hundred individuals attended the one-day session. Data collected included a list of over 150 change-related projects, challenges faced by change agents, and opportunities to improve change processes in the future.

Q5 Internal Documents (whole department container)
What do system-wide communication documents (E) reveal about
the process and depth of the change across the department (C)?

This activity explored the exchanges across the department over the previous year to identify key differences and recommend future communications strategies. This activity examined the ways in which departmental leadership and staff had communicated with each other in writing about the redesign efforts, the integration of services, and the improvement of outcomes for clients. One hundred seven clusters of related documents were reviewed, including official management communications, meeting minutes, newsletter articles, and change initiative reports. The source and audience of each communiqué, in addition to its timing and core messages, were analyzed.

Assessment of Findings

Each component of the assessment generated a rich source of qualitative data about the patterns emerging from the redesign efforts and about the conditions that were or were not facilitating coherent change across the system. At the conclusion of each activity the evaluators completed a preliminary analysis. Summaries of data were then presented to a Redesign Team, who further refined the analyses and provided interpretations from their perspectives of the context and history of the organization. A detailed report of each component was prepared to reflect the data and analysis. The detailed reports were presented to an executive committee at the conclusion of each activity, and interim actions were defined and recommended for immediate implementation based on the findings from each component. Finally, the detailed reports were posted electronically so that all staff had access to the findings from each of the assessment activities. At the end of the project a summary report was produced and distributed. Table 8.1 summarizes these findings.

Through these means of documentation and broadcast reporting, the project not only assessed the conditions (CDE) for self-organizing, it also helped shift the conditions toward different patterns by establishing new containers, differences, and exchanges across the department.

What Patterns Emerged?

Similar patterns appeared to some extent in each one of the five question-based assessments: management levels, individual employees, service delivery processes, change initiatives, and the department as a whole.

Recommendations for action were based on five behavioral rules. These rules were based on the CAS notion that self-organizational behavior is often the result of interacting sets of simple behavioral rules. The V-shaped flight of birds, for instance, is the product of three rules: (1) Fly toward the center. (2) Match the speed of the flock. (3) Don't bump into others. In order to frame

Table 8.1. Summarized Findings

	Container	Differences	Exchanges
Vertical Alignment			
Design	Management levels	Concerns and processes	Decision making
Findings		Focus on tactical rather than strategic decisions Massive concern for involving others Unclear accountability and autonomy	
Networks of Meaning			
Design	Individuals	Key concerns and stories	Essay responses to questions
Findings			25% response rate shows desire to connect Confidentiality concerns Similarities among stories indicate shared discourse Negative essays twice as long as positive essays
Horizontal Alignment			
Design	Work groups	Input and output to processes	Individual mapping
Findings		Matrix map of integrating connections Assessment of new and productive connections Distinctions among more and less integrated functions Dependence on external and internal partners	
Common Language of Change			
Design	Change initiatives	Barriers and successes	Large group training session
Findings			Learning about others' projects Recognizing similar challenges across SSD

(continued)

Table 8.1. (continued)

	Container	Differences	Exchanges
			Celebrating accomplishments
			Recognizing progress Defining a common change process and language about change
Internal Documents			
Design	Department	Audience and message	Formal written discourse
Findings		Intranet as primary medium has limited success Face-to-face contact with supervisors is missing Focus on redesign process rather than outcomes	

SOURCE: Glenda Eoyang. Used with permission.

all the conditions for self-organizing, a complete set of simple rules must define container(s), differences, and exchanges that will contribute to the desired system-wide pattern. The CDE-based assessment identified five potential rules for reshaping the self-organizing processes of Cope County. Although these rules appear very high level, the evaluators' report lists ways in which the rules can be integrated into the department's practice. For more details, see Royce Holladay and Kristine Quade (2008) and Eoyang (2007).

Pattern: Many exciting changes in service process, delivery, and outcomes are already being realized from the redesign.

Rule: *Build success for yourself and others (D)*. This rule focuses on the significant differences (D) needed for the group to further support people toward success in whatever way they choose,

Pattern: Staff members understand and support the vision of integrated service delivery and improved outcomes for clients, but they are anxious and confused because they do not have a clear picture of the path that will lead the department into this different future.

Rule: *Develop people and processes that improve outcomes (D).* This rule acknowledges that there will be different routes to achieve the outcomes and that people's different routes need to be supported.

Pattern: Individuals across the organization are feeling the natural discomfort related to large-scale organizational change. Structural and staffing changes have left individuals feeling disconnected from each other and from the organization.

Rule: *Stay connected (E).* This rule acknowledges that all kinds of exchanges (E) must be supported, including personal and institutional, internal and external, with peers and with management, across silos, and among teams.

Pattern: This new organizational form—beyond silos—presents a new landscape of opportunities and accountabilities. Managers and staff at all levels are unclear about how to develop skills they need to be successful in this new way of working.

Rule: *Learn your way into a shared future (C).* This rule provides the shared glue (C) that holds the organization together. As staff focus on a shared future, they come together across their differences to form a coherent whole.

Pattern: An agile organization requires efficient decision-making processes that use knowledge from all levels of the organization. Today in the department, decision making is slow, concentrated at the top, and not transparent. No process exists to resolve conflicts so that we can move ahead together. As a result, the tremendous adaptive potential of departmental staff has not yet been realized.

Rule: *Decide and trust others to decide (E).* Decisions are key exchanges (E) in bureaucracies, as in other organizations. This rule states the expectation that decisions must be made at appropriate levels, and, once made, the decisions must be executed.

Given the similarity of the patterns, one might ask whether assessment of all five containers was necessary. Though the systemic patterns could be discerned after the fact in data collected from patterns within each container, the five-part design is preferable for a variety of reasons. First, multiple activities allowed the team to triangulate the patterns as they emerged, so a shorter list of more significant patterns could be articulated clearly. Second, each activity involved more and different staff members as integral parts of the assessment effort. This increased sense of engagement was a key outcome of the assessment process. Third, not all of the identified patterns appeared equally strongly in all of the dimensions. Depending on the subset of activities included, one of the major patterns might not have appeared to be significant. Finally, the redesign effort was viewed from a variety of quite distinct perspectives. Data collected and analyzed from any one of these would have been suspect. This diverse and broad-based design helped establish credibility for the findings and commitment to the recommendations.

REFLECTIONS ON THE CDE MODEL

The CDE approach is distinct from standard consulting practice in at least four ways. First, the CDE assessment design makes the emergent patterns manifest, so that everyone involved in the project is able to see and name them. Second, participants can see underlying dynamics that could inform their work in a wide variety of contexts. Third, patterns can be captured at multiple levels of analysis (management levels, individuals, service delivery processes, change initiatives, and department-wide). Fourth, the CDE model describes dynamical relationships that lead to recommendations for action to shift self-organizing patterns as they emerge (Eoyang 2007).

Reflecting on the use of the CDE model, Holladay and Quade (2008) make the following points:

The CDE model is applicable in organized, self-organized and unorganized situations. For instance:

- In organized situations, the Eoyang CDE can help you find ways to invigorate and rejuvenate the organization by decreasing constraints in the C, the D, or the E.

- In self-organizing situations, the Eoyang CDE can be used to help shift the conditions toward greater adaptability by shifting the C, D, or E appropriately.

- In unorganized situations, the Eoyang CDE will help you find ways to organize the random unpredictability that exists due to the level of constraint, helping to influence the conditions that will lead to self-organization.

However, there are some traps. Tips for avoiding them follow.

When using a CDE analysis to design an intervention, it is easy to come up with a number of ways to intervene. How do you decide which one to use? The answer is to pick the simplest one first and try it and see how it works. There is no secret or special way to know what to do—just do it, and then watch for results.

When the CDE analysis reveals that a particular challenge is focused in one of the conditions, try an intervention in a different area. For example, if the difficulty emerges as an exchange problem, try a difference intervention or try shifting the container. Sometimes individuals will resist change that seems to be "attacking" or in judgment of what exists, and going to a different condition may alleviate that resistance. Additionally, a subset of a system can establish patterns to sustain itself, in spite of the overall needs of the system. These patterns set up a self-perpetuating effect in the system that make specific conditions difficult to shift. By moving to another condition, you bypass the resistance.

Identify the containers that you wish to observe, influence, or change, then identify the differences and exchanges within that single, identified container. Thinking of two containers at once will make the task appear more complicated than it has to be.

Because your issues may be massively entangled across levels in the organization, what appears as a difference at one level will be a container at another level. For example, if you are looking at all the people in the organization as the container, then a difference that could make a difference would be "experience." However, if you are looking at all the experienced people in the organization, then experience becomes the container, and "degree or level of expertise" could become a difference that matters.

When you shift one condition, the resultant change will likely be fast, so be ready to move.

When you shift one condition, it will impact all the others, so you don't have to do all three at once. You can change one condition and then observe how the others adjust. Because these changes happen quickly, the cycle time is short, and the next attempt to shift one of the conditions can be based on the results of the last shift.

If the sticky issue is occurring at one place in the organization, try an intervention at the level either above or below. For example, if a team is interacting in unhealthy ways, look at what management is asking of the team, how management is interacting, and/or how the individuals are functioning in getting their jobs done.

A caveat: There is a tendency to use exchange interventions first because we know them best, but other conditions may be more effectively shifted.

NOTE

Our thanks to Glenda Eoyang for permission to draw on her PhD dissertation and other work; to the American Evaluation Association and EdgePress for permission to extract from *Systems Concepts in Evaluation: An Expert Anthology*; and to Royce Holladay and Kristine Quade for permission to quote from *Influencing Patterns for Change: A Human Systems Dynamics Primer for Leaders*.

REFERENCES AND FURTHER READING

Eoyang, Glenda. 1996. *Coping with chaos: Seven simple tools.* Circle Pines, MN: Lagumo.
Eoyang, Glenda. 2001. *CDE model: Conditions for self-organizing in human systems.* Unpublished doctoral dissertation. Cincinnati: The Union Institute and University.
Eoyang, Glenda. 2007. Human Systems Dynamics: Complexity-based approach to a complex evaluation. In *Systems concepts in evaluation: An expert anthology*, ed. Bob Williams and Iraj Imam, 123–139. Point Reyes, CA: EdgePress / American Evaluation Association.
Holladay, Royce, and Kristine Quade. 2008. *Influencing patterns for change: A Human Systems Dynamics primer for leaders.* Minneapolis, MN: CreateSpace.
HSD Institute Web site. http://www.hsdinstitute.org.

9

ASSUMPTION-BASED PLANNING

What are the key assumptions underpinning the achievement of a plan?

What can be done to assure that these assumptions are sustained?

What can be done to make the plan more robust to assumption failure?

THE PRINCIPLES

Assumption-Based Planning (ABP) helps an organization to prepare for changes in its environment that could disrupt its plans. It is systemic because it explores the interrelationships, perspectives, and boundaries of an established plan to ensure the viability of that plan.

ABP was developed by the RAND Corporation to help the U.S. Army with its mid- and long-range planning in uncertain environments.

The method lies somewhere between planning and strategy and in some ways addresses Henry Mintzberg's comment that most strategic planning processes result in bad plans and poor strategy. It is based on the idea that plans fail because inadequate attention is paid to monitoring a plan's underlying assumptions. All plans contain assumptions—but those assumptions are unstable. Some assumptions are correct, some assumptions are incorrect, and some assumptions become correct or incorrect during the period of a plan. Like many assumption-oriented methods (see Chapters 2, 6, or 16), ABP identifies key assumptions and closely monitors them over time. What makes ABP unique is the way it actively protects the plan from assumption failures.

DETAILED DESCRIPTION OF THE METHOD

There are five steps to ABP (see Figure 9.1):

1. Identify Important Assumptions

An *assumption* is an assertion about some characteristic of the past, present, or future that underlies a plan. Locating assumptions is not always easy; implicit assumptions are especially hard to identify—but are often the most important.

An assumption is *important* or *load-bearing* if its negation would lead to significant changes in a plan. The importance of assumptions is commonly judged along two dimensions, certainty of the assumption being justified and influence of the assumption on the plan (see Chapter 6, "Strategic Assumption Surfacing and Testing," and Chapter 16, "Scenario Technique"). Important assumptions tend to be high on influence and low on certainty. The importance is further refined in step 2.

2. Identify Vulnerabilities of Assumptions

There are three activities in this step. The first sets the planning time horizon (e.g., one year, fifty years). This is an important and often ignored component because it sets the boundaries of vulnerability of an assumption. You may not be interested if an assumption is vulnerable over a decade if your planning horizon is only three years.

To find out which assumptions may be vulnerable within the planning time horizon, you next identify elements of change in the environment that could happen within the time horizon and thus nullify the assumption. An *element of change* is an event or condition that

- represents a change from today;
- is plausible within the planning horizon;
- is related to the situation and the plan.

The third activity is to identify the vulnerabilities. These are assumptions that will be invalid if the elements of change occur. There can be more than one way in which a single assumption can become invalid.

You end up with a series of vulnerable assumptions and "elements of change" pairings (see Table 9.1 in the case application). It is easy to have a

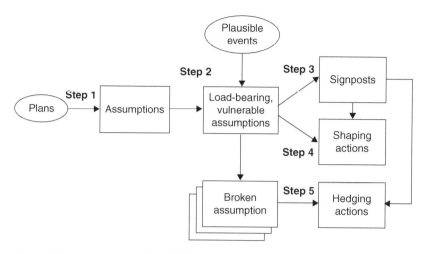

Figure 9.1. Assumption-Based Planning Steps
SOURCE: James A. Dewar, *Assumption Based Planning: A Tool for Reducing Avoidable Surprises* (Cambridge: Cambridge University Press, 2002).

long shopping list of pairings, and how many to carry forward to the next stage is a judgment call. Some assessment of risk, impact, and ranking may be useful.

3. Define Signposts

ABP is designed to plan within futures that contain important uncertainties. Despite these uncertainties, it is possible to erect *signposts* that indicate that the status of the assumption is changing. Signposts are mechanisms for monitoring the uncertainties in an organization's future and help an organization perform shaping and hedging actions (see steps 4 and 5). The signposts generally flow from the "elements of change" statements.

It is critical to ensure that the signposts clearly indicate that an assumption is becoming vulnerable. It is also important that the signposts associated with an assumption are as accurate and unambiguous as possible—which is not always an easy task with some assumptions.

4. Define Shaping Actions

A *shaping action* is an action designed to take control of the uncertainty. These actions, if successful, guarantee that the plan remains unmodified. Shaping actions steer events either toward the maintenance of the assumption or to prevent an assumption-threatening situation to occur (see Taking Shaping and Hedging Actions below). Most often these shaping actions are externally focused, seeking to influence the environment rather than the organization.

5. Define Hedging Actions

A *hedging action* is more internally focused, helping prepare an organization to cope with an assumption failure.

Hedging actions help an organization preserve important options despite the possibility that an assumption will fail at a certain point. Arriving at a hedging action is based on rethinking the organization's plans as though an important assumption had already failed. Often this is best done by visioning or scenario approaches (see Chapter 16), where those in the organization can imagine situations where the assumption had failed.

A hedging action is different from a shaping action because it involves re-planning. These plans can make the organization less vulnerable to assumption failure or can create backup plans should failure occur. Hedging actions, however, must be both relevant to the scenario they seek to address and feasible (i.e., within the organization's existing capacity).

A. J. Dewar, Carl H. Builder, William M. Hix, and Morlie H. Levin (1993) warn against constructing too many scenario and too many hedging actions. For instance, if there were five assumption and "elements of change" pairs, it is theoretically possible to have over 3,000 different combinations of pairs for which to develop hedging actions. Step 5 then becomes a mess of options. In practice, Dewar et al. consider that you can identify strong hedging actions by considering one action for each pair rather than for combinations of pairs. So if you have five assumption and "elements of change" pairs, you would consider only five sets of hedging actions—one set for each pair. Another suggested coping strategy is similar to the strategy for assumption prioritization in Strategic Assumption Surfacing and Testing (see Chapter 6), balancing the risk of ignoring the assumption with the likely cost of developing a hedging or shaping action.

An important issue to consider is that poorly executed hedging actions can undermine shaping actions. Dewar et al. (1993) give the example of being cornered by a wild animal. An appropriate shaping action is to hold your ground and look fierce, but this can be negated by the perfectly reasonable hedging action: slowly backing away.

Taking Shaping and Hedging Actions

Dewar et al. (1993) suggest posing three questions when deciding whether to take a shaping or hedging action in the near future:

1. How soon could the assumption fail?
2. How easily can the violation be foreseen?
3. How much time will be required for an action associated with the violation to be realized?

Based on the answers, two sets of hedging and shaping actions can be determined, one short term and the other longer term.

CASE APPLICATION OF ASSUMPTION-BASED PLANNING

ABP was used by RAND to assist the U.S. Army in its long-range planning by providing an alternative to the army's tradition of using trend analysis. Trend analysis was felt to be too dependent on the assumption that you can predict the future using current trends. (You could consider therefore that adopting ABP was a hedging action against the failure of this assumption!) This case application summarizes the work RAND undertook on the AirLand Battle–Future Umbrella Concept (ALB-F) (Dewar et al. 1993).

Identify Important Assumptions

The team identified twenty-three assumptions that underlined the ALB-F: fifteen explicit and eight implicit assumptions. The key assumptions included the following:

1. The army will continue to play a primary role in maintaining global stability.
2. The United States will have at least rough parity in surveillance assets, long-range weaponry, and mobility.
3. Most army operations will be covered by ALB-F.
4. The long-range systems will be militarily effective.

Identify Vulnerabilities of Assumptions

The time horizon was set to twenty-five to thirty years (i.e., up to 2020 from the baseline of 1990). Participants were asked to imagine they had been asleep for thirty years and on waking up could ask ten questions about that world. Using Delphi technique, participants came up with the elements of change that could be the basis of a future world scenario (Table 9.1).

Define Signposts

From the above list of assumptions, four separate scenarios were developed and explored. Each scenario assumed that one of the assumptions had been wrong. Signposts identified how you would know that the assumption had been wrong. For instance, in terms of the military effective-

Table 9.1. Potential Elements of Change

Question	Element of change/Assumption
Is the United States still maintaining the role of world policeman, either unilaterally or predominantly?	The Army will continue to play a primary role in maintaining global stability
Has the United Nations become a cohesive body with sufficient military capacity to enforce sanctions?	
Is there a nation with a military force that could be construed as a threat to the United States or its national policy?	The United States will have at least rough parity in surveillance assets, long-range weaponry, and mobility
Is there a competitive military superpower that can destroy the United States?	
Did the Army take on more domestic missions?	The predominance of Army operations will be covered by ALB-F
Are there any severe threats to the global environment that could lead to US intervention for protection of the environment?	
Have there been substantial breakthroughs in weapons, propulsion, and transportation technologies? Are projectile weapons still the predominant force on the battlefield?	The long-range systems will be militarily effective

SOURCE: James A. Dewar, Carl H. Builder, William M. Hix, and Morlie H. Levin, "Assumption-Based Planning: A Planning Tool for Uncertain Times" (RAND Corporation, 1993), http://www.rand.org/pubs/monograph_reports/2005/MR114.pdf.

ness of long-range weapons, signposts included the development of conflicts that required more hand-to-hand encounters. In terms of the United States' key role in sustaining global stability, a signpost for that assumption being incorrect was the emergence of a strong, independent UN peacekeeping force.

Define Shaping Actions

Shaping actions were easier in those scenarios where the army had a degree of control. For instance, in terms of keeping parity, army investment in research and development is clearly an effective shaping action. For those scenarios over which the army had little control (e.g., global stability), it wasn't possible to identify strong shaping actions.

Define Hedging Actions

For each of the four key assumptions, further scenarios were built around each negated assumption. Then hedging strategies were developed for each. For instance, in terms of the United States losing its primary role in global security, scenarios were developed that raised the possibility of the army becoming more involved in domestic affairs (e.g., drug control, civil disobedience, border control) and taking a minor role in international peace keeping. Thus hedging actions were conceived that reorganized the army into a series of small combat forces that could have greater flexibility and impact on the international scene, while building a large but well-trained "reserve" force that could be rapidly deployed on domestic issues. Since these were all areas over which the army had some control, shaping actions were developed to help bring about these hedging actions (highlighting the somewhat recursive nature of ABP).

REFLECTIONS ON ASSUMPTION-BASED PLANNING

Dewar et al. (1993) consider ABP to be most effective when a plan is largely complete. In the early stages of a plan there are simply too many options and uncertainties. Since "choices" are a good source of assumptions, they argue that there is little point in using ABP until those choices have been decided. ABP is really what you do when you have a plan.

According to Dewar (2002), the strengths and weaknesses of ABP are:

Pros / Advantages

ABP works well in very uncertain times. For the simple reason that in certain times assumptions are likely to be more stable.

ABP generates relevant scenarios systematically. Dewar argues that in most scenario planning, scenarios are not generally "complete"; they do not cover all the organization's planning challenges. However, he states that the focus of ABP on load-bearing and vulnerable assumptions "provides greater confidence that the most important scenarios have been considered.

ABP ties actions to specific assumptions. All organizations perform "shaping" and "hedging" actions; however, in ABP these are linked to specific assumptions. Thus, as the assumptions change, the implications for action are more obvious.

ABP relates to any and all plans. All plans contain important assumptions that can be risky if they fail.

Cons / Challenges

ABP requires an initial plan or concept. ABP is a post-planning process. Although most actions are informed by assumptions, they may be fleeting. A plan has some form of commitment over time—and thus hedging and shaping actions have more impact.

ABP produces fragments, not complete strategies. ABP has no means of synthesizing the helping and shaping actions. The actions are determined on the basis of individual assumptions, not on any overall comprehensive strategy. Hedging and shaping actions can reinforce each other or can work against each other. For instance, Dewar gives the example of a plan to develop environmentally friendly transport. A shaping action that advertised electric vehicles as the *only* sensible solution to energy and environmental concerns would be contradicted by a hedging action that continued research on fuel-cell and hybrid alternatives to electric vehicles. From a planning standpoint, both of these are plausible and rational actions. Together, however, they ruin the coherence of the overall strategy by potentially working against each other.

ABP handles threats better than opportunities. ABP in its traditional form is fundamentally about seeking out and avoiding risks of failure. It has little

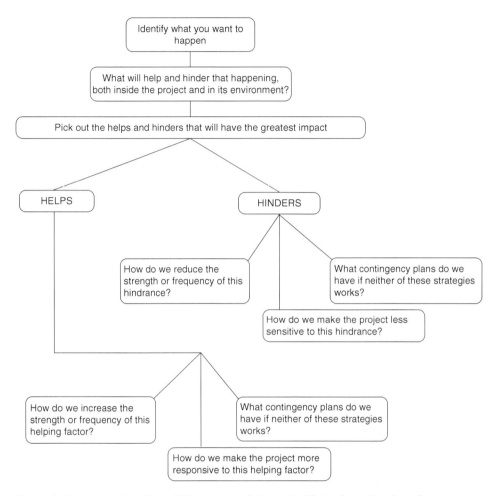

Figure 9.2. Assumption-Based Planning and Force Field Analysis Combined

to say about promoting opportunities, even though those opportunities also contain assumptions. Bob Williams's modification of ABP specifically addresses this issue (see Variations and Modifications below).

You cannot ensure that all load-bearing assumptions have been identified by ABP. When acting in uncertain times and within unknowable environments, you can never be absolutely sure that you have identified all your key assumptions. Plans always have unintended or unanticipated consequences when they are enacted. However, combining ABP with other methods—

including those in this book—can help explore these unknown and unknowable regions.

VARIATIONS AND MODIFICATIONS
In order to address some of the weaknesses of ABP, especially the difficulty some people have in identifying assumptions and the "risk" rather than "opportunity" orientation of ABP, Bob Williams developed a variation of ABP that incorporates ideas from Force Field Analysis. Force Field Analysis was developed by Kurt Lewin as a means of judging the relative importance of forces that push you toward a goal or away from a goal. It is a simple notion that has been hugely influential in the planning, organizational development, and social science fields (see Figure 9.2).

Notice how this modification reframes the "hedging" and "shaping" actions to make options for helping or hindering plan achievement more explicit.

NOTE
Our thanks to the RAND Corporation for permission to use material from "Assumption-Based Planning: A Planning Tool for Uncertain Times."

REFERENCES AND FURTHER READING
Dewar, James A. 2002. *Assumption Based Planning: A tool for reducing avoidable surprises.* Cambridge: Cambridge University Press.
Dewar, James A., Carl H. Builder, William M. Hix, and Morlie H. Levin. 1993. Assumption-Based Planning: A planning tool for uncertain times. RAND Corporation. http://www.rand.org/pubs/monograph_reports/2005/MR114.pdf.
Williams Bob. A Strategic Planning Tool. http://users.actrix.co.nz/bobwill/abp.pdf.

10

CYNEFIN

How are we framing the situation: as simple, complicated, complex, or chaotic?

What are the implications of this framing for how we manage a situation?

What are appropriate ways of managing a situation on the basis of this framing?

WHAT IS CYNEFIN?

Management theory and practice in the past few decades have often factionalized into two distinct camps. There are those who seek to treat all situations as if they were simple irrespective of the actual nature of the situation (e.g., results-based management, management by objectives). Then there are those who regard everything as complex, notably those influenced by complexity theory.

More recently, a third way has evolved: those who argue that managing everything as if it were simple is ineffective, and managing everything as if it were complex is inefficient. Cynefin is an example of this more recent trend.

Developed by David Snowden and Cynthia Kurtz when they were at the IBM's Institute of Knowledge Management, Cynefin identifies four behaviors a situation can display: simple, complicated, complex, and chaotic. This terminology is not new; the systems literature has used it for decades. However, in Cynefin the behaviors and the properties that underpin these four states are not entirely drawn from systems theories or even theories of chaos and complexity. Cynefin draws heavily on network theory, learning theories, and third-generation knowledge management.

Crucially, compared with many network and complexity approaches, Cynefin also takes an epistemological as well as an ontological stance. Similar to the Soft Systems and Critical Systems traditions (see Chapters 14 and 19), Cynefin explores how people perceive and learn from situations. So, for instance, an ontologically "complicated" aspect of a situation could be seen, epistemologically, by you as simple and by me as complex. Our different framing provides different but valid ways to manage the situation. More on that later.

DETAILED DESCRIPTION OF THE METHOD

According to the Cynefin model, every situation has structural elements that display behaviors on a continuum between "order" and "chaos" (see Figure 10.1).

However, in practice this apparent continuum hides four different structural relationships that Snowden draws primarily from network theory (Kurtz and Snowden 2003):

> *Simple* aspects of a situation have weak connections *between* elements but a strong link to a central control element. This is a classic command-and-control scenario. These aspects are sometimes referred to as the "known" aspects of a situation.

> *Complicated* aspects of a situation have strong connections *between* elements, but each element still has strong links to a central controlling element. These aspects are sometimes referred to as the "knowable" aspects of a situation.

> *Complex* aspects of a situation have strong connections between elements but no central controlling element: a classic distributed network.

> *Chaotic* aspects of a situation have weak connections *between* elements and no centralizing organizing core.

Thus two dimensions emerge, one about centrality (weak/strong) and one about connectivity (weak/strong). The framework is often displayed in the form illustrated in Figure 10.2.

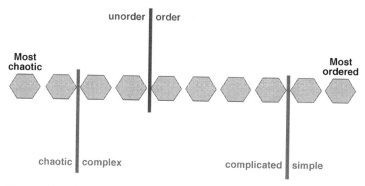

Figure 10.1. Continuum Between Order and Chaos
SOURCE: Brian Donaldson (Donaldson Associates) and Shankar Sankaran (University of Technology, Sydney, Australia).

Simple Aspects of a Situation

The emphasis on centrality and the relative looseness between connections implies the following:

- Clarity of dynamics. Anyone can see the things the way they are.
- Very simple linear patterns of cause and effect. If I do X, then Y will almost certainly happen. Predictability depends on knowing X and what you are doing with it.
- Things are "known." There is a known right answer within the current context.

Take a small school in an isolated rural area. It has been left money by a wealthy benefactor to provide a library. The library building needs a concrete floor, a corrugated iron roof, and wood-framed walls, exactly the same as all the other building in the village, many of which were built by their occupants. The construction of the block is thus a simple exercise, building on the known knowledge and expertise within the village.

Complicated Aspects of a Situation

The influence of centrality is offset somewhat by the tightness between the elements. This implies the following:

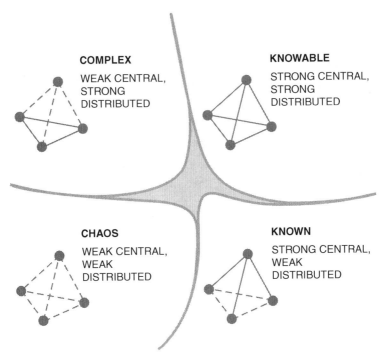

Figure 10.2. Cynefin Framework
SOURCE: Cynthia F. Kurtz and David J. Snowden, "The New Dynamics of Strategy: Sense-Making in a Complex and Complicated World," *IBM Journal of Research and Development* 42, no. 3 (2003): 462–483. Reproduced with permission of IBM and Cognitive Edge.

- The situation is "knowable." While the center may not have all the answers, answers are accessible via the strong network links between elements.
- The relationship between cause and effect can be known from the input and the detail. Y is predictable if you know X and the details of the relationships between the elements.
- Effects may be separated from causes in time and space.
- Expertise is important because knowledge of how to exploit the network is important. Indeed, Snowden sometimes calls this the zone of the expert.

To return to the school library, although members of the village have the knowledge and skills to construct the building, there are matters that require some external expert help. There are building regulations to be followed as well as conditions laid down by the education authorities. Moreover, local people have very little idea of what a modern library facility can offer; few have actual experience of libraries, and even they recognize that libraries are more than just books these days. But the answers are out there somewhere—it's a matter of finding them.

Complex Aspects of a Situation

Since there is little centralized force, the nature of the strong interrelationships between elements implies the following:

- Behavior is highly context dependent.
- Behavior is highly dependent on the starting conditions. Different starting conditions will result in different behaviors.
- The nature of the interrelationships can be determined only during or after the event. X may result in Y or Z or A, but you will be unable to predict which outcome on the basis of knowing X or any of the details.
- The key to understanding what might be going on is by observing patterns of behavior over time rather than single results.

One of the terms of the gift is that the library, although based in the school grounds, will be freely accessible to all members of the village and anyone else who is passing through the area. Although the school has some experience of community use of facilities, the degree of access required under the gift breaks new ground, locally and indeed elsewhere. There is a rich brew of issues: security, safety, management, access, finance, control, participation, standards, religious beliefs, and others—all of which interlink in ways that nobody can work out in advance.

Chaotic Aspects of a Situation

Chaos means there are no patterns that can be observed, no previous experience to rely on. The weak relationships between elements of the situation and the absence of any centralizing core means almost anything can happen for almost any reason. For instance, the gift is located in a bank that defaults

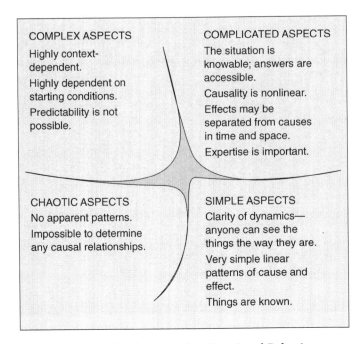

COMPLEX ASPECTS

Highly context-dependent.

Highly dependent on starting conditions.

Predictability is not possible.

COMPLICATED ASPECTS

The situation is knowable; answers are accessible.

Causality is nonlinear.

Effects may be separated from causes in time and space.

Expertise is important.

CHAOTIC ASPECTS

No apparent patterns.

Impossible to determine any causal relationships.

SIMPLE ASPECTS

Clarity of dynamics— anyone can see the things the way they are.

Very simple linear patterns of cause and effect.

Things are known.

Figure 10.3. Cynefin Framework—Situational Behaviors
SOURCE: Modified from Cynthia F. Kurtz and David J. Snowden, "The New Dynamics of Strategy: Sense-Making in a Complex and Complicated World," *IBM Journal of Research and Development* 42, no. 3 (2003): 462–483.

during construction of the building. This was unexpected. What can be done? Who will pay the outstanding bills? No one knows—at least immediately— but some response is necessary.

These four aspects are summarized in Figure 10.3.

Cynefin as a Tool for Managing Situations

Cynefin provides a number of strategies for intervention. We describe three: one focused on interrelationships, one focused on perspectives, and one focused on boundaries.

INTERRELATIONSHIPS: MANAGING EFFECTIVELY

Cynefin suggests four main strategies for managing interrelationships, each strategy corresponding with simple, complicated, complex, and chaotic aspects of the situation (see Figure 10.4).

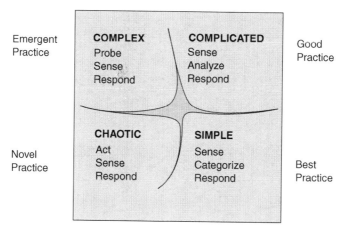

Figure 10.4. Cynefin Framework—Appropriate Responses
SOURCE: Modified from Cynthia F. Kurtz and David J. Snowden, "The New Dynamics of Strategy: Sense-Making in a Complex and Complicated World," *IBM Journal of Research and Development* 42, no. 3 (2003): 462–483.

Simple Aspects

The most appropriate ways of managing simple aspects of a situation are the following:

1. Sense (i.e., collect sufficient data to identify the characteristics of this aspect of a situation)

2. Categorize (i.e., identify where these characteristics fit within the known world)

3. Respond (i.e., pick the proven appropriate response to that category)

Thus "best practice" (i.e., context-free application of methods from one situation to another) is the most effective, efficient, and efficacious approach to managing such situations.

To return to the school again:

Sense: What is required is a cement floor, corrugated iron roof, and wood frame structure.

Categorize: There are many examples of this construction in the village, and a lot of skill around in building them. Errors in the construction are easily identified and corrected.

Respond: Members of the village community build the library.

Complicated Aspects

In management terms, influence and a degree of predictability are possible; while the center may not "know" and thus control, it is able to exploit the strong networks to assess what the appropriate responses are. Thus:

1. Sense (i.e., collect sufficient data to identify the characteristics of this aspect of a situation)

2. Analyze (i.e., get the networks to find out the information and use expertise to evaluate and choose the most appropriate means of response on the basis of that information)

3. Respond (i.e., pick the most appropriate response to that category)

Thus "good practice" (i.e., context-modified application of methods from one situation to another) is the most effective, efficient, and efficacious approach to managing such situations.

In terms of the design of the library:

Sense: The relationships between the various regulations are not locally known, but there are experts who can provide advice. There are many different views about what constitutes a modern library but plenty of experience and views about this.

Analyze: Identify the people and other information sources that provide the necessary advice on how to handle all the regulations.

Respond: Apply this knowledge and expertise to the local situation. Establish a consultative process about options for the library. Choose between the various options based on expert opinion and drawing on other networks of information.

Complex Aspects

In terms of seeking to handle such situations (*manage* is not really the appropriate term), it is wise to tread cautiously and to evaluate constantly. Snowden and Boone (2007) suggest several strategies:

- Keep discussion open.
- Set clear boundaries within which the elements can operate and self-organize.

- Stimulate attractors to help improve centrality.
- Encourage dissent and diversity—they improve the ability to spot patterns emerging.
- Be very careful about starting conditions and monitor for emergence.

Thus:

1. Probe. Kurtz and Snowden (2003) have this to say: "Decision making creates probes to make the patterns or potential patterns more visible before taking action. We can then sense those patterns and respond by stabilizing those patterns that we find desirable, by destabilizing those we do not want, and by seeding the space so that patterns we want are more likely to emerge. *Emergent* practice (i.e., practice in this situation emerges from experiments within this situation)."

2. Sense (i.e., collect sufficient data to identify the patterns of behavior that could be attributable to the probe).

3. Respond (i.e., on the basis of what seems to be the right thing to do to enhance the patterns that are deemed to be "good" and dampen down the patterns that are deemed to be "bad"). Thus this domain calls for emergent practice.

In terms of exploring what an open access library means in practice:

Probe: Try two or three strategies or combinations of strategies— volunteer staffing, paid staffing, pass key access, timetabled access, access controlled via the local store.

Sense: Watch the results, spot the patterns that emerge, and see what works best for whom.

Respond: Build on what works, avoid what did not, and continue probing and sensing.

Chaotic Aspects

Kurtz and Snowden (2003) suggest three strategies when confronted with chaotic aspects of a situation claim that the appropriate response to chaotic situations is essentially to assert a strong central attractor, hold your breath and see if it does any good, and then make an appropriate response to that.

Thus:

1. Act (i.e., a strong response designed to shock that aspect of the situation back into some form of order, or at the very least triage to staunch the bleeding)

2. Sense

3. Respond

Chaotic Response

In terms of the bank collapse:

Act: Stop work and pay no bills.

Sense: Observe what happens (e.g., bank gets a bailout, creditors seek outstanding money).

Respond: Depending on what happens and in which order, move cautiously.

Relationship Between Simple and Complex

It is easy to be complacent about simple aspects of a situation. Everything is known, everything is predictable. In fact, Snowden deliberately placed this category next to "chaos" in the Cynefin quaternary. Closer inspection will reveal why.

A simple situation has a centralizing force with weak relationships between elements. Remove that centralizing force, and you are left with a situation that has only weak interrelationships—the condition of chaos. The necessary strong interrelationships between elements that characterize the complicated and complex zones cannot be achieved overnight (and provision for this possibility is often strongly discouraged in purposefully simple systems). In the absence of those interdependencies, a simple situation has only one direction to go: into chaos.

The community knows how to build the library. It has done similar things before many times. It is simple. And then part of the building collapses. What had been until then a simple situation, the removal or collapse of the central focus or attractor, the central authority (i.e., local knowledge), tips the situation not into complicated or even complex zones but into chaos. What made it collapse? Could more collapse? Is the insurance adequate? No one knows, at least immediately, thus destroying the centralized notion of adequate community skill. That self-confidence in community skill will take time to rebuild (i.e., make complicated) or develop (i.e., treat as complex).

Perspectives: Ontology and Epistemology

So far Cynefin has been described as an essentially ontological tool; in its own terms a process of sensing, categorizing different aspects of "real life" behavior, and responding accordingly. However, Cynefin in practice has a strong epistemological orientation. The critical point about the Cynefin framework is not that "real life" necessarily behaves according to the four domains, but that these domains provide us with a framework for explaining and making sense of behavior.

Frequently, when using the Cynefin framework, different people put the same aspect of a situation into different domains. That means they are observing and making sense of the situation in different ways. Both may well be correct (indeed, soft system [see Chapter 14] considers that perspectives help determine the dynamics of a situation). Managing this is a matter of allowing both framings to enter into a dialectic—instead of working out which one is "right," allowing both to be right, and the solution to any problems associated with that situation emerge from that debate. Cynefin provides two ways of addressing this dialectic.

One is best highlighted by an example. During a workshop focused on resolving issues of rural elder care, the same aspect of the situation was placed in both the complex and the complicated zones by different people. When looking at it, one person turned to another and said, "*That's* why we are disagreeing with each other over how to handle this issue. You see it as complex and I see it as complicated. Let's talk about that." In other words, part of the problem they were experiencing was that they were imagining the same aspect from two different understandings of what was going on. And this, in part, explained why they were having difficulty resolving or managing the situation: "Oh, so you were managing it as if it were complicated, and I was managing it as if it were complex—no wonder we were clashing over strategies." In this particular case, the two protagonists were able to come up with a means of resolving the issue from both perspectives (see Figure 10.5).

The second way is by adding what Kurtz and Snowden (2003) call "the fifth domain": the domain of disorder.

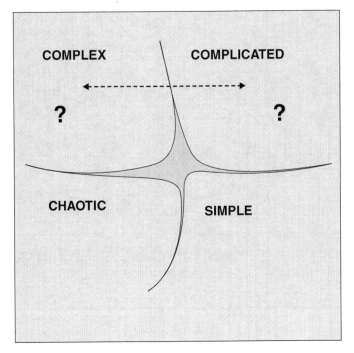

Figure 10.5. Cynefin Framework—Perspectives
SOURCE: Modified from Cynthia F. Kurtz and David J. Snowden, "The New
Dynamics of Strategy: Sense-Making in a Complex and Complicated World," *IBM
Journal of Research and Development* 42, no. 3 (2003): 462–483.

Take a look at the diagrams in this chapter, and you will notice a gray area
in the middle. This is a domain of disorder. Snowden argues that this domain
is critical to understanding conflict among decision makers looking at the
same situation from different points of view.

Kurtz and Snowden (2003) state:

Often in a group using the Cynefin framework, people agree on what the ex-
tremes of the four domains mean in the context they are considering, but disagree
on more subtle differences near the centre of the space. . . . As a result, individuals
compete to interpret the central space on the basis of their preference for action.
Those most comfortable with stable order seek to create or enforce rules; experts
seek to conduct research and accumulate data; politicians seek to increase the
number and range of their contacts; and finally, the dictators, eager to take advantage of a chaotic situation, seek absolute control. *The stronger the importance of
the issue, the more people seem to pull it towards the domain where they feel most*

empowered by their individual capabilities and perspectives [emphasis added]. We have found that the reduction in size of the domain of disorder as a consensual act of collaboration among decision makers is a significant step toward the achievement of consensus as to the nature of the situation and the most appropriate response.

In terms of the library example, some people are inherent borrowers of ideas from elsewhere and would tend to see the management of this open access resource as a complicated issue. And then there are the folks who just like to try things out—who would tend to consider the management of the resource in complex terms. Are you able to identify which one you tend to favor? How you and your colleagues handle this goes to the heart of Cynefin as both an ontological and epistemological tool.

Boundaries: Changing the State of Situations

Managing complex aspects of a situation is resource intensive, complicated aspects somewhat less so, and simple aspects least of all.

Anything is easier than chaotic. Thus, if it is possible to "nudge," say, a complex aspect of a situation into being merely complicated, then this is probably more efficient, effective, and efficacious than trying to manage it as a complex aspect. Can an aspect of a situation identified as "complex" (and thus requiring being managed using probe-sense-respond) be shifted into the complicated domain (and thus managed more easily using sense-analyze-respond)? Kurtz and Snowden (2003) argue these things can really be achieved only at or close to the boundaries between domains. If we can move an aspect of a situation a small distance across the boundary from one domain to another, we have made the management task more efficient. To "nudge" something from the complex to the complicated domain, you should seek some means of strengthening the centrality of the situation—a focus of some kind. To nudge something from the complicated to the simple requires loosening the interdependence of the relevant elements of that situation. (See Figure 10.6.)

For instance, after experimenting with various ways of managing access to the library (i.e., the complex domain), it is found that a pass-key access seems to work better than the others, but it does not quite work with visitors to the area. Then someone recalls reading that a village elsewhere handled access to

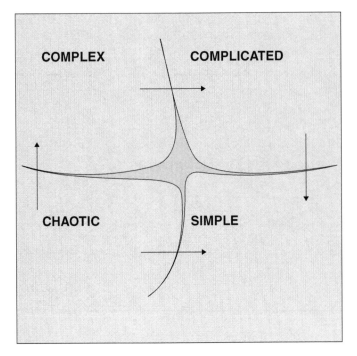

Figure 10.6. Cynefin Framework—Boundary Nudging
SOURCE: Modified from Cynthia F. Kurtz and David J. Snowden, "The New Dynamics of Strategy: Sense-Making in a Complex and Complicated World," *IBM Journal of Research and Development* 42, no. 3 (2003): 462–483.

a visitors' center by having the pass key stored at the local gas station, which was open twenty-four hours a day. After a bit of research was done, the solution seemed to fit and was applied—thus moving that aspect of the situation into the complicated space.

Indeed, the suggested strategy for chaotic situations (act-sense-respond) can be seen as pushing the situation into the simple space. Triage makes a chaotic situation simple, at least for a time and for long enough to work out what might actually need to be done.

CASE APPLICATION OF CYNEFIN

A medium-sized professional body in the United States experienced considerable expansion over five years. Its annual conference had expanded from fewer than 1,000 to more than 7,000 attendees, placing great strain on the conference organization. Traditionally the selection of papers at the conference was light handed, and the number of presentations was small enough to use small venues and for people to get a handle on the whole affair. Now the conference spread over several separate venues with many parallel sessions. Dissatisfaction with the conference was rising, so a workshop was arranged toward the end of one conference to investigate what could be done.

People's assessments of the current conference were categorized into the four main Cynefin domains:

Simple

   Developing the conference schedule

   Registration process

   Checking into hotels

   Obtaining electronic copies of conference presentations

   Locating where sessions were

Complicated

   Selecting which session to attend

   Arranging to meet up with friends

   Sharing of knowledge

   Application of new ideas from conference

   Satisfaction with conference

   Environmental friendliness of conference

   Finding local places to eat

Complex

   Sharing of knowledge

   Application of new ideas from conference

   The impact of the conference theme on participants

   Development of new professional relationships

   Satisfaction with conference

   Development of new themes within conference

   Tailoring presentations to the audience

Chaotic

    Traveling between conference venues

Based on these experiences and the way in which people handled these dynamics (including the conference participants, organizers, and venue managers), the following conclusions were made.

Interrelationships

Overall, the simple and complicated aspects of the conference were being handled well, but the spread-out nature of the venues, the style of the sessions, and the crammed program did not encourage the interactions necessary for the development of professional relationships. There was little ability to experiment (i.e., probe), and the consequences of doing so were that participants often found themselves in the wrong place without any means of correction. The strong message that came out of this assessment was that if the conference organizers want to improve professional relationships then the design of the conference needs to reflect on how to assist and support "complex" more emergent processes of professional development within the constraints of a multisite conference.

    There was usually a major failure in the venue transport process at some stage (i.e., something that was simple became chaotic), and there was a shared view that it was never handled very well. Rather than "act-sense-respond," the organizers tended to "probe-sense-respond" (i.e., tinker rather than act), but the conference was almost over by the time any possible solution emerged.

Perspectives

The ability of the conference to influence professional practice was seen by some as a complex process and by others as a complicated one. Those who saw it as complicated tended to evaluate the conference more favorably than those who saw it as a complex process. Responses formed an interesting pattern. Very experienced and very inexperienced conference goers tended to see the conference's professional practice influence as a more complex aspect of the conference than those who could best be described as "mid-career" professionals. Compared with the newcomers, these folks knew where to go to find out information, either professional or organizational—the situation was knowable to them. The densely packed program was frustratingly constraining for the more experienced, who really wanted to chew the fat and try things out with other colleagues, something very difficult when there is only five minutes for questions at the end of a jammed session, or whizzing between venues. Personal probes to resolve the issue were frustrated by the rigidity of the conference agenda, and such interactions had to be organized outside the conference schedule. Midcareer conference goers had a much clearer idea of whom and what they wanted to see and hear, so they were relatively happy with the conference organization. Clearly this has implications for the future viability of the conference if newcomers do not return, old-timers stop coming, and midcareer people depend on both for their information.

Boundaries

Given how spread out the conference was, meeting up with friends was clearly a complicated process. However, as the conference proceeded, various innovations, both official and unofficial, were introduced to enable people to identify if friends were attending and track them down. A dating service was set up so that schedules could be aligned and people found. A Twitter page was established. A couple of rooms were set aside for informal meetings to take place. Thus some parts of the complicated aspect of the conference were nudged over the boundary to become a simple aspect of the conference.

During a plenary session, organizers of the next year's conference suggested some possible themes and organized a session for these themes to be discussed and investigated in terms of their popularity and feasibility—thus pulling the issue of future conference planning, initially a complex activity, more toward and over the "complicated" boundary.

REFLECTIONS ON CYNEFIN
Pros / Advantages

Cynefin sprang fully formed on the world in 2003 and was rapidly adopted by organizational consultants, social researchers, and evaluators in many parts of the world. It has had a substantial impact on the action research field in particular. The reasons for this are relatively simple. Cynefin has combined in an accessible way two specialized fields (network theory and complexity theory) that individually have sometimes struggled to be applied broadly.

Although the framework has been described so far in terms of project design and project management tasks, it is also useful for research and other forms of evaluative inquiry.

For instance, in his work on Developmental Evaluation, Michael Q. Patton (2010) explores what this means for evaluation (see Table 10.1).

Table 10.1. Decisions in Multiple Contexts: An Evaluator's Guide

	The Situation	The Leader's Job	The Evaluator's Job	Evaluation Challenges
SIMPLE	High agreement about the problem and what to do; high certainty that the right action will produce the desired results; clear, direct, linear, predictable, and controllable cause-and-effect pattern. What needs to be done is known.	Sense, categorize, respond. Know what is known. Manage based on facts. Advocate for and implement best practices.	Validate best practices. Monitor implementation of best practices to assure high fidelity, adherence, and quality. Report departures from best practices and implications of those departures, especially implications for outcomes.	Assuring that best practices fit new contexts (different from where the practices were originated and validated). Detecting unanticipated consequences and context-specific implementation problems.
COMPLICATED	Some differences of opinion about the problem and what to do. Expertise needed. The necessity of coordinating many areas of technical expertise and many actors introduces uncertainty about attaining desired outcomes. More than one effective way possible. Cause-and-effect linkages are context-contingent: discoverable with careful analysis, but neither obvious nor certain. Contingencies discernible (known unknowns).	Sense, analyze, respond. Find needed expertise to identify good practices. Listen to and assess conflicting expert advice. Use monitoring and evaluation to track what unfolds as good practices are tried.	Validate good practices and options with attention to context and system contingencies. Convert expert advice into a testable theory of change. Evaluate and report unfolding cause-and-effect complications and their implications. Systems thinking.	Designing a reasonable test of the theory of change. Understanding the system(s) and context(s) within which action unfolds. Detecting and measuring both outcomes and contingencies. Facilitating interpretation of less-than-certain findings.

Table 10.1. (continued)

	The Situation	The Leader's Job	The Evaluator's Job	Evaluation Challenges
COMPLEX	High uncertainty about how to produce desired results and great disagreement among diverse stakeholders about the nature of the problem and what, if anything, to do. Results highly dependent on initial conditions; nonlinear interactions within a dynamic system. No right answers; key variables and their interactions unknown in advance. Each situation is unique.	Probe, sense, respond. Foster dialogue, creativity, and innovation. Watch for and interpret emerging patterns. Be flexible and adaptive. Make time for and engage in reflective practice to capture, understand, and interpret what is emerging.	Identify and document initial conditions and monitor what emerges. Provide ongoing, timely, and rapid feedback about what is emerging. Track incremental actions and decisions that affect the paths taken (and not taken). Facilitate regular reflective practice about what is *developing*. Embed evaluative thinking in the innovative process.	Keeping up with the rapid pace of change in turbulent and dynamic environments. Managing a flexible, emergent design. High level of ongoing interaction and communication. Combining creative and critical (evaluative) thinking in support of innovation. Facilitating interpretation of emergent findings. Staying developmentally focused.
CHAOTIC	High conflict among stakeholders; extreme uncertainty about what to do. Turbulence and volatility make pattern detection unreliable and undecipherable. Dynamic interactions hard to follow, not even sure what to pay attention to. Unreliable information. What to focus on is unknown and a matter of great debate. Tense, stressful decision environment.	Act, sense, respond. Try things out and see what happens, watching for anything that works. Manage what is manageable to establish some degree of order. Don't yield to panic.	Distinguish better and worse data; some information may be better than none, but interpret cautiously. Find those parts of the action where evaluation can make a short-term contribution.	Acknowledging data inadequacies. Being open and opportunistic about finding data. Avoiding defaulting to the simple in an effort to exercise control and create the illusion of certainty where none exists.

SOURCE: M. Q. Patton, *Developmental Evaluation* (New York: Guilford Press, 1990). Reproduced in edited form with the permission of Guilford Press.

Cons / Challenges

Cynefin has its critics, both in the complexity and knowledge management fields. Most of these criticisms concern Cynefin in terms of a wider debate between emerging paradigms and theories of knowledge management. Although not the concern of this chapter, they are relevant to those who wish to dig deeper into Cynefin. Critics within the complexity field identify its incomplete use of complexity theory, and those within the knowledge management field argue its validity.

The main problem with application is common to many systems approaches. It is important to get the scale right (i.e., group, organization, institution) and be relatively consistent within the analysis. If the unit of analysis is, say, sustainable agriculture in Canada, then it is not helpful to include a unique aspect of a single farm in Manitoba in one of the quadrants.

However, the main weakness is also one of the strong points of the approach. The terms used within Cynefin—sense, categorize, patterns, knowable, known—are capable of many meanings. While this ambiguity allows users the freedom to use the framework as a heuristic, it can create problems when using it in a strictly ontological way.

SOME MODIFICATIONS AND ADDITIONS TO CYNEFIN

Cynefin forms part of a much larger set of methodologies, methods, and techniques that have emerged from the networked organization Cognitive Edge. Some of these approaches are open source under a Creative Commons license; some are familiar tools in organizational development, community work, and applied social science; and some are proprietary to Cognitive Edge.

Cognitive Edge's focus is primarily on the "complex" domain, an example being their micronarrative data analysis tool SenseMaker. SenseMaker helps identify small, weak patterns emerging from probes so that responses can be made much earlier than by traditional pattern-matching methods. Typically, respondents to an intervention are asked to create small micro-narratives about their experience (e.g., a visit to a museum, the services provided by refugee camp managers). These are usually no more than three or four sentences. Based on that narrative, respondents are then given a series of tasks or posed a series of questions that enable them to analyze their own experience; this self-analysis is a distinctive feature of the Cognitive Edge approach. That analysis is then processed, usually through SenseMaker, which allows managers and researchers to identify small trends emerging in real time. Large amounts of data can be collected, analyzed, and responded to very rapidly, theoretically allowing cycles of probe-sense-respond to occur in days rather than the traditional weeks associated with most applied or market research.

NOTE

Our thanks to Michael Patton, IBM, and Guilford Press for permission to use their material.

REFERENCES AND FURTHER READING

Cognitive Edge Web site. http://www.cognitive-edge.com/.

Kurtz, Cynthia F., and David J. Snowden. 2003. The new dynamics of strategy: Sense-making in a complex and complicated world. *IBM Journal of Research and Development* 42, no. 3: 462–483.

Patton, Michael Q. 2010. *Developmental evaluation*. New York: Guilford Press.

Snowden, David. J., and Mary E. Boone. 2007. A leader's framework for decision making. *Harvard Business Review*. November: 69–76.

11

SOLUTION FOCUS

What would it be like if the problem suddenly disappeared?

Who should be doing (or stop doing) what to reach that ideal situation?

How can these actions be supported, and by whom?

Which elements of the solution take place already?

WHAT IS SOLUTION FOCUS?

Solution Focus is an approach to positive change within people, teams, or organizations. Focusing on solutions is fundamentally different from conventional approaches to problem solving that are based on the belief that focusing on problems (by analyzing, reacting to, and talking about them) is the best way to solve them. It sidesteps the often futile search for the causes of problems and heads straight for solutions.

Problem analysis and diagnosis are so widespread in Western thought and have been successful in so many areas that investigating their roots is an almost automatic response. Detailed understanding of a problem is conventionally considered a prerequisite for finding a solution, and this thinking also informs the approach of specialist problem solvers like consultants or evaluators.

Yet, while this problem focus still has its due place in many domains (e.g., engineering), it can be less useful when the issues involve interaction between people. Here a better understanding of a situation considered problematic often only leads to more insights about what is going wrong but might not be helpful in finding a way out. And the more one talks about problems, the bigger they tend to become—"Problem talk creates problems, not solutions" (de Shazer 1988).

Solution Focus is based on two fundamental assumptions: there is not necessarily a logical connection between problem and solution, and the route to the solution depends on the solution, not the problem. Therefore attention is placed on identifying a different "ideal" situation that will "dissolve" the problem. And on the changes required to arrive at this new situation, which are usually differences in behavior and interaction of the people involved.

The method has its origins in systemic (family) therapy and was developed in the 1970s by Steve de Shazer and his partner Insoo Kim Berg at the Brief Therapy Center in Milwaukee. Their "Solution Focused Brief Therapy" combines, in a stunningly simple approach, earlier findings from communication theory (notably by the Mental Research Institute in Palo Alto) and Milton Erickson's techniques for hypnotherapy:

- At the core is the "miracle question," where the client is asked to assume that the problem has disappeared overnight and to subsequently imagine the details associated with this change (What will be different for you? What or how will others notice?)

- The miracle question is embedded in a sequence of solution-oriented questions that systematically guide the client to depart from a problem toward the imagined solution.

- The therapist's role is to support the client on this imaginary route, to safeguard against flashbacks of problem-loaded thinking, and to assure that a sufficient level of detail is elaborated and all relevant context factors are taken into account.

The Solution Focus approach has spread to many other domains, including organizational development and management consulting. While therapy is for individuals and families, solution-focused consulting is used as a change process for organizational groups of every size, from small teams to large business units.

DETAILED DESCRIPTION OF THE METHOD
AND HOW IT FUNCTIONS

The following description of Solution Focus is a synthesis of the version that was developed by U.K.-based consultants Paul Z. Jackson and Mark McKergow and published in their book *The Solution Focus: The SIMPLE Way to Positive Change* (2002).

Their model is based on six principles and according to their acronym is called SIMPLE:

Solutions, Not Problems

The solution is imagined as a situation in which the problem does not exist anymore. The client is encouraged to describe details of a desired situation, where everything is somehow working exactly as he or she wishes. Solution talk, that is, discussing where and how elements of the solution are already happening, is encouraged from the very beginning.

In Between: The Action Is the Interaction

All change occurs from someone's point of view. What some may consider a way forward or a solution, others might regard as the status quo or problematic. Therefore, solutions must be co-constructed by the people involved, and aspects of a solution are thought to be located between them rather than belonging to only one party. This interactional view is a link into systems thinking, and solution focus explicitly builds on two systems approaches: the design view (e.g., System Dynamics) and the emergent view, whereby behavior of complex systems is not based on intentional design but emerges from interaction between individual components.

Make Use of What's There

A solution is considered an emergent property; its seeds are already there and can be used—provided they are noticed. And change happens all the time. It can be guided and amplified by identifying useful interactions and turning them into building blocks for constructing a solution. For this a resourceful attitude is needed—everything that is within reach of the client can turn out to be a resource toward the solution. Even resistance on the way toward the solutions should be used as a resource; it is a sign that the best way to cooperate has not yet been found and something needs to be done differently.

Possibilities: Past, Present, and Future

Instead of investigating what does not work, participants focus their attention on what works or has worked. Exceptions from a problem situation are interpreted as concrete possibilities, which provide hope and motivation for reaching the solution. Examining the differences between times when the problem happened and other times can embrace the past, the present, or the future. But care should be taken to specify the differences in behavior or interaction that accompany these exemptions, which is often difficult because our memories are flawed and perception is selective or does not sufficiently appreciate important aspects. Possibilities are always to be found; the skill lies in recognizing and applying them.

Language: Simply Said

The language used should be kept simple, in order to facilitate understanding between the participants, make communication more precise, and enable participants to reach consensus. Practical, everyday words that lend themselves to describe observable events or objects are preferred and expert jargon or abstractions avoided. This also means using participants' words as much as possible and paying attention to key words or metaphors that they apply.

Every Case Is Different

Solution focus is an approach to change, not a set of prefigured methods to fit every case. It offers a set of tools and principles applied in a flexible way, to find out what works in the respective case, seeking actions that have enough "fit" to begin the desired change process. This is easier if you adopt a beginner's mind and act solution focused but not "solution forced"—that is, forcing people to set their mind on solutions when they are not ready and rather want to do something else, for example, talk about problems.

The Solution Focus Process

Even though there is no fixed route that applies to every situation, the following six-step path is typical, each step focused around a specific tool and a set of corresponding questions.

1. Platform

This starting point for change is established early on and is frequently derived from the problem. By reframing a problem into a platform, a shift in perspective takes place: the issue is not so much problematic as a set of circumstances that provides the point of departure. An important aspect is to identify the customer or a customer for change, someone who is willing to act differently to start or stop doing something.

2. Future Perfect

From this platform attention is shifted directly to a situation without the problem, as desired and imagined by the customer for change. But this future should be immediate, not distant and defined in concrete terms, by naming specific details and useful differences. This allows defining the direction of progress and the steps leading in this direction.

3. Counters

What counts in moving toward this desired state is identifying where the solution, or part of it, happens already and identifying what helped create or sustains this solution. These factors can identify the skills, resources, expertise, or past achievements and collaborations that will facilitate the solution.

4. Affirm

It is important to affirm the factors that count. Often aspects that might contribute toward a solution are neglected, and it is important to give feedback on people's qualities, skills, capabilities, and attitudes, which are considered valuable. These compliments have to be sincere, expressed unpatronizingly, and based on direct observation.

5. Small Actions

So far the steps have been directed at finding out what works. Now it is time to do something and see what happens. This can be by either doing more of what works or stopping what does not work and trying something else instead. It is crucial to identify small actions that do not take a big effort, are easy to identify, and are close to the present situation. But these actions must be carried out by the customer for change and make an immediate difference. These effects loop back to the counters, as any progress made is a further counter toward a solution and allows a fresh look at further affirmations and choices of next small steps.

6. Scale

Connecting all these elements is a scale for measuring progress toward the desired future. Scales (e.g., from 1 to 10) form a simple tool for assessing differences, offer an intuitive logic that is readily accessible, and are easy to establish. But again, it is specificity that matters: the various points on the scale and the differences that are observed should be described as concretely as possible.

CASE APPLICATION OF SOLUTION FOCUS

This case describes a workshop with key actors of a Regional Development Agency in rural Austria., with the aim of jointly preparing the agency's midterm strategy. During the months preceding the workshop tensions between some of the actors had built up, and there was a big risk that the workshop would be overshadowed by mutual accusations and blame. Therefore the facilitators chose to apply the Solutions Focus approach, hoping that in this way the prevalent problem-focus could be overcome. The workshop lasted for two days and involved fifteen participants, who included the agency's director, key staff, and some members of the agency's board.

Platform

The director briefly described the situation: the agency was successful, and the team generally worked well together, although recently tensions had risen between agency staff and some board members, in particular mayors who were opposed to some of the activities carried out by individual staff members. He pointed out that these criticisms had not been communicated directly, and due to other commitments the critics had not come to meetings lately. Some staff members who had been criticized were only recently appointed and were not yet well known in the area.

The workshop began with personal introductions, aiming to break the ice and reveal more information. Participants described personal achievements outside their job, which increased knowledge about each individual. Some discovered things they had not known about each other before. Others commented on the achievements presented, and these compliments created a positive atmosphere of mutual appreciation.

Participants then described the current situation in the agency, by acting out one of the recent critical incidents in a role-play (where some of the actors were invited to slip into a different role than their own). It became apparent that participants felt they were in two camps. On one side was the agency's staff, pressured by daily troubleshooting, deadlines, unreliable partners, and other issues that built up a backlog of tasks and further stress. On the other side were the board members, out in the municipalities, who felt that the agency's staff did not respond to their demands, and who were also faced with criticism from their community members about some of the agency's recent activities (which apparently had been poorly communicated). It was surprising to see how little each group had been aware of the particular stress of the others.

The Future Perfect

Workshop participants gave an indication of their preferred future by presenting their objectives, which were written on cards, displayed to the others, and clustered to form coherent themes. Broadly, the overall themes were:

- Clear targets for the agency's core domains of action
- Open communication about difficulties and problems
- A sense of belonging together in working for the region's future

In small groups the participants then drew poster-sized pictures of the future perfect. The drawings revealed a great deal more detail, for instance:

- More development projects than currently planned
- Board members actively supporting agency staff
- Involving new people in the agency's activities, in particular the young
- Winning a national award for innovative actions at the regional level.

Counters

To elicit counters, participants were asked how much of the vision was already happening or to list their currently successful methods. This revealed that some of the board members had supported agency staff for quite a while, which in turn had also led to more community involvement in their actions. New approaches had led to situations where young people were enthusiastically taking part in activities. For instance, one staff member reported that by organizing a "future day" in one municipality, in collaboration with the young farmer association, many ideas were developed and communicated to the municipal council (which had approved funding for some of them).

To make their counters more robust, the group was asked to play the part of skeptics to each other's claims and to request evidence in sufficient detail to substantiate them. A convincing example of the benefits for building up the support of board members was the story of a staff member who routinely met with or called up three of the board members to capture their concerns and ideas on matters relating to a specific project, and thus gradually consolidated their support for that project.

Scaling

For other parts of the future perfect, the counters were more scarce and the evidence was less compelling. The participants scaled each of their drawings to indicate the current position, which not only indicated what still lay ahead but also showed the difference between various situations.

The picture for involving young people, for example, was rated as 3, because this was taking place only in some instances. But having identified a counter and having learned from other positive experience, they now felt there was good potential for moving up the scale. The picture for support by board members was rated 7, because the board worked well with most of them already, and thus it seemed only a minor step to resolve existing tensions and obtain support from board members who were currently reluctant to provide it.

Small Actions

A number of team-building activities during the two days instantly provided first steps for moving toward the preferred future. Individuals whose relations had been strained recently were deliberately paired or grouped together in small teams and given tasks where they could experience a sense of joint achievement. This not only led to positive feelings but also improved interpersonal communications, which in most cases continued after the workshop.

Thus the two days together laid the ground for more constructive future relationships.

Affirming

On the morning of the second day, one of the participants read in the newspaper about the call for proposals for a national rural development award. Participants instantly decided to use the workshop for screening the requirements, and at the end decided that one of their most successful projects in the past year would fit well into one of the categories. They formed an ad-hoc working group to prepare the proposal and defined who else would be needed for this endeavor. This sudden opportunity worked as an amplifier, affirming the positive spirit that had gradually been building up.

At the final session of the workshop, each participant told the others what they brought—or intend to bring—to the agency, to which the listeners added some compliments. Thus the workshop ended with a streak of affirmative intentions and positive feelings between participants and the common goals. Thus the participants explicitly built a resource bank for the agency's future.

More Small Actions

At the lunch break on the second day, inspired by an energizing morning session on defining future strategic goals, there was a sense of openness to change and the feeling of collaborative power. Then someone proposed taking a fresh look at the projects that had caused so many problems lately to see what could be done to change the situation. The participants listed these projects and (either individually or in pairs) took responsibility for one of them. They immediately sat together and decided who else should be called upon to take a closer look at the critical incidents involved and to explore solutions for them.

In this way, a mechanism was triggered (almost spontaneously) to improve the current situation, and several smaller groups were established to undertake this in a structured and collaborative way. These groups met in the weeks following the workshop, and although it was not possible to resolve all outstanding issues, at least the ground was laid for bringing forth solutions and overcoming the tensions that had prevailed in the weeks before the workshop.

At the staff meeting following the workshop, the director held a brain-storming session, inquiring about techniques the staff members could apply or about experience (of others) they could build upon to improve the situation in the former "trouble projects." And at the next board meeting (two months after the workshop) each of the groups was invited to report on their progress. It was remarkable to see how quickly the agency had moved up the scale toward the future perfect.

REFLECTIONS ON THE USE OF SOLUTION FOCUS

Solution Focus is a powerful and proven approach to bring about change. It provides a practical way to overcome problems and to avoid becoming locked in a problem-focused mode of thought. And it takes an explicit systemic view by recognizing and making use of interaction patterns and identifying solutions by changing perspectives.

The approach can be applied in many different areas where relations between people matter, from private encounters, leadership, and team development to (large) organizational change processes. It is essentially a refined art of conversation, which can be readily applied provided that some fundamental principles are observed. Its use is particularly recommended for situations marked by negative experiences from the past or situations where an emotional burden weighs on the relationship between the involved parties.

Solution Focus can also be usefully applied in evaluations but means a drastic departure from the problem-solving attitude normally applied. It can be rather helpful with formative evaluation styles that do not only seek to inform change but already initiate change during or through the evaluation work. Or in cases where a more detailed analysis of the causes of a problem is inappropriate, for example, because the problem at hand has already existed for a long time or because the parties involved are tangled up in this problem very closely and over a long period of time.

Pros / Advantages

The focus on solutions (instead of problems), the future (instead of the past), and what is going well (rather than what went wrong) leads to a pragmatic—and often very rapid—way of making progress.

Although it assumes that solutions start with a sudden change ("miracle"), Solution Focus has a minimalist approach, advocating changing as little as possible. This has benefits in terms of time, cost, and effort and takes the path of least resistance. Energy, enthusiasm, and cooperation are frequent side effects of this different approach to problem situations.

Solution Focus is not just positive thinking; it is about taking action to achieve a desired state. And it is more than best practice, because the intention is not to copy others but to focus on finding an appropriate solution for the situation at hand. Although the approach is simple, it is not simplistic in the sense of finding a simple solution and quickly applying it. Its practice is not that easy and requires skill and creativity—and the solutions found can be rather complex.

Always seeing the solution as rooted in the reality of the particular circumstance avoids imagining things that are not there—or bringing in change proposals that are not shared by those expected to carry them out.

Cons / Challenges

Nevertheless, there are a number of challenges or pitfalls involved in practicing Solution Focus, some of which are deeply rooted in our cultural traditions of dealing with problems.

- Falling back into problem talk:

  During the process there is a strong temptation to shift the focus toward describing problems, searching for their causes, or personalizing them by blaming individuals. But problem talk tends to make problems even larger, with more causes and explanations—and rarely reveals what to do next. Instead, solution talk leads to stories of possibilities. Indeed, key actions are often not directly connected to the problem situation or might involve seemingly unrelated people.

- No customer for change:

  Frequently people not only blame others for problems but also expect someone else to solve them. Therefore finding individuals who are willing to change a situation is often one of the first tasks in the process. A specific danger to be avoided is external actors (e.g., consultants, evaluators) acting as their own customers of change. But there are also cases where several customers exist, which might require dealing with conflicting views and interests.

- Trying to solve an unsolvable problem:

    Describing solutions in vague or fuzzy language can make them unachievable. Solutions must be defined in precise terms (specific visible or audible features). A solution described as what is not wanted must be turned around to describe what the customer for change really expects.

- Resistance and short-term fixes:

    Solutions must be sustainable. Therefore, damaging interventions should be avoided, in particular decisions that encounter resistance or are against important values of the customer or a customer. The way forward is with affirmative attitude: accept and appreciate what is there (even if one is skeptical) in order to build cooperation, not to foster resistance.

Last, but not least, Solution Focus requires skilled facilitators or consultants who are capable of engaging in—and maintaining—a solution-focused conversation, asking useful questions in an appropriate manner, and spotting or exploring the nuances of the differences at work.

VARIATIONS
Appreciative Inquiry

Appreciative Inquiry is a structured process for mobilizing energy from previous success for further change, which can be carried out at various scales (from individuals up to large groups). The approach originated in the late 1980s in the United States in the field of community development and subsequently in organizational development.

The Appreciative Inquiry process is carried out in four steps:

1. Discovery: personal experiences are assessed with respect to characteristics and conditions bearing on past successes.

2. Dream: perspectives for the future are imagined or a vision is developed; previous experience with success and achievements is explicitly taken into account to ensure that future developments will fully exploit existing potential.

3. Design: the vision is made more concrete, with reference to the partners and the required types of communication and interaction, as well as appropriate supporting conditions.

4. Delivery: finally, the goals and measures that are required to realize and achieve the vision in the short and medium terms are established.

The "appreciative interview," as the core tool, poses inspiring questions that demonstrate respect for existing qualities, reveal new potential, and generally encourage a learning process. The process of inquiry and the process of transformation take place simultaneously; change can begin by posing the first question.

Appreciative Inquiry is a relatively simple procedure that has been utilized in many change projects. It can be applied rather flexibly and adapted to suit different situations and group sizes. Due to the consistent orientation toward success, the positive energies of all actors are bundled and directed toward future change. It is similar to Solution Focus but is geared toward larger change processes and places more emphasis on affirmation.

Solution Focus Constellations

Systemic Structural Constellations (SySt) were developed in Germany by Matthias Varga von Kibéd and Insa Sparrer. They are rooted in traditions of role-play, psychodrama, and systemic family therapy, notably Virginia Satyr's family sculptures. In this approach social systems are represented by "constellations," that is, spatial arrangements of people as seen by a client. The positions and relative distance of these representatives illustrate the relations to each other (or with respect to a certain issue). This way, crucial aspects like proximity, distance, and exclusion are directly felt by the representatives and expressed nonverbally.

The basis of this transverbal language is "representative perception," the assumption that the differences in the bodily perception of representatives represent differences in the simulated system. But these perceptions are independent of individual feelings and relate strictly to spatial relations and configurations. This can be particularly helpful in situations where dependencies, personal prejudice, and animosities block new insights. Since positions can easily be changed, the approach is well suited for experimenting with different options and exploring new solutions. The goal of such group simulation is to "reconstellate" in order to generate new ideas for steps to be taken in the original system.

Insa Sparrer has lately combined SySt with elements of Solution Focus, in particular, solution-focused interviews (Sparrer 2008): either parts of this interview (e.g., goal, miracle, exceptions) are translated into a constellation, which is then rearranged with the aim of improving the representatives' situation, or the interview is held with representatives who are positioned in a constellation that has been carried out beforehand. The advantage of this combination is a more intense experience, the possibility to test actions and enhanced transparency of the solution. In addition, absent conflict partners can be integrated via representatives, and dialogues between conflict partners can be acted out by changing perspectives in a lively "as-if" form.

Constellations have proven to be an effective way of working with problems in families or organizations and are quite popular in continental Europe, where a new profession of "constellation workers" has emerged. They are a rapid way (sessions last only up to two hours) to make mental maps explicitly visible and to initiate change by activating conscious as well as unconscious elements that affect relationships. Expert support is needed if one wants to go beyond gaining new insights and to arrive at effective new solutions.

Positive Deviance

Positive deviance is a method that focuses on solutions that are already occurring. It is based on the observation that in every community there are certain individuals or groups whose uncommon behaviors and strategies enable them to find better solutions to problems than their peers, while having access to the same resources and facing similar or worse challenges. It has been used extensively in developing countries, especially on health issues.

NOTE
The account of the methodology closely follows the description in P. Z. Jackson and M. McKergow (2002), *Solution Focus: The SIMPLE Way to Positive Change*. Our thanks to the authors for their support and valuable comments.

REFERENCES AND FURTHER READING

Cooperrider, David. L. 1999. *Appreciative inquiry*. San Francisco: Berrett-Koehler.

De Shazer, Steve. 1988. *Investigating solutions in brief therapy*. New York: W. W. Norton & Company.

Elliott, Charles. 1999. *Locating the energy for change: An introduction to appreciative inquiry*. International Institute for Sustainable Development. Available for free download at http://www.iisd.org/pdf/appreciativeinquiry.pdf.

Jackson, Paul Z., and Mark McKergow. 2002. *Solution Focus: The SIMPLE way to positive change*. London: Nicholas Brealey.

Sparrer, Insa. 2008. *Miracle, solution and system: Solution-focused systemic structural constellations for therapy and organisational change*. Cheltenham: SolutionsBooks.

See also the following Web sites:

Centre for Solutions Focus at Work: http://www.sfwork.com.

Positive Deviance Web site: http://www.positivedeviance.org

SOLWorld. The group of Solution Focus practice in organizations: http://solworld.ning.com.

12

VIABLE SYSTEM MODEL

What are the operational, coordination, management, strategy, and governance needs of the situation in order to deliver on its purpose?

What information is needed at each level of the situation to achieve the purpose?

How does information flow through the situation?

Is the right information available at the most appropriate level of a situation's hierarchy of tasks?

WHAT IS THE VIABLE SYSTEM MODEL?

The Viable System Model (VSM) illustrates the minimum requirements that must be placed on social systems if they are to prove enduring and capable of development. The aim is to bring enterprises and organizations into a condition such that they attain their optimum performance capacity and to render these enterprises and organizations able to survive in the long term, in other words, to be viable.

In the 1970s, the British cyberneticist Stafford Beer explored the viability conditions of living systems, such as biological organisms, to see if they could relate to sociocultural systems, such as organizations and enterprises. He found a number of organizational requirements that must be in place if the system is to prove viable. The model he developed was finally called the Viable

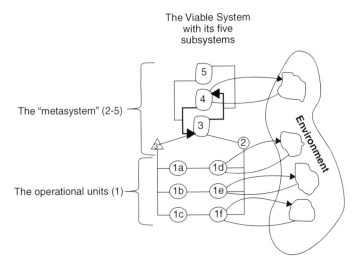

Figure 12.1. Subsystems of VSM and the Corresponding Steering Levels
SOURCE: Robert Lukesch. Used with permission.

System Model (Beer 1979). Its most well known form is a diagram composed of mutually interlocking and "nested" systems that depicts the necessary and sufficient conditions for the viability of social systems in general (see Figure 12.1).

VSM has three elements that interact: the operation system (that does the basic "work"), the metasystem (that holds the different units of the basic "work" together), and the environment (within which the system remains viable).

A central aspect of VSM is the principle of recursion. This principle states that, in a constellation of systems that are themselves composed of subsystems, each system, regardless of the level on which it is situated, will display the same structure. This means that systems that are structured according to this principle of recursion will not be the pyramid-type structure familiar from organizational theory. Rather, such a hierarchy is more like mutually interlocking and "nested" systems that resemble the well-known Russian Matryoshka dolls.

DETAILED DESCRIPTION OF THE METHOD
AND ITS FUNCTIONING

The classic representation of a viable system depicts five subsystems (for reasons of simplicity, these subsystems are referred to as "systems") (See Figure 12.1) . Susanne Tepe and Tim Haslett (2002) provide a succinct description of VSM, and it is reproduced in an edited form below.

The Structure of the VSM

System 1 is construed as the system that actually "does" what the system does. This would generally be construed as the operational units of an enterprise. This system is capable of autonomous adaptation to the environment and optimization of ongoing business (Schwaninger 2001). It interacts with System 3 in a continual feedback loop of receiving resources in return for accountability for their use (Beer 1985)—it is commonly called the management system. Within an enterprise there are several Systems 1 that communicate with each other as well as with their respective System 3 (see later). System 1 is strongly influenced by the environment in which it exists.

System 2 provides information, communication, and processes for issues common to all Systems 1. It is used to coordinate the various System 1 units by providing stability and conflict resolution through reducing choice and attenuating variety from the environment (see later for explanation of variety). It reflects managerial policies and decisions but does not make them. This system is usually described as information systems, internal service providers, and coordination teams but also includes cultural elements such as standards of behavior (Schwaninger 2001).

System 3 is essentially the interface between System 1 and the policy makers in System 5 (see later). Its primary function is to control the activities of the Systems 1 by managing the "resource bargain" that ensures that System 1 performs the functions that the organization has deemed appropriate. Robert. L. Flood and Michael. C. Jackson (1991) describe this as interpreting the policy decisions of higher management and ensuring effective implementation of policy through allocating resources to the parts of System 1. In doing so, it provides the control function that ultimately maintains internal organizational stability. In other words, System 3 is usually called "Management."

System 3 contains a special function described as System 3*. This function investigates and validates the information flowing between and among the systems. This "auditing" provides information to System 1 about its own functions but independently provides this information to Systems 3 and 5 (Beer 1985).

System 4 acts as an intelligence function that monitors the environment and helps the enterprise adapt and plan for the future (Vidgen 1998). System 4 primarily communicates with the System 5 policy makers, but each viable group within the organization needs its own intelligence to interpret how the environment affects their part of the organization.

System 5 is responsible for policy, or "what are we going to do." It establishes policy in light of competing demands between the present and future and between internal and external perspectives (Schwaninger 2001). Beer (1985) describes how legal and corporate requirements flow from senior management in return for accountability from Systems 1 and 3.

Recursiveness

As mentioned earlier, recursiveness is an important feature of VSM. Each viable organizational unit has embedded within it all five system structures of the entire enterprise; the Russian doll analogy. For example, an operating plant as System 1 in the corporate view should have a complete Systems 1–5 structure within it. The senior manager of the operating plant would be construed as the policy maker or System 5 in their own plant. The operating plant would have its own management team responsible for control and access to services that provide coordination and intelligence-gathering (Espejo et al. 1996).

This recursive structure ensures that down to the smallest viable work group, each unit has the policy, intelligence and information, control, and coordination services to do the work that needs to be done according to its environment. This provides the organization with the ability for the small groups to make "policy" about how to handle the problems they encounter in their jobs and provides the flexibility to survive in complex and rapidly changing environments (Espejo et al. 1996). Yet, if higher-level Systems 5 have been conveying policy clearly, these lower levels of recursion will understand the corporate goals and apply them to their own circumstances.

Requisite Variety

Variety is also an important concept in VSM. Variety is the total number of possible states of a system. For a system to be viable there must be a match between the variety of each system, especially between the metasystem (Systems 2–5) and the operation system (System 1). Each of an organization's systems must provide, reduce, or amplify the variety of its own activities and information flows so that they match the variety and complexity of the systems around them (Beer 1985). Any variety not controlled in this way is construed as "residual variety" and must be "managed" by the organization. If this residual variety is not managed, then the organization risks being overwhelmed by the complexity and ceases being viable. The way in which organizations control variety is critical. Often organizations try to decrease variety of the operational system (System 1) by imposing more rules, less innovation, fixed work patterns, and tight management. However, self-management and delegation at the operation level is also a strategy for reducing variety because it allows the operational system to limit its own variety directly without overloading the metasystem.

CASE APPLICATION: OCCUPATIONAL HEALTH AND SAFETY

A large, diverse, complex organization became concerned about several factors (Tepe and Haslett 2002):

- Their Occupational Health and Safety (OHS) computer reporting system was being underutilized.
- Workers' compensation costs were increasing dramatically.
- Senior management and the OHS professionals were becoming concerned about the ability to show that accountability and responsibility for OHS were being properly executed.
- All this was becoming a corporate governance issue.

The "Ideal"

A VSM-oriented audit of an organization's occupational health and safety used the following "ideal" template to compare what should be happening in a "viable" system with what was actually going on.

System 1

System 1, as the operational unit within the organization, is where most safety issues occur and are controlled. Systems 1 at all levels of the organization implement the policies defined by System 5 and resourced by System 3. System 1 is accountable to the organization for its OHS performance. In addition, it uses sufficient variety to control the safety risks it encounters in operations.

System 2

System 2 provides the information systems, OHS service functions, and cultural norms that underpin the OHS activities. These activities differ depending on the type of organization and the recursion within the organization, and they are owned by the organization itself or acquired from an external service provider.

System 3

System 3, the control system or management, will interpret the policy decisions (from System 5) concerning OHS for the System 1 units and ensure that adequate resources are available for compliance with policy. They monitor OHS performance by the operational units. System 3* provides additional independent audit information concerning compliance with the OHS policies and regulations.

System 4

System 4 monitors the environmental changes in the OHS regulations and in community attitudes, and it influences the organization to adapt to these. All levels in the organization have OHS intelligence appropriate to their activities.

System 5

OHS is clearly a legal and corporate issue for which System 5 establishes policy. This policy is communicated throughout the organization in order for the lower levels of the organization to reflect this policy in the context of their own activities.

Recursiveness

The concept of recursive structures means that every viable unit within the organization is responsible for responding to safety issues within the unit and environment, including accessing appropriate OHS information and services and acquiring intelligence and performance feedback about the internal and external environments. Yet every viable unit does this in light of the OHS policy conveyed from the higher recursions in the organization. The audit function in System 3*, with its independent reporting to management, ensures that this occurs.

Variety

The information that flows through the enterprise provides the method for monitoring safety performance. Information concerning safety events and audit data flows from System 1 to the other systems as proof of performance and evidence of accountability. System 2 uses this information to interpret the services required and to affirm the organization's attitude to safety. System 3 uses the information to determine the adequacy of performance and adjust the resources for OHS. System 4 compiles summary safety performance reports and compares these to the needs reflected by the environment. This information is provided to System 5, which determines if performance is adequate or if policy needs to change in response to the environmental trends. The task ensures that the requisite variety of each level (in this case, its ability to absorb and respond to information) is in balance with the others.

The Reality

When the organization and its OHS functions were examined in light of this "ideal" VSM, it was not clear if there was any relationship between the reality and the model! There were very few structures in the "ideal" model that were visible in the OHS function of the organization:

- There was no clear policy concerning OHS coming from the most senior managers. Policy was being developed by the corporate OHS group and, while there was some consultation with Systems 1 representatives, the policy did not have the authority expected. While the most senior managers did convey responsibility for OHS to management, there was no feedback on their performance. In short, there was little visible System 5 activity and clearly no ability of the senior management to feel that they understood the OHS of their organization; for example, there was no visible corporate governance on OHS.

- There was little gathering of information concerning the OHS environment, and when it was done, it was not used to inform policy because the policy area was misaligned. Some monitoring of regulation was done, but the results tended to be provided to lower levels in the organization. This was a good idea but was not able to improve the corporate policy and governance of the whole organization. It appeared that in the corporate OHS function, System 4 was aligned to the lower recursions in the organization, leaving the corporate System 5 without an intelligence-gathering function.

- Management were clear in their responsibility for OHS, but because the most senior management did not require or provide feedback on performance, there were various levels of commitment to and resources for OHS.

- There were no OHS audits done on a departmental or organizational basis, so there was no independent information concerning OHS performance given to management; but then management did not ask for it, either.

- The corporate OHS group provided services to the whole of the organization, but without any clarity of purpose and in a very piecemeal manner, primarily because there was no clear policy or requirements from the senior management.

- The operating units were very keen to provide good OHS performance but were under-resourced and uncoordinated. Each was developing their own creative manner to achieve what they thought were the desired outcomes. There was a lot of very good work being done, but because there was no clear direction, each took a different path, a different focus, and a different way of measuring success.

In summary, there was very little concordance between the existing OHS function in the organization and what a VSM would expect. A variety of approaches were used to sort out the problems, including Soft Systems Methodology (see Chapter 14), Balanced Scorecard, and the Carver model of organizational governance. VSM was used as a means to highlight who should produce the policy, who must receive performance feedback, who makes resource decisions, and how important intelligence about the environment is.

The VSM concept of recursive structures is particularly important in the context of OHS. While most operations personnel would recognize that they need their own set of services intelligence about the environment and performance feedback, few would admit that they develop their own policy. Most would say this comes from "The Top." However, the model recognizes that each unit develops their own decisions about what to do, and this is consistent with the reality of OHS in organizations but is never mentioned in OHS management system texts. If this one assumption alone is made explicit, the VSM will have served a useful purpose. The VSM was helpful in defining the next steps for the implementation of a robust OHS system in the organization. The VSM could also be used to add further detail to the computer system that provides performance feedback and audit data; the intention is to align the feedback with the VSM.

In addition, VSM was used to define the organizational structure for the corporate OHS function. More recognition is being given to the need to provide environmental intelligence and policy support to the most senior management committee. This group is likely to be "separated" from the OHS functions that provide information and support to the lower recursions in the organization.

REFLECTIONS ON THE VIABLE SYSTEM MODEL
Pros / Advantages

The Viable System Model (VSM) is one of the few systems methods that specifically focuses on both the structure and process of information flow through organizations (CHAT is another; see Chapter 13). It is unique in identifying what kind of decisions needs to be made where on the basis of what kind of information. It is applicable as a diagnostic tool as well as a design tool. Conceptually it is relatively simple to grasp, although the notion of variety can initially be difficult to understand.

Cons / Challenges

In common with other methods from the cybernetics stable, its weak point is dealing with perspectival, cultural, and power issues (although see the St. Gallen variation below). The example in the previous section is a case in point—there were historical, managerial, motivational, and cultural reasons that prevented the open, honest, and accurate provision of information about safety issues (Tepe and Haslett 2002). However, as in that case study, these issues can be addressed using other systems approaches, such as Soft Systems Methodology for perspectival issues (see Chapter 14) and CHAT for motivational issues and dealing with conflicting motivations (see Chapter 13) and Critical Systems for dealing with power issues (see Chapter 19).

Another challenge for VSM is, given the emphasis on information for decision making, how to deal with uncertain and unknowable conditions, both within the system and in the environment.

FURTHER VARIATIONS
St. Gallen Management Models

The St. Gallen Institute in Switzerland is a leading European proponent of VSM. Over the years, VSM has provided the base for a series of management models used extensively throughout Europe, especially German-speaking countries. St. Gallen has pushed the "old" VSM model, which was essentially about the *management* of information, toward an appreciation of what is needed—structurally, functionally, and culturally—to make *sense* of information.

The St. Gallen management models use VSM to distinguish between three different levels of management: operative, strategic, and normative.

System 1 represents the operational units. Systems 2 and 3 comprise the way in which these units collectively operate in an optimum manner; securing synergies and appropriate resource allocation. Thus it is considered the *operative* level of management.

System 4 comprises the means by which the whole system engages with its future, especially with its long-term future. Thus it is called the *strategic* level of management (e.g., research and development, knowledge generation).

System 5 comprises the means by which the competing demands of the present and future are balanced. It holds the entire system to the highest values, norms, and rules. It is thus called the *normative* level of management.

In early versions of the St. Gallen model, these three distinctions were further broken down into three organizational aspects: structure, activities, and culture (see Table 12.1).

Table 12.1. St. Gallen Management Model: Management Levels and
Organizational Aspects

	Structures	Activities	Culture	Primary Focus (Schwaninger 2001)
S5 Normative	Corporate constitution	Corporate policy	Corporate culture	Legitimacy (ability to fulfill the claims of all stakeholders)
S4 Strategic	Organizational structures Management systems	Programs	Problem-solving attitudes	Effectiveness
S1–3 Operative	Organizational processes Disposition systems	Tasks	Performance and cooperative attitudes	Efficiency

SOURCE: Adapted from Markus Schwaninger, "Intelligent Organizations: An Integrative Framework," *Systems Research and Behavioural Science* 18 (2001): 137–158.

In more recent times, these basic concepts have evolved into the "New St. Gallen Management Model" that seeks to blend these nine concepts into issues that relate to making sense of the organizational development and renewal, specific management, business, and support processes and in particular the ethical and pragmatic relationships with an organization's environment.

The 1234-Model, a Scheme for Designing Managing Structures (Robert Lukesch)

This model has used the principles underpinning the St. Gallen management model to support intermediary organizations in setting up their managing structure. Intermediary organizations fulfill—at least partly—public functions, but are not necessarily made up as public institutions; they represent "hybrid" forms placed between public and private organizations. The St. Gallen management model is applicable for both nonprofit and profit-making organizations, and it can also be used to reflect public governance structures.

The 1234-model consists of four components (see Figure 12.2):

1. Organization
2. Steering entities
3. Steering levels
4. Steering functions

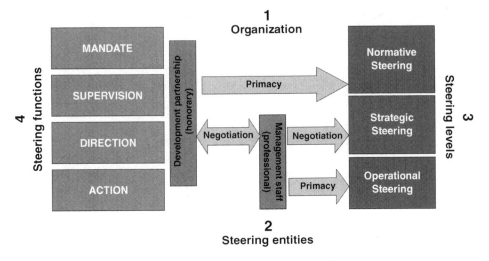

Figure 12.2. Basic Model for Steering Structures of Intermediary Organizations (1234-model)
SOURCE: Robert Lukesch. Used with permission.

In detail:

Organization may range from a small nonprofit organization, a firm, a political party, up to large networks and governance arrangements; larger structures might require further differentiations and subdivisions according to place, type of activity, or other criteria (in order to avoid "understeering").

There are two *steering entities*, the "honorary" partnership, often called "owners" in the widest sense of the word (shareholders in a firm, the electorate in a political system, the general assembly of an association, or others), and the implementing structures, the managing staff, who are employed or contracted as professionals.

There are three *steering levels* (relating to the St. Gallen model above):

• *Normative Steering* relates to the long-term vision, the guidelines, and the general operational principles. They constitute the ethical basis for joint activities and provide a consistent common goal. Normative steering endows the cooperation system with meaning. It is embodied in visions, value and mission statements, political programs, and ethical codes.

- *Strategic Steering* relates to a medium- to long-term programmatic horizon, which indicates what should be achieved, with which stakeholders, and in which way it should be pursued. Strategic steering does not aim at "quick wins," but on building up competencies and social capital, focusing on model-like, dynamizing activities of highest priority. This level of steering is embodied in programs and guidelines, midterm goals, and determined core processes.

- *Operational Steering* refers to "everyday business" of an association, a firm, a party, a religious congregation, a soccer club, or a municipality. It is embodied in the chain of activities defined as core processes generating the intended output of the organization. This is where value is added and where the organzation regenerates itself.

In direct connection to the three steering levels, there are up to four kinds of steering *functions*. How many of these functions are present and how they are configured constitutes the touchstone of success or failure of any collaborative structure or process.

- *Mandate*: The mandate comes "from the people" (e.g., in a political system), from the co-owners (of firms), from a general assembly (of a nonprofit organization), or from target groups; in some cases the mandate is delegated to representatives (e.g., corporate members of a national consumer protection association) or limited to one-off events (e.g., a planning workshop). The function of "mandate" can easily be forgotten in the hodgepodge of everyday activities, but the price for this can be either technocratic self-assertion of the management staff or lack of legitimacy of the overall endeavor. In larger collaborative projects, the mandate is borne by democratically elected people or their highest administrative delegates. If the mandate function is not properly fulfilled, the collaborative project inevitably lacks public legitimacy, thus hampering its potential impact and sustainability (see Chapter 19). The mandate is the connecting link between the operating system and the intended end user or beneficiary.

- *Supervision*: Representatives of political, administrative, scientific, financial, civil society, and other bodies fulfill this function in a way that could be compared to a company board of directors. The corresponding bodies provide guidelines, embed the enterprise into the larger societal environment, and make decisions that neither derail the enterprise nor produce dissatisfying results. These bodies are often called supervisory or monitoring committees or advisory committees.

- *Direction*: This is the level at which most management decisions are taken and which hosts the "face" or "speaker" of the enterprise to the outside world. Sometimes "honorary" and "professional" agents share this steering function; in enterprises, the professionals prevail, whereas in nonprofit associations this steering function is often carried out by "steering committees." If things go wrong, they are usually the first ones to be replaced.

- *Action*: Loosely speaking, the direction function ensures that the right things are done. The action function ensures doing things right. Consequently, this is the domain of the management staff, mostly employees (although in small or local nongovernmental initiatives, they may all be volunteers). In larger collaborative projects, be they NGOs, firms, political parties, governance arrangements, or intermediary partnerships, there will always be a professional (employed or contracted) manager and his or her staff. Sometimes they might count on the support of voluntary people (development projects, nonprofit initiatives such as private schools). Individual members of supervisory or direction bodies should not be involved in this steering function. Detail management and interventionism from higher-level decision makers always create problems. Actions have to be carried out within the frame of relevance set by the direction, whose main tasks are to provide the necessary resources and to check the achieved results against the objectives.

NOTE

Our thanks to Susanne Tepe and Springer for permission to quote extensively from Susanne Tepe and T. Haslett (2002), "Occupational Health and Safety Systems, Corporate Governance and Viable Systems Diagnosis: An Action Research Approach." Our thanks as well to Robert Lukesch for material on VSM and the St. Gallen management models, as well as permission to extract extensively from an as yet unpublished paper on his 1234-Model.

REFERENCES AND FURTHER READING

Beer, Stafford. 1979. *The heart of enterprise.* New York: Wiley.

Beer, Stafford. 1985. *Diagnosing the system for organizations.* New York: Wiley.

Carver, John. 1997a. Designing policies that make a difference. In *Boards that make a difference: A new design for leadership in nonprofit and public organizations.* San Francisco: Jossey-Bass.

Carver, John. 1997b. A new vision for governing boards. *Boards that make a difference: A new design for leadership in nonprofit and public organizations.* San Francisco: Jossey-Bass.

Checkland, Peter, and Jim Scholes. 1999. *Soft Systems Methodology: A 30-year retrospective.* New York: Wiley.

Espejo, R., W. Schuhmann, M. Schwaninger, and U. Bilello. 1996. *Organizational transformation and learning: A cybernetic approach to management.* New York: Wiley.

Fitch, Dale. 2007. A cybernetic evaluation of organizational information systems. In *Systems concepts in evaluation: An expert anthology,* ed. Bob Williams and Iraj Imam. Point Reyes, CA: EdgePress / American Evaluation Association, 61–74.

Flood, Robert L., and Michael C. Jackson. 1991. *Creative problem solving: Total systems intervention.* New York: Wiley.

Kaplan, R. S., and D. P. Norton. 1996. *The balanced scorecard.* Boston: Harvard Business School Press.

New St. Gallen Management Model. http://www.ifb.unisg.ch/org/Ifb/ifbweb.nsf/wwwPubInhalteEng/2B1E1A1BE163DC5BC1256A5B00512DD8?opendocument.

Schwaninger, Markus. 2001. Intelligent organizations: An integrative framework. *Systems Research and Behavioural Science* 18: 137–158.

Schwaninger, Markus. 2006. *Intelligent organizations: Powerful models for systemic management.* New York: Springer.

St. Gallen Institute. http://www.sgmi.ch/htm/357/en/Homepage.htm.

Tepe, Susanne, and Tim Haslett. 2002. Occupational health and safety systems, corporate governance and viable systems diagnosis: An action research approach. *Systemic Practice and Action Research*15, no. 6 (December): 509–522.

Umpleby, Stuart Anspach. 2006. The viable system model: Research program in social and organizational learning. The George Washington University. Document prepared for the *International Encyclopedia of Organizational Studies.*

Vidgen, Richard. 1998. Cybernetics and business processes: Using the Viable System Model to develop an enterprise process architecture. *Knowledge Process Management* 5, no. 2: 118–131.

Walker, Jon. The Viable System Model. http://www.esrad.org.uk/resources/vsmg_3/screen.php?page=home.

PART THREE

LEARNING ABOUT SITUATIONS

Only Connect ...
 E. M. Forster

13

CULTURAL HISTORICAL
ACTIVITY THEORY

WHAT IS CHAT?

Cultural Historical Activity Theory (CHAT) was developed by the historical philosopher Alexei Leont'ev at Moscow State Lomonosov University during the 1960s. It is based largely on Lev Vygotsky's particular theories of cognition and learning. Vygotsky believed that learning takes place as a social activity within a "zone of proximal development." Unlike Piaget, who believed that humans learned while passing through developmental stages that are largely context free, Vygotsky believed that learning was more influenced by social conditions and conventions (i.e., zone of proximal development).

CHAT was developed by cognitive psychologists, whose orientation is quite different from the way in which most systems thinkers have engaged with the field. Cognitive psychologists focus on understanding how we develop understandings of the real world, draw meanings from that understanding, create learnings from those meanings, and are motivated to respond to those learnings. These cognitive "mental models" correspond to how we think about the real world and engage with it, not necessarily how the world actually works in a physical or biological sense. Their claim for legitimacy in the systems field is: if the point of systems thinking is to gain new insights and meanings, then we should develop systems models that reflect how we actually develop insights and meanings. In other words, if the way we gain insights of the real world from systems models is essentially a cognitive rather than physical process, then the systems models we develop should be based on our understanding of cognitive processes.

Activity theory was the basis of much research in Russia, especially in the areas of play and learning. However, while Piaget went on to influence the educational field, Vygotsky has until recently been more influential in the organizational development field. Activity theory in organizational development was promoted by the work of Yrjö Engeström's team at the Center for Activity Theory and Developmental Work Research at the University of Helsinki and Mike Cole at the Laboratory of Comparative Human Cognition at the University of California–San Diego.

DETAILED DESCRIPTION OF THE METHOD

A CHAT-based inquiry combines three components:

- A systems component that helps us to construct meanings from situations
- A learning component: a method of learning from those meanings
- A developmental component that allows us to expand those meanings toward action

These three components are constructed from seven basic propositions. Five relate to establishing the systems component, one relates directly to learning, and the final proposition relates to development.

Out of each proposition flows a set of questions that we can pose of the real world.

The Systems Component
Proposition One: The Fundamental Proposition
Activity theory is based on the proposition that learning is a social and cultural process, not simply a biological process.
The proposition means that in different situations (e.g., food production, design, factory, accounts), thinking and learning will be practiced and achieved in different ways, and those ways are not likely to be readily transferred from one person, team, or organization to another. Learning is not that simple; your learning, your knowledge is merely my information until I make sense of it in my own context.

Figure 13.1. Proposition Two

Proposition Two
"Activity" is what happens when human beings operate on their environment in order to satisfy a need. It is fundamentally driven by motivation (see Figure 13.1).

The needs we are seeking to satisfy are the *motives* for the activity and are what make sense of what is happening, rather than the *actions* we are undertaking. The same actions may have different motives. For example, a newspaper chief reporter may seem to be pressuring a team of journalists to work faster because of a desire to have the newspaper out on deadline, but she might also do this because she wants to look authoritative and impress the editor.

Similarly, there are many different actions we might take to satisfy the same need. For example, one social worker might try to become more innovative by reading books, while another might set up a discussion group with other social workers to achieve the same end.

Diagnostic Questions for Proposition Two

- What can we *observe* happening?
- What needs are those actions serving?
- Do the actions seem to fit the needs? Or might there be some other, unstated needs determining the action?
- How well suited are the actions we can observe to the desired needs? If there is a misfit, why is it happening?
- What does this tell us about the motivations that link the actions to the goal?

Proposition Three
Information must flow through the activity system in order to achieve the desired result (see Figure 13.2).

There are two types of information:

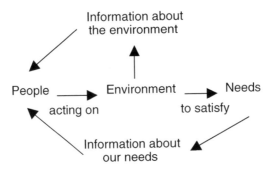

Figure 13.2. Proposition Three

1. Information about our needs (What are they? Have they been satisfied?) comes from within ourselves and involves an internal dialogue, either personally or interpersonally.

2. Information about the environment (What resources are there that can help me meet my needs? What do I have to do with those resources in order to succeed?) comes from outside through our senses.

Both types of information require internal mental processing to make sense of them.

There are also two main types of information we get from the environment, and they subdivide. The main categories of information we receive look like those shown in Figure 13.3.

Language, whether written or spoken, is indirect because it consists of symbols that describe the "real world" as seen by others rather than the real world itself that we experience directly through our senses—seeing, hearing, or feeling. Language consists of symbols, but it also consists of other people's interpretation of reality. This is where many communications problems lie. You may have perceived what is going on incorrectly or may have interpreted what you saw in very personal ways. However, I can also misunderstand the words that you used to describe what you experienced.

In any focused group activity, all four sources of information are vitally important to performance. Yet, often for practical reasons, many individuals, teams, and program participants get their information unequally and may

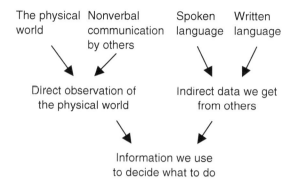

Figure 13.3. Proposition Three Expanded

have different internal resources and perceptions for making sense of the information.

When we "decide what to do," we place the information we have gathered alongside our needs and figure out how to use one to satisfy the other. In other words, we *think*.

Diagnostic Questions for Proposition Three

- What information is available to the stakeholders, and where is it sourced?

- What information that the stakeholders need to achieve their goals is not available? Why not?

- Where are stakeholders getting their information? If it is filtered through other people, is it being distorted in this process? If so, why and how? Do stakeholders have any verification strategies for indirect information?

- What values and assumptions are underpinning the ways in which the stakeholders are processing and analyzing information?

- Is information from some sources given more weight than from others simply because of the power and status of the source?

Proposition Four
We use tools to manipulate our environment and to get information from the environment. The tools we use mediate (or shape) the way we do the work.

Humans are tool users. A tool is anything we use to help us manipulate the environment to meet our needs. We also use tools to obtain necessary information from the environment. This definition means that language is a tool, as are concepts and mental models. When someone opens a book or a computer file to get information, the book or the computer is being used as a tool for work. But the written language is also part of the tool. Exactly the same thing happens when someone asks a question of another. In this case, the spoken language is the tool, and in a way so is the person whom the other person asks.

But while physical tools enhance our physical capabilities and conceptual tools enhance our mental capabilities, they also have embedded in their design the ideas and assumptions of the people who developed them, which means they also always have limitations. For example, the desk (a tool) I am sitting at as I write this is not mine. The position of the height adjustment lever assumes that the desk user is right handed. But I am left-handed. Similarly, every project or program has embedded in its design assumptions the developers have about the users' world. For example, business planning manuals make assumptions about how business processes are carried out. However, I often find that these business planning methods are not aligned with ways of successfully managing my own business. To improve my business, I need to find more appropriate tools. Alternatively, I can take the basic ideas and insights I gain from the planning manual and alter or modify them to be more appropriate for my historical, social, financial, and cultural context.

So while we use tools to manipulate the environment, the nature of the tools we use also shapes our own thinking about what to do and how to do it (see Figure 13.4).

Diagnostic Questions for Proposition Four

- Are the tools in use well suited to addressing the stated need?
- In what ways are the tools in use constraining or influencing the way the work is done?
- Do stakeholders have sufficient skills to use the available tools effectively? (This includes the questions of literacy and language proficiency, including technical language proficiency.)

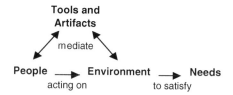

Figure 13.4. Proposition Four

- Are some stakeholders privileged over others in the use of the tools? Does this matter, or is it merely a sensible division of labor?

Proposition Five
The human systems—social, cultural, and organizational—within which we work to satisfy our need also mediate the ways in which we conduct our activities.

It is not only the tools we use that shape how we approach the way we work toward satisfying our needs. Humans are social beings, and mostly we have to come together in some form of organization to undertake the activities that will address our needs.

Furthermore, the nature of our social relationships and the ways in which an organization is structured are the product of the cultural and historical traditions and experiences that have been transmitted to individuals and groups by those who went before. Finally, those cultural and historical perspectives also play a large part in determining not just *how* we work to satisfy our needs, but also *why* we work. Our motivation again. The authors want to change the world with this book, but our independent and shared histories and cultures determine why we want to change the world with this book. Our motivation.

This principle can be shown diagrammatically as in Figure 13.5.

This is the basic structure of an activity system. It consists of elements, listed in the words in the diagram, actions and tasks. It also requires information flows. An activity system is a basis for structural analysis of a team or organization or program and its work.

For practical purposes, the structure of an activity system can be expressed in a slightly different form, as shown in Figure 13.6:

Figure 13.5. Activity System Model

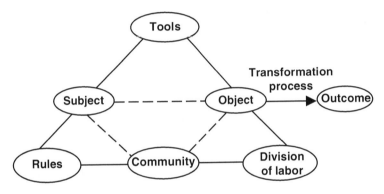

Figure 13.6. Revised Activity System Model

Where:

- Object: the purpose and motives that define the activity
- Subjects: the person or people who carry out the activity
- Outcome: both intended and unintended results of carrying out the activity
- Tools: both physical and non-physical instruments that are used in the conduct of the activity
- Community: the community in which the subjects carry out that activity

- Rules: the formal and informal rules that the community imposes on the subject
- Division of labor: relationships in the community that determine the roles that subjects have in carrying out the activity (Hassan 2002)

The key difference is the expansion of "needs" into two components. One, the object, describes the motivations that drive us to satisfy our needs, and the other, the outcome or goal, is the result or consequence of our actions driven by those motivations. In an activity system, all actions are driven by this motive and directed toward achieving a result.

Thus, an "object" describes the motives or drivers that help define and focus the activities within the system and help direct them toward the outcome (or goal). The following case study is driven by the motivation to run a food distribution business in a manner directed at the result of environmentally and socially sustainable agricultural practices.

In an Activity Systems–based inquiry, the first task is to identify the object or objects – the purpose(s) and motive(s) driving the activity. It is the core unit of analysis of the system. Activity Systems always have multiple objects, some of which are held by the whole system and some of which are held by one or many of the actors in the system. However, there is usually a superordinate object or set of objects that constitute the explicit purpose of the system, why this system is valid. Motivations, ethics, or core values are good places to start looking for a system's objects.

It is important to understand that even at the superordinate level the explicit objects can often be in tension with one another. For example, an airline may have a desired result of delivering passengers to their destination. However, two formal motivational objects, "safe travel" and "profit," implies that operational trade-offs will sometimes need to be made between profit (e.g., operating in a cost-efficient manner) and safety (e.g., diverting or climbing away from storms—thus burning more fuel and potentially causing expensive disruptions to schedules and crew shifts). But at the tacit level, tensions between objects almost always produce multiple levels of tension that are not always explicit. The most widespread class of these are the personal objects of individuals and groups who work with or in the system. One social worker is a solo parent and needs to put food on her table. She complies with organizational rules to keep her job. Another social worker of independent means is motivated by the opportunities to empower young adolescents. He represents their interests strongly. All this is unproblematic until, say, both are asked to jointly manage a contested foster situation. How the system handles these contradictions, as we shall see, is key to how a successful activity system operates.

Analyzing these multiple objects, and surfacing the tacit or unspoken ones, is an essential first step in a CHAT approach. Such analyses help us understand why people do things the way they do and why those observable actions often seem to be in conflict with the stated objects of the system.

Diagnostic Questions for Proposition Five

- What are the underlying motivations that underpin all other aspects of the activity system (i.e., objects, purpose)? Who is motivated to do what for what reason?

- What are the consequences or outcomes of these motivations? What goods, services, or social conditions are being produced (i.e., outcome, goal)?

- What raw materials and prerequisite conditions are required for the activity to start from? What are the processes by which the raw materials and the prerequisite conditions are transformed into the outcomes?

- What physical and mental tools are needed for the work? What knowledge and skills are needed? Are they present?

- Who are the different kinds of people needed to do the work?

- What are the formal rules (manuals, standard operating procedures, etc.) that promote or constrain the way in which the activity proceeds?

- What are the informal (cultural) rules that promote or constrain the way in which the work proceeds?

- What are the organizational structures that shape the way the work is done?

- What other systems must supply inputs in order for the work to proceed? What other systems use the product of our systems' work? How are all these systems connected to our system?

- What information must flow around the system for it to operate effectively? Where is the information needed kept, and where must it go? Is the information flowing as required?

Learning

Proposition Six: The Learning Proposition

When the tools, rules, community, and organization operate as expected, those within an activity system proceed by conducting standardized tasks with predictable results. But the system will often be interrupted by unanticipated events (disturbances) or surface underlying tensions between elements of the system (contradictions). When a team, program, or organization encounters these, it will flounder unless it is able to learn *how to deal with these issues. Thus disturbances and contradictions in system components allow us to learn about the "real" world.*

Disturbances and contradictions are fundamental concepts in CHAT. Disturbances are almost always the visible manifestations of systemic contradictions. Even natural disasters such as droughts are risks around which informed choices were made about the location of farming activities. If a drought that is within normal climatic ranges occurs and it is unplanned for, then that represents a failure of the activity system—it should have been able to handle those plausible contradictions.

The management literature and most management practice tends to regard disturbances negatively. Much effort goes into preventing them from happening. Consequently it is socially unacceptable in most organizations to make contradictions explicit. They are ignored. However, CHAT approaches consider that contradictions provide the opportunity for learning and innovation; thus they should be sought out and made explicit. If disturbances are seen as irritations—"problems" to be overcome—then it is unlikely that stakeholders will progress beyond "fire fighting." But CHAT points to disturbances and contradictions as potential springboards for learning, innovation, and development.

There are four possible sources of contradictions (see Figure 13.6):

1. *Within* components of an activity system (e.g., between rules)
2. *Between* components of an activity system (e.g., between rules and object)

3. *Between Activity Systems* (e.g., a tool used in an organization's object to have a safe working environment, and another tool used to support the same organization's object to be profitable)

4. *Historical disturbance*—between what is now and how it used to be (i.e., between a newly introduced tool and an old rule)

As stated earlier, the most difficult contradictions to use as springboards for growth are those that are "invisible" or "undiscussible." An invisible contradiction is one that is so much part of the team's everyday life that the members do not even recognize it as a difficulty. Invisible contradictions include anything that is "taken for granted" and especially covers cultural assumptions about how things are done and how relationships are managed.

Undiscussible contradictions are those that nobody ever talks about because they are embarrassing, uncomfortable, or culturally difficult to confront. Gender and racial issues in teams, or offensive personal habits of politically powerful program stakeholders, are all examples of undiscussibles. Nobody is willing to talk about them openly, but they may be seriously impeding progress toward the goal, toward satisfying the need.

Surfacing invisible or undiscussible contradictions and stimulating a developmental dialogue around them is the most potentially valuable service that a CHAT-based intervention provides.

Diagnostic Questions for Proposition Six

• What contradictions are there within the system? What have been the consequences? How have people responded? How could they have responded?

• What generalizations do people make about the performance of the system? What exceptions are there to those generalizations? What learnings are there from these "small" contradictions?

• What disturbances—unanticipated events—have happened ? What were the consequences? What are the potential learnings?

• What are the historical underpinnings of these contradictions and disturbances? How is the "past" interacting with the "present"; the "old" with the "new"?

- What events and circumstances remain undiscussible? Between whom are they (un)discussible? What rules, roles, tools, objects, and histories mediate these undiscussibles?

Proposition Seven: The Developmental Proposition
When a contradiction's potential as a springboard is triggered by
the actions of system participants, they enter a "Cycle of
Expansive Learning."

The Cycle of Expansive Learning is a central concept in activity theory and concerns how new knowledge—that is, innovation—can occur and be nurtured.

Why "Expansive Learning"?

"Learning" because the introduction of the "new" situation developed to resolve a contradiction will set up further contradictions between what currently "is" and what emerges as a result of the intervention. This leads to further opportunities for learning, and so on. Thus it is a cycle of learning. However, expressed like this it is little different from the traditional action learning cycle. The difference is its expansive nature.

"Expansive?" Figure 13.7 (essentially combining propositions six and seven) demonstrates that learning can be "expansive" because the consequences of action may lead to further contradictions within the system (e.g., "new tool" imposed on "old rules"), or even beyond the boundary of the existing system (i.e., between Activity Systems) and thus expand the possible boundary of learning beyond the initial focus of the inquiry. Expansive learning is the process by which the learning from disturbances and contradictions builds cumulatively; applying learnings and learning from that application creates opportunities for deeper learning.

Diagnostic Questions for Proposition Seven

- What is the history of how current activities came to be as they are now?
- What kinds of weaknesses exist in the relationships between the elements of the system?
- What is missing that is needed?
- What is not working as well as it might? What relationships are not working as they should?

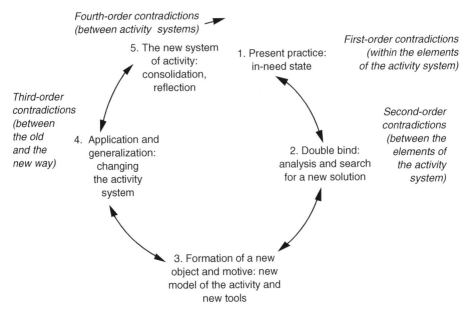

Figure 13.7. Cycle of Expansive Learning
SOURCE: Yrjö Engeström. Used with permission.

- What strengths are there in the system? Are they being used as well as they could be?

- What potential for growth and development is there in the system? What is desirable? What weaknesses and deficiencies need to be rectified before the potential can be tapped?

- How could possible changes impact on the existing activity system? What are the learning opportunities and how can they be enhanced?

- Are adjacent Activity Systems likely to be affected? If so, in what way, and how can these learnings be exploited?

Notice here how history is critical to a CHAT analysis and intervention. We cannot understand what is happening in a work system now without understanding how it came to be.

CASE APPLICATION OF CHAT

Whole Fruit began in 1985 as a not-for-profit business, although built on the shell of a much older for-profit workers' cooperative. The principles of worker involvement in the company are still an important aspect of the way it goes about its job, largely through a desire to maintain a stable and happy workplace.

Its mission is to develop marketing and educational activities that strengthen ecological family farms; to increase public access to the benefits of a local farm system by serving as a broker (i.e., intermediary between producers and retail markets) for small- and medium-scale family farmers in Oklahoma. Oklahoma is a state that imports most of its fruit supplies (see http://www .noble.org/ag/Horticulture/FreshFruitOkla/index.html). Formally this is expressed as the following goal: "to accelerate the movement toward a locally based and locally controlled food system in Oklahoma."

Whole Fruit has had a bumpy ride over the past twenty years. Originally, it hoped to be self-sufficient, but cut-throat competition and other events have made the possibility for self-sufficiency unrealistic, even though "making money" is a major driver in the organization. Whole Fruit has now morphed into two services: trader and consultant.

It is an ambitious company that has established a strong brand via its promotional and other activities. Much of its success has been developed through very close relationships with farmers and retailers. For instance, whatever the circumstances, it tries to ensure that farmers get a fair price, whatever the difficulties the firm is experiencing.

On the other hand, it demands and closely monitors the quality of the product from the growers and closely monitors the quality of the product that is delivered to the retailers. The quality control process is shared among the farmers, contractor, Whole Fruit, and retail staff—it involves a lot of work.

Growth is important to Whole Fruit, and it has grown significantly over the years, partly as a matter of principle and partly to gain economies of scale. Initially Whole Fruit established the contract for supplies and the farmers did the deliveries. However, one of the consequences of growth was that the retailers were demanding more frequent deliveries from farmers—and individual farmers were unable to do this themselves. The response was that Whole Fruit raised capital to purchase the means of delivery—it invested heavily in warehousing and trucks to solve this problem. This required new approaches to quality control.

This increased capacity allowed it to develop relationships with larger retailers and to grow substantially. A particular retailer was very enthusiastic about the product and began to become a significant, almost dominant, customer. At some stage, Whole Fruit reached the point where it became more visible (and a more significant threat) to larger, much larger, competitors. Eventually one of the larger suppliers persuaded this large customer to drop Whole Fruit. It was done just before the main delivery season when all its contracts were established and the growers were growing the crops. The cash flow consequences were disastrous, as were the implications for Whole Fruit's relationships with farmers and retailers.

To sustain these relationships (for instance, it chose to keep the relationship going with the retailer who dropped it), it had to reduce costs and very fast. It made its delivery staff redundant, sold the trucks, and leased out its warehouse. Slowly the firm began to recover, and the relationships with farmers and retailers were sustained. However, it meant redesigning—again—the quality control methods.

This experience highlighted that despite the organization's growth, unit costs were not reducing. Whole Fruit needed to be twenty to fifty times bigger to get the economies of scale that would allow it to withstand significant disturbances. It also began to realize that it needed to be able to trade all year round, not just for six months of the year when produce was available. This meant vastly expanding its product range, considerable capital expenditure, and extending considerably the network of trading relationships. This, however, could negatively impact on the service toward existing growers. As a result, Whole Fruit pursued alternative strategy—something that sustained existing relationships but was also low investment, high margin, and low maintenance. It started a business consultancy service.

You have been asked by a large foundation that has supported this project for ten years to evaluate Whole Fruit. Ostensibly the foundation wants to judge Whole Fruit's performance against its formal stated goal. More candidly it is concerned that the continuous financial crises and changes of direction display a lack of prudent business knowledge and poor management. There is a concern that the foundation is throwing money down a bottomless pit without any real impact. These are perspectives through which the foundation wants you to evaluate Whole Fruit.

So let us unpick this story within a CHAT context. This is not a full analysis; the observations are based only on the data presented. A full study would uncover a richer array of viewpoints, meanings, contradictions, and perspectives.

KEY DIAGNOSTIC QUESTION: WHAT IS THE OBJECT?

Whole Fruit's object is actually quite complex, but at the core there is a clear motivational driver: it wants to be a business whose practices are ethically driven by sustainable agricultural and community principles. Whole Fruit is committed to an idealized food production system that it wishes to operationalize.

Proposition Two
"Activity" is what happens when human beings operate on their
environment in order to satisfy a needs state.

The "need" is a combination of the object (see above) and the consequence (goal). The goal is a locally based and locally controlled food system in Oklahoma that increases public access to high-quality, locally grown food.

Overall, the actions described in this case study are oriented toward this goal and consistent with the object. However, clearly there are other adjacent Activity Systems directed toward goals that both help and hinder the activity system achieve the goal. For instance, in order to sustain year-long operation, Whole Fruit began to work with Californian citrus farmers (who may have other objects and goals) and later starts a national consultancy service. These are not entirely consistent with local produce locally distributed. Depending on what we are trying to investigate, these could be seen as a separate activity system or part of the same activity system.. These boundary decisions are a critical aspect of Activity Systems inquiry.

Proposition Three
Information must flow through the activity system in order to
achieve the desired result.

Observed actions may be puzzling in terms of the object(s) because people are acting on inadequate or distorted information. Deficiencies may be due to inadequate information and knowledge management or because actions are interpreted through the culturally biased lenses of people who handle information. In either case, such distortion represents a tension in the system.

There are limited data about information use in this case study. The most important information described in the case study relates to sustaining high-quality produce throughout the activity system. This is only tangentially related to the object or even the goal; it relates more to the organizational rule of high-quality produce.

One area of information flow that relates directly toward the Whole Fruit object was the behind-the-scenes discussions between the major retailer and their major supplier. It demonstrated a contradiction between Whole Fruit's object and those of the two key stakeholders. Had information been flowing through the system earlier (i.e., before the farmers had planted their crops), or had Whole Fruit "read" the information that was flowing slightly differently, or had the potential contradiction been observed earlier or had the boundary of the activity system been drawn more widely, then the disturbance to the activity system may have been much less significant.

Proposition Four
Tools mediate (or shape) the way we do the work.
Inappropriate or inadequate tools for the object(s) are tensions in the system. The variety of tools used in this activity system is large. The critical tools appear to be the following:

- Methods of delivery and storage (e.g., transport and warehousing)

- Methods of assessing the quality of the produce at various stages in the value chain

- Whole Fruit itself, since it brokers the relationship between producers and retailers

- The foundation, since it provides a mechanism for bridging gaps between what farmers receive, what retailers are willing to pay, and what it costs to run Whole Fruit.

Clearly there have been some issues over time about the ability of stakeholders to use the quality control tools—issues that have flowed largely from the systems response to disturbances, which we will discuss shortly.

Proposition Five
The human systems—social, cultural, and organizational—within which we work to satisfy our need also mediate the ways in which we conduct our activities.

The critical rules in this activity system include the following:

- The system must grow.
- The business must be profitable.
- Whole Fruit should have a stable workforce.
- Whole Fruit must become independent of foundation money.
- Farmers must get a fair price for their produce.
- Retailers must pay a fair price for their supplies.
- The relationships between farmers, retailers, and Whole Fruit are to be good and constructive.
- Whole Fruit must be "worker friendly" and a good place to work.
- High-quality produce is essential.

Many of the struggles that Whole Fruit wrestled with involved disturbances that created contradictions between previously compatible rules. For instance, to sustain most of the "social goal" rules, Whole Fruit eventually had to abandon the rule that it should become independent of external grants. The other interesting thing about these rules is that they point Whole Fruit toward expansion of the original "object"—enlarging notions of sustainability and fairness. If that was the case, then it is almost inconceivable that Whole Fruit would ever reach the steady state that the foundation and some of its management envisaged.

The "division of labor" (DoL) has changed several times, largely as the result of disturbances elsewhere in the system (see the following list).

DoL One

- Farmers produce and deliver.
- Retailers purchase.
- Whole Fruit brokers and assesses quality.

DoL Two

- Farmers produce.

- Retailers purchase.

- Whole Fruit brokers, assesses quality, picks up produce, stores produce, and delivers.

DoL Three

- Farmers produce.

- Retailers purchase.

- Whole Fruit brokers and assesses quality.

- Other parties pick up produce, store, and deliver.

Propositions Six and Seven: Learning and Development

The first major disturbance was between the "growth" rule and the "division of labor" structure. The system became too big to sustain the historical way in which produce was distributed. Whole Fruit sought to resolve this disturbance by reorganizing the structure of the system and becoming the storer and deliverer of produce.

The new efficiencies within the system led to the ability to supply large quantities to a single retailer. The next disturbance occurred as a consequential contradiction between the "growth" rule, the "information" tool, and some aspects of the overall "object." Responding to some contradictions of its own (within an adjacent activity system), the major retailer dumped Whole Fruit at short notice—something that the systems information tools were unable to pick up, possibly because of an overreliance on the "good relationship" rule.

Within the system, Whole Fruit was confronted by a massive and simultaneous set of contradictions. There were contradictions within system elements (especially between rules, and between the superordinate object) and between system elements (e.g., between division of labor and objects, between rules and tools) as well as some historical contradictions (the potentially bad relationship with the major retailer and past relationship with that retailer).

Whole Fruit responded essentially by changing the community of practice: it altered the relationship between the rules and roles by essentially changing the division of labor. It laid off staff and changed the way in which food was stored and delivered. In that way it expanded the community of practice and kept the good employer rules (by altering whom it employed). Thus the solution allowed the rules, tools, and object to remain largely untouched.

However, as with any cycle of expansive learning, this resolution created further disturbances. The new division of labor created tensions within rules and tools around the rule of maintaining high quality. A new set of tools had to be developed, which also allowed the quality rule to be "expanded" slightly and is probably now best expressed as "keeping quality consistent in a changing environment."

The other consequence of this massive disturbance was to focus Whole Fruit on other contradictions within the activity system, in particular, the rule of being free of foundation money, and survive under its current business model. This led to a profound reassessment of the activity system and Whole Fruit's role within it and outside it. While the consultancy operation can be seen within the existing object of sustainable agriculture, it might now be more valuable to expand the inquiry and explore how Whole Fruit is seeking to work within two or three different Activity Systems. For instance, "business sustainability," once regarded as a rule, may now be best considered an end in itself—effectively becoming an object with its own and perhaps contradictory sets of goals, rules, roles, and tools. Much will depend on key decisions about who are the clients of the consultancy arm and what their own motivations might be. Will the consultancy be aimed at other "sustainability"-oriented organizations (inside or outside the agricultural sector), or to any small business within the produce distribution sector? Either way, the lessons of CHAT can help Whole Fruit make those choices.

This narrative has been largely diagnostic, but it also may be used in any future planning and strategizing for Whole Fruit. In terms of evaluation, it has provided an alternative framework—focusing primarily on understanding what opportunities Whole Fruit had to learn from the changing situation and their response to it. In terms of the original stated goals of Whole Fruit, it is possible to see failure—it has at times had to wrestle with disturbances to the "object" in order to survive. On the other hand, the twists and turns of Whole Fruit's experience and its ability to learn and adapt create significant potential lessons for the sustainable agriculture movement as a whole. So instead of withdrawing funding from Whole Fruit because it was not achieving financial independence, the foundation could well learn about running businesses that promote agricultural sustainability by continuing to support such a smart operator in such a complex and changing environment.

REFLECTIONS ON THE USE OF CHAT
General

CHAT has been used in a variety of quite specific areas. It is extensively used in areas where there is a shared set of critical activities that nevertheless may serve different goals and different motivations. Perhaps the most obvious examples are in high-risk industries such as nuclear power, the airline industry, railways, and the oil industry, where balancing high risk and high reward is essential. CHAT has also been used in the evaluation of higher education (since it is fundamentally about understanding how people learn under multiple objectives).

Pros / Advantages

The main benefit of CHAT is that it has brought the world of systems concepts to the world of learning. In doing so it has provided some intellectual grunt to those systems advocates who believe that systems ideas can promote deeper understandings and meanings. CHAT also helps people acknowledge that there are substantial benefits in acknowledging and embracing "contradictions" rather than ignoring them or explaining them away.

CHAT also helps us understand why unanticipated events happen. It is not because people are essentially incompetent or not committed to organizational goals. It just means that they may have other goals and objectives that for reasons of motivation, history, or role may take precedence at unexpected times.

The focus on "contradictions" has also meant CHAT has been used to understand how some teams are more innovative than others. Indeed, many argue that innovation is fundamentally about dealing with contradictions—and CHAT provides a structure and theory to allow us to understand how innovations occur.

Cons / Challenges

A CHAT-based approach can be quite labor intensive. The subtleties of unacknowledged contradictions can occur almost unnoticed within a meeting of, say, project workers. Keen-eyed and keen-eared external observers, armed with video cameras, are often used to identify and deconstruct those vital moments.

The jargon of CHAT often gets in the way. It is a set of highly abstract constructs that take a while to get your head around. This is especially the case with the notion of "object." Current management practices are so used to thinking about "result" as a driver that switching the focus to the motivational forces that underpin the goal is a major disturbance in itself.

SOME VARIATIONS AND MODIFICATIONS
Change Laboratory

The Center for Activity Systems and Developmental Work Research in Helsinki, Finland, developed a workshop-based version of CHAT. The purpose of the method is to help a work team or the members of an organizational unit to encounter the problems they face in their daily work and systematically analyze the systemic causes of these problems and design and implement a new form for the activity to overcome the root cause of daily problems.

The Change-Laboratory is a space that offers practitioners a wide variety of instruments for analyzing disturbances and bottlenecks in the work practices. It is a diagnostic tool that allows for constructing new models and tools and for putting them on trial. Since it involves all key stakeholders in the diagnostic and development activities, it also provides a means of cooperation between expert interventionists and local practitioners (Edutech Wiki).

Communities of Practice

The idea of communities of practice is primarily associated with the work of Etienne Wenger and Jean Lavé, whose work on situated learning has been extremely influential in knowledge management and educational circles in the past decade or so. Like activity theory, the theoretical ideas underpinning communities of practice are based on Vygotskyian notions of learning being a social and socially constructed activity contained within a "zone of proximal development." Indeed, the two fields can be seen as two sides of the same coin, where the rules and roles associated with a shared object constitute a community of practice.

Contradiction Analysis
Chapter 15, "Dialectical Methods of Inquiry," has a section that draws from the ideas underpinning Proposition Six of CHAT.

NOTE
Our thanks to Phil Capper and Web Research for permission to draw heavily on the paper "Activity Theory as a Design Principle for Team Development Processes."

REFERENCES AND FURTHER READING
Capper, Phil, O. Harvey, R. Hill, and K. Wilson. 2004. Activity theory as a design principle for team development processes. Available at http://www.webresearch.co.nz/.
Center for Activity Theory and Developmental Work Research. University of Helsinki. http://www.helsinki.fi/activity/.
Edutech Wiki. http://edutechwiki.unige.ch/en/Change_laboratory.
Hassan, H. 2002. An activity-based model of collective knowledge. Proceedings of the 36th Hawaii International Conference on System Sciences (HICSS'03).
Laboratory of Comparative Human Cognition. University of Southern California. http://www.lchc.ucsd.edu/index.html.
Work, Education and Business Research (WEB Research). http://www.webresearch.co.nz/.

14

SOFT SYSTEMS METHODOLOGY

What are the different ways in which a situation can be framed?

How does each of these ways, on its own, provide a means of comprehending how a situation behaves?

What are the implications for any changes to the situation?

WHAT IS SOFT SYSTEMS METHODOLOGY?

Soft Systems Methodology (SSM) was developed by Peter Checkland in the late 1960s at the University of Lancaster in the United Kingdom. In his years as a manager at ICI, a major British plastics company, he had become increasingly disillusioned with the application of systems engineering ideas to management problems. In particular, he identified that the formal definition of a particular management problem often failed to provide guidance to its resolution.

Checkland's key insight was, at the time, revolutionary. Existing systems methods assumed that a given set of interrelationships would be understood by everyone in roughly the same way. His experience as a manager, however, told him that this was not so; different people within a situation are working to different objectives, based on different perspectives. These differences influence their behavior and thus the dynamics of a situation. Thus, addressing a situation regarded as problematic required an understanding of the multiple perspectives that people brought to that situation.

Implicit in this approach is the idea that merely observing a situation and then mapping or modeling it will lead to fewer insights than identifying the different ways a situation can be appreciated and modeling or mapping each of those ways.

Consider, for instance, a rock concert. Say that the particular band had a history of concerts that ended in riots, and you—as promoter or local mayor or police—wish to avoid that. But first the puzzle. How is it that a riot can be a product of something as ostensibly harmless as entertainment?

Checkland would argue that a rock concert can in fact be considered, appreciated, and perceived (i.e., framed) from a variety of different standpoints, such as the following:

- Entertainment
- Employment for musicians
- Machismo of security personnel
- Tribal identity (e.g., heavy metal fan)
- Drug dealing
- Enterprise for promoters
- Merchandising (T-shirts, DVDs)
- Marketing (e.g., Pepsi)
- Fund raising (e.g., benefit concerts)
- Publicity (e.g., Live Aid and world poverty)
- Underage drinking

Making sense of just one of these perspectives, especially the formal "entertainment" perspective, will not explain the riots or help plan a riot-free concert. Only understanding all of these perspectives and the dynamics of how these perspectives play out provides a way to do both.

The problem is that wrestling with all these perspectives as a whole can be a confusing task. Checkland's great contribution was to propose separating out these perspectives and appreciating them individually, working out the logical consequence of taking each perspective and comparing that with the messiness of the real situation. Out of these comparisons between perspectives and the real world emerge ideas for improvement.

Checkland describes the approach in the following way (Checkland and Poulter 2006):

1. You have a perceived problematical situation that

    • will contain people trying to behave purposefully;

    • will be perceived differently by people with different worldviews.

2. So make models of purposeful activity as perceived by different worldviews.

3. Use these models as a source of questions to ask of the problematical situation, thus structuring a discussion about changes that are both desirable and culturally feasible.

4. Find versions of the to-be-changed situation which different worldviews could live with.

5. Implement changes to improve the situation.

6. Be prepared to start the process again.

Although originally conceived as a problem-solving tool, SSM has developed over the years to be oriented toward learning and insight. Because the methodology is exploring a situation from different perspectives, soft systems is inherently multivoiced. It tends to work better when a range of participants are involved, although it is not essential.

DETAILED DESCRIPTION OF THE METHOD
Overview

Soft systems is a methodology. However, it is generally described in the form of a seven-step method. Checkland has consistently argued that this method does not have to be followed strictly or even in the order described below. Rather, it should be considered a heuristic, an approach, that informs your process of inquiry. Indeed, Checkland has developed an alternative version, described in this chapter in the section "Variations."

However, the classic seven-step approach reveals most clearly the concepts that underpin the methodology and forms the basis of the explanation in this chapter. Five of these steps focus on the actual situation of interest, and two steps depend entirely on thinking systemically and conceptually about that situation. (See Figure 14.1.)

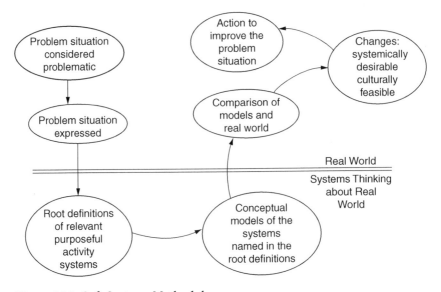

Figure 14.1. Soft Systems Methodology
SOURCE: Peter Checkland and Jim Scholes, *Soft Systems Methodology in Action: A 30-Year Retrospective* (New York: John Wiley and Sons, 1999). © 1990, 1999 John Wiley and Sons Ltd. Reproduced with permission by the publisher.

Step 1: Identify the issue you wish to address.

Step 2: Develop an *unstructured* description of the situation where the issue lies. How the situation *is*.

Step 3: Identify key perspectives through which to view the situation.

Step 4: Develop ideas of how the situation *ought* to behave from the point of view of each perspective.

Step 5: Compare perspectives and compare each perspective with the situation (i.e., compare *ought* with *is*).

Step 6: Out of the various insights that step 5 throws up, develop ways of addressing the issue that are both desirable and feasible.

Step 7: Implement.

The success of the approach depends on being able to separate the *systems thinking* stages from the *real world* stages. This separation sets up a series of tensions and dialectics. There are tensions between how the *real world* is (steps 1 and 2) and *systems thinking* about that real world as it might be (steps

3 and 4); the tension between the messiness of the real world situation and clarity of taking a single perspective on the situation and the tension between the different perspectives. All these tensions provide sites for creative thinking (steps 5, 6, and 7). Handling these tensions is a somewhat more difficult task than it sounds and is perhaps the most common reason for the failure of soft systems approaches.

Steps 1 and 2: The Situation Defined

The first step, very much in the real world, is to acknowledge, explore, and define the situation in some way. Peter Checkland talks about the "problem situation," as the original purpose of developing SSM was a problem-solving one. However, the situation can be any that is of interest and presents a puzzle of some kind.

The first task is to decide what it is you are actually exploring. At this stage you do not define the problem but merely explore the situation that is of interest to us. Indeed, Checkland argues that defining the problem too early is a key mistake.

This is an arbitrary starting point, and it may shift—for instance, at some stage you may choose to open out the boundary of the situation to sweep in more aspects of the situation. At this stage you are also not particularly constrained by any formal definitions or organizational boundaries. You collect as much data as you can, qualitative, quantitative, by whatever method seems appropriate—survey, observation, measurement.

Having done this research, step 2 "expresses" the issue in some way. Checkland calls this a *rich picture* for two reasons. First, the situation needs to be expressed in all its *richness*. Checkland provides some guidelines as to what should be included:

- Structures
- Processes
- Climate
- People
- Issues expressed by people
- Conflicts

Second, almost everyone's experience is that the best way of doing this is in a *picture* form (often despite their inclinations). There are many ways that this can be done: mind-maps, conversation maps, sketching. However, it is important that the picture should not structure the situation (as in a logic model or process chain). The whole point of a rich picture is to reflect as much going on as possible without privileging, predetermining, or presuming a particular perspective or point of view.

Figure 14.2 is a rich picture of a distance learning situation.

Step 3: Root Definitions of Relevant Systems

Step 3 moves out of the *real world* and into the world of *systems thinking*. Checkland calls this the *root definition* step because it is the "root" out of which everything else grows. It can be the most challenging part of the methodology.

The first task is to draw out different ways of appreciating or understanding the situation through different perspectives. Checkland calls these perspectives *holons*: plausible, relevant, purposeful perspectives that are represented in the real-world activities.

Consider again the rock concert:

- Employment for musicians
- Machismo of security personnel
- Tribal identity (e.g., heavy metal fan)
- Drug dealing
- Enterprise for promoters
- Merchandising (T-shirts, DVDs)
- Marketing (e.g., Pepsi)
- Fund raising (e.g., benefit concerts)
- Publicity (e.g., Live Aid and world poverty)
- Underage drinking

All these are perfectly valid purposeful perspectives, or holons. They may not be shared by all stakeholders or participants in the situation, and a single participant may align himself or herself with several perspectives. For instance, the performer may have a stake in the drug dealing, tribal identity,

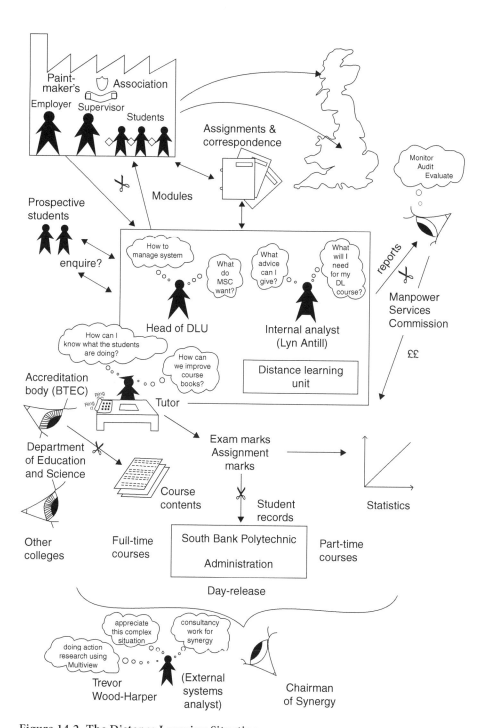

Figure 14.2. The Distance Learning Situation

SOURCE: A. T. Wood-Harper et al., *Information Systems Definition: The Multiview Approach* (Oxford: Blackwell Scientific Publications, 1985). © 1985 Blackwell Publishing Ltd. Reproduced with permission by the publisher.

merchandising, and employment aspects of the concert, all vying for her attention.

The next task is to select each perspective and process it via a structured and rigorous model development process. The model centers around a Transformation (T), a change in state that is implied by the perspective chosen.

Checkland (1993) developed the mnemonic CATWOE to help guide the process of model building:

- *Customers* who benefit from a transformation
- *Actors* who enable the transformation to take place (e.g., decision makers)
- *Transformation*, the change in state implied by the perspective
- *Weltanschauung* that gives the transformation some meaning (e.g., why this transformation is a good thing to do; why this transformation makes sense)
- *Owner* to whom the "system" is answerable and/or could cause it not to exist (e.g., holders of key resources, elected representatives, sponsors)
- *Environment*, important factors that must be taken as "given"

In constructing CATWOE, it is important for everything to be built up from the transformation (T). One way of ensuring this is to construct the CATWOE in the following order:

1. Transformation
2. Weltanschauung
3. Customer
4. Actors
5. Owners
6. Environment

So in terms of a rock concert, from the perspective, or holon, of "tribal identity":

1. Transformation: feeling part of a wider community (e.g., fans)
2. Weltanschauung: identity, a core human need
3. Customer: audience members

4. Actors: musicians

5. Owners: concert sponsors, Pepsi

6. Environment: rules of the venue that may enhance or constrain that sense of identity (e.g., noise, alcohol, capacity, seating, or standing); history of the band's approach to their fan base

The next task is to form a statement of the relevant system. Checkland suggests that one way of structuring these elements is in a statement such as the following:

PQR: a system to do P ("what") by way of Q ("how") in order to R ("why")

So in terms of a rock concert holon of tribal identity,

A system by which audience members (C) satisfy a basic human need (W) by feeling part of a wider community of fans (T) by listening to musicians (A) within a live music event subsidized by Pepsi (O), in a seated venue with a band that encourages adulation by audiences (E).

Of course (and this is critical to the entire SSM approach), even the same perspective can have different CATWOE components. Consider what would happen to CATWOE or the root definition if we identified "musician" as the "customer," or "local council" as the "owner." We might end up with very different CATWOE, different root definitions, and ultimately a different model. This is why SSM is a very iterative approach: you keep trying things out and see how that changes your assessment of the situation.

Checkland recommends keeping the elements of CATWOE roughly in scale. For the same holon, an "owner" could be a particular individual, part of an organization, an organization as a whole, or perhaps an entire sector. These different levels of scale need to be matched throughout the CATWOE So, for instance, the transformation will be quite different at the level of a "worker" than the level of an entire industrial sector. Getting the scale appropriately balanced (i.e., a relevant system) is one of the arts of SSM.

Step 4: Developing the Model

Using the root definition, you draw a conceptual model using systems conventions. There are many ways of modeling a system, and by today's standards Checkland's original convention (see below) might seem a little primitive and rather overly focused on activities rather than consequences of activities. However, in practice it is a remarkably good method for constructing simple models. Like many who believe that insights flow from simple rather than complicated models, Checkland supports the model having as few elements as possible. The point of the model is essentially to compare the logical consequence of the root definition with the existing situation. It is not to predict or simulate complex interrelationships. It is modeling for insight, not prediction (see Chapters 1 and 2).

Checkland recommends that beginners follow the process below (Checkland 1993):

1. Using verbs in the imperative, write down activities necessary to carry out the transformation (T in CATWOE). Aim for 7±2 activities that are at the same *scale*.

2. Select activities that could be done at once (i.e., are not dependent on others).

3. Place these activities in a line, and then those that are dependent on these first activities in a line; continue until all are accounted for.

4. Indicate the dependencies.

5. Rearrange to avoid overlapping arrows where possible. Add a means of assessing performance (i.e. evaluation) and include the aspects of the environment identified in CATWOE.

6. Finally, check whether your model demonstrates the following systems properties:

   • An ongoing purpose that may be determined in advance (purposeful) or assigned through observation (purposive)

   • A means of assessing performance

   • A decision-taking process

   • Components that are also systems (i.e., the notion of subsystems)

   • Components that interact

   • An environment (with which the system may or may not interact)

   • A boundary between the system and the environment (that may be closed or open)

- Resources
- Continuity

Checkland recommends you do not spend much time in initial model building. The modeling in the case study below took about twenty minutes from the root definition stages. He considers it better to undertake the comparison step, have the discussions, gain insights, and return to the model, rather than spend a long time on the initial model building. This reinforces his belief that the SSM process is about cycles of discussion, debate, and learning rather than producing the "ideal" solution the first time. However, the speed is not at the cost of rigor. Checkland recommends the model to be closely inspected in ways that increase the rigor of the overall inquiry. For instance:

- Does the diagram come wholly from the root definition and CATWOE with no other extraneous features and ideas added? The rigor of the method depends on this. The modeling process is *not* an idea-generation process but a logical process of assembling and linking features that flow only from the definition *and nothing else*.

- Is the model a "system" or a collection of boxes with lines between them? Does the model include all the features that make it a system? In particular, does the model have a means of monitoring, assessing, and responding to its own performance?

- For those CATWOE that include multiple items (e.g., multiple owners), how would the model and definition look if only one were used?

- What alternative or additional W's are there, and what implications does that have for the defined system and model?

- Has context (i.e., a description of the particular state of system or its environment) been confused with environment (given factors that interact with the system but are not part of it)?

Once you have asked yourself these questions and modified the model, you may think you can move on to the next step, comparing the model with reality. But that would be to miss one of the really powerful parts of SSM. It is wise to do one more thing before moving on. Run through process again, using different CATWOE based on different perspectives (holons) or at different scales (i.e., subsystems of the model you have just developed). This is where you start getting real insights into the complexity of the situation.

Running through several different CATWOE and models will help you explore what recurring themes might emerge or what contradictions might be between the models.

Models can be constructed for each of these perspectives, and the activities identified in the models compared and contrasted with each other (e.g., do they reinforce each other, do they work against each other, which is likely to bring greatest leverage).

You do not *have* to produce multiple models, but SSM really comes into its own when you do. Although ideally they should be developed, like all models, collaboratively with a range of stakeholders, there are times when it is useful to do them just by yourself.

Steps 5 to 7: Back in the Real World

Now comes the time to step back into the real world and compare the model or models with reality. This is the real powerhouse of the methodology, where insights are drawn from these comparisons and ideas for improvements determined.

Step 5: Compare Model and Real World, Gain Insights

Checkland suggests four ways of comparing the model and the real world:

1. Unstructured discussions
2. Structured questioning of the model using a matrix approach
3. Scenario or dynamic modeling
4. Trying to model the real world using the same structure as the conceptual model

The second is the most common, often using a matrix that looks at each component of the model and asks:

- Does it exist in the real world?
- How does it behave?
- How is its performance identified and measured?
- Is this process any good?

So in the following case study, we would look at the models produced and the basis of those models (i.e., CATWOE and the root definitions) and consider what actually does happen in the real world. What is present, and what is missing? What behaves similarly, and what does not?

The biggest and most common mistake you can make at this step is to confuse reality with the models. People often say, "But it is not the purpose of a project or program to do this" or "This is not how I see it." They confuse the point. A holon is a perspective on the system; it is a way in which some people might see the program. The purpose of this step is to develop insights.

Step 6: Develop Desirable and Feasible Interventions
At this point the methodology tends to stop being sequential and starts swinging back and forth through all seven steps of the methodology in order to gain the greatest leverage. On the basis of this analysis, possible interventions are explored. Assessing the feasibility of these interventions is an important aspect of the methodology, and Checkland suggests several ways of doing this:

1. Run through the model again using different CATWOE, different perspectives, different scales (i.e., model subsystems)

2. Undertake different systems-based analyses (e.g., system dynamics, VSM, CHAT)

3. "Owner analysis": Who fundamentally has the authority to take action?

4. "Social system analysis": How do the various roles, norms, and values present in the real world relate to the conceptual model?

5. "Political analysis": How is power expressed in the situation being studied?

Run through the model again using different CATWOE, different perspectives, different scales (i.e., model subsystems).

As already discussed, comparing the model's different systems with "reality" may start to reveal areas of contradiction and synergy that suggest possible strategies.

Undertake different systems-based analyses.

Checkland does not regard his methodology as exclusive. Depending on the situation, you could use a variety of systems-based approaches, for instance, soft systems combined with System Dynamics (see Chapter 2) or Critical Systems Heuristics (see Chapter 19) or Strategic Assumption Surfacing and Testing (see Chapter 6).

The owner, social system, and political analyses

The owner, social system, and political analyses were early additions to the original methodology and a response to initial criticism that the methodology neglected key cultural factors that determine the feasibility of suggested improvements. Although these analyses are placed in step 6. Checkland argues that these analyses should run parallel to the entire investigation, informing each step.

Step 7: Action to Improve the Situation
This is where the methodology comes full cycle and ideally starts a new cycle of deliberation.

CASE APPLICATION OF SOFT SYSTEMS METHODOLOGY*
Governments commonly fund community organizations to provide social, cultural, and welfare services. It is, however, a contested activity. There are often rivalries between organizations for limited resources. Experience of governing and managing the activities might be limited, leading to substandard practice. The relationship between the funding agency and the community organization may be tense. The funding process can be highly politicized, which means that the activities of these organizations are closely scrutinized and become political footballs irrespective of the quality of the services they provide. In fact, partly because of these issues, the government agency became a funding *brokerage* agency, helping organizations get funding from other sources rather than funding organizations directly.

In this particular case, organizations were providing services to marginalized and discriminated communities. The services were controversial—with

Note: Like many applications of soft systems methodology, this case is not a slavish cranking of the methodological handle. It tends to emphasize multiple perspectives more than the classic SSM and has somewhat less emphasis on the rigors of step 5.

media reports highlighting some notable failures. The government agency chose to frame the issue in terms of the quality of management and governance of the community agencies. Consequently they hired consultants who would work with these community agencies to identify management and governance problems. The consultants would also provide a report on each organization to the funding agency, a controversial part of the intervention. Mindful that this was likely to be an expensive project that could result in some negative publicity, the government agency chose to pilot the idea and called in some evaluators to assess its success and how best to expand the pilot scheme.

Because of the complexity, the evaluators were unconvinced that the issue (or at least the potential solution) was just about management quality and that evaluating only the impact of the consultancy work on management quality may not provide adequate insights on how to expand the pilot project successfully.

After some initial exploration with stakeholders and the construction of a rich picture, six possible holons were considered relevant to assessing the worth of the project:

1. *Red flag.* In this perspective the project can be seen as giving advance warnings to the government agency of organizations that are likely to cause trouble.

2. *Management and governance.* In this perspective the pilot project can be seen as about improvements in the governance and management of organizations.

3. *Confidence in the sector.* The perceived problems with the organizations were affecting the way in which the entire community sector was performing. Everyone was suspicious of everyone else, traditional forms of networking and sharing had dropped away, skills were no longer exchanged between organizations. So from this perspective the projects is about confidence in the sector overall.

4. *Consultant testing.* From this perspective the project is about consultants who can work effectively with marginalized groups and organizations.

5. *Role definition.* From this perspective the project is about brokering funding (the new way) versus direct funding (the old way).

6. *Policy.* From this perspective the project is an evidence base for policy development

Note that these holons are all plausible perspectives through which the program could be viewed. They are also largely independent of each other but have the potential to directly affect the behavior of those within the system.

Here are root definitions developed for each of these perspectives.

Holon: Red Flag   *A system of organizational assessment by consultants (A) supported by a government agency (O) that provides the key staff in the agency (C) with early intelligence about potential problems instead of late intelligence when the problem has become public (T) and consequently politically difficult to solve because the social program is treated with public suspicion (W).*

Holon: Management and Governance   *A system by which the performance of culturally based organizations (C) is improved (T) within the conventions of not-for-profit governance (W) from the intervention by consultants (A) paid by a government agency (O) in an environment where there is tension between the suspicion of the quality of these organization and the belief that local people are best positioned to deliver locally relevant services (E).*

Holon: Confidence in the Sector   *A system that as a result of the consultants' work (O) improves knowledge sharing (T) between sector organizations (C) and (A) because the image of a competent sector is important (W) within a situation that is highly politicized (E).*

Holon: Role Definition   *A system whereby a government agency (C and O) is changed from a source of money to not-for-profit agencies into a facilitator and broker working on behalf of those not-for-profits (T) by the actions of an independent consultancy (A). This change of role is consistent with the agency's belief in self-help and sustainability (W) and legitimized by legislative responsibilities (E).*

Holon: Consultant Testing   *A system by which the government agency (O and C) and local organizations (C) gain new understandings about which consultants (A) can work successfully within a culturally appropriate*

framework (W) that helps ensure better analysis and resolution of the problems (T) created by externally imposed contract criteria (E).

Holon: Policy   *A system by which the work of consultants (A) working collaboratively with community agencies (O) generates evidence (T) for the government agency (C) that wishes to intervene constructively when organizations get into difficulties (W) in a situation that is highly politicized (E).*

Fairly crude models of each holon were developed (step 4) and checked for the appropriate systems properties (step 4). When these were compared with "reality," the program was judged to be performing well from the perspective of most key holons, with the appropriate processes and structures in place (step 5).

There were, however, some important exceptions that assisted in the development of step 6. These essentially related to the "role definition" holon. There were problems with the internal ability of the government agency to carry out the facilitator role and the ability of other government agencies (who also provide funding and support to these community organizations) to accept that changed role. The political, social, and cultural analysis also revealed that some agency staff found it difficult having a role as both an advisor (i.e., facilitating) and as a funder (i.e., deciding whether to give money to the organization). The ability to make funding decisions within local communities gave agency employees (who were locally based) a privileged role within their community that was threatened by the move to a more facilitative role. As recommended by Checkland, some of these issues were teased out using another systems approach, CHAT (see Chapter 13).

This issue formed the major change between the pilot projects and the full rollout (i.e., step 7). All the issues were addressed before the rollout, including much more substantial training of funding agency staff and greater liaison between the funding agency and other possible sources of funding.

Two important systemic issues flow from this. First, the policy makers would have missed a vital aspect of the project if they had solely focused on the "formal" identification of the problem. Second, new people were brought into the system; the system boundary was expanded to include funding agency liaison staff and equivalent staff in other agencies.

REFLECTIONS ON SOFT SYSTEMS METHODOLOGY
Pros / Advantages
Soft systems is a very flexible approach. It is possible to cherry-pick the methodology. CATWOE and the "root definition" steps can expose very important insights and highlight unspoken assumptions. It is possible to work with the basic principles: separating out "is" from "ought," following through the logic of a perspective without reference to "reality," the idea that perspectives affect not only the way we "see" a situation but also the way in which we react to that situation—without recourse to the seven-step process. Indeed, Checkland himself promotes the principles more than the methodological practice. In fact, just posing the questions at the beginning of this chapter is often enough to get powerful discussions going.

Cons / Challenges
It is easy to generate interest in soft systems approaches but more difficult to sell the methodology itself. There are various reasons for this.

First, SSM is far from "soft" in its approach. It demands a degree of rigor that belies its apparently commonsense approach Some people find the rigor of distinguishing between thinking systemically and thinking about the real world especially difficult to handle. This has led to "softer" applications of soft systems than intended by Checkland. Indeed, his most recent book (Checkland 2006) was at least partly aimed at correcting common misunderstandings and misuses.

Another challenge is the contradiction with the multiple objective ideas that inform SSM with the fashion for "results-based" management, where a single perspective and a single result dominate the discourse. Indeed, in the case application, the major problem encountered was the reluctance of the program instigators to "see" the program through any other perspectives except their own. SSM works best when all key stakeholders are able to openly acknowledge the value and worth of getting to grips with the implications of alternative perspectives. As C. West Churchman stated, "systems thinking starts when you first see the world through the eyes of another."

This leads to a further challenge with soft systems. Since it is impossible to look at every perspective from every angle, when is it appropriate to stop?

How do you stop a soft systems approach going completely out of control? The answer is to stay focused on what is truly relevant to the problem situation. Is the perspective relevant and important? If it is, then leaving it out may well lead to a quicker solution to the issue—it may just be the wrong one.

SOME VARIATIONS
There are several variations of SSM.

Checkland's Variation
These days, Checkland considers the methodology more of a heuristic than a method. In other words, the important aspect is not proceeding sequentially through the seven steps but moving forward and backward through the seven steps, gaining insights each time. For instance, the ideas that flow from activities in step 4 may bring further elements to include in step 2 that can further help identify new perspectives for step 3.

Midgley and Reynolds's Variation
Gerald Midgley and Martin Reynolds, who are primarily associated with critical systems (see Chapter 19), made two apparently small but very significant changes to CATWOE:

1. They replaced C with two concepts, B for beneficiaries and V for victims (BATWOVE).

2. B and V can include *ideas* as well as *people*.

These are highly significant changes that increase the dialectical edge of SSM to a considerable degree. Some people find it difficult to identify stakeholders or ideas that *ought* to be disadvantaged in order to address a situation, but the insights derived from doing so are very powerful.

Bob Dick's Variation
Bob Dick, an action research thinker and practitioner, became interested in the various dialectics that underpin SSM (Dick, 2002). In doing so, he reframed SSM into a workshop-based method comprising four stages, one for each key dialectic.

The four dialectics are the following:

1. Between the situation as it is and the perspectives that can be attached to that situation

2. Between these perspectives and the possible ways of addressing the situation from each perspective

3. Between these possible ways of addressing the situation (i.e., the *oughts*) and the actual situation (i.e., the *is*)

4. Between the plan that emerges from the deliberation and the implementation of the plan (i.e., between steps 7 and 1)

The workshop runs in the following way:

Participants are divided into four small teams. Team 1 discusses the situation (whatever it is) and captures it as a rich picture diagram (i.e., steps 1 and 2).

Team 2 then identifies the different perspectives through which this situation can be viewed. It discusses these perspectives with Team 1. When the key perspectives are agreed between the two teams, Team 2 completes the tasks in step 3 of the methodology—the root definitions. If more than one perspective seems important, then multiple teams can take one perspective each.

Team 3 is under instructions to forget the way in which the situation operates in reality. Team 3's only task is to devise ways of achieving what Team 2 identified but without any reference to reality. At first they try on their own. Then, in discussion with Team 2, they check that their creativity will deliver what the Team 2 identified (i.e., step 4).

Team 3 then presents its ideas to Team 1. Together they discuss how well these transformations achieve the outcomes and how feasible it would be to do it that way. Team 1 is encouraged to treat this as a cooperative exercise in which it is as encouraging of Team 3 as possible (step 5).

Team 4 has been listening to this conversation between Team 3 and Team 1 and noting possible changes to the way things are currently done. Team 4 decides what changes are feasible and desirable. Team 4 then discusses these with Team 1, who then develop plans for implementation (step 6).

NOTE
Our thanks to John Wiley & Sons Ltd. for permission to reproduce material from *Soft Systems Methodoloy in Action* by Peter Checkland and Jim Scholes.

REFERENCES AND FURTHER READING
Checkland, Peter. 1993. *Systems thinking, systems practice: A 30 year retrospective*. New York: John Wiley and Sons.

Checkland, Peter, and Jim Scholes. 1999. *Soft Systems Methodology in action: A 30-year retrospective*. New York: John Wiley and Sons.

Checkland, Peter B., and John Poulter. 2006. *Learning for action: A short definitive account of Soft Systems Methodology and its use for practitioners, teachers and students*. New York: John Wiley and Sons.

Dick, Bob. 2002. *Soft Systems Methodology*. Session 13 of Areol—action research and evaluation on line. http://www.uq.net.au/action_research/areol/areol-session13.html.

Patching, David. 1990. *Practical soft systems analysis*. London: Pitman.

Williams, Bob. Soft Systems Methodology. http://users.actrix.co.nz/bobwill/Resources/ssm.doc.

Wood-Harper, A. T., et al. *Information systems definition: The multiview approach*. Oxford: Blackwell Scientific Publications, 1985.

15

DIALECTICAL METHODS

OF INQUIRY

What are the different ways in which people see or can see a situation?

What are the exceptions or contradictions to the way in which people see or can see a situation?

How can exploring and making sense of these differences enhance our understanding of a situation?

WHAT ARE DIALECTICAL APPROACHES TO INQUIRY?

Dialectics is the use of opposing viewpoints to gain meaning. It has deep philosophical roots: in Western traditions reaching as far back as Socrates and even to Heraclites; in non-Western traditions to Jain and Vedic philosophies.

In more recent times, other dialectical traditions (e.g., Marx and Hegel) have made their way into techniques and methods associated with and used by systems practice.

Dialectics has been a core aspect of modern systemic inquiry for at least half a century. For instance, Vickers's concept of an appreciative system as "a set of readinesses to distinguish some aspects of the situation rather than others and to classify and value these in this way rather than that" is essentially about contrasting perspectives. Appreciative systems helped establish the conditions that led ultimately to the emergence of Soft Systems (Chapter

13) and Critical Systems (Chapter 19) approaches that are explicitly dialectical (Ramage and Shipp 2009). Dialectics are also a feature of CHAT (Chapter
12), circular dialogue (Chapter 18), and SAST (Chapter 6).

The next section describes three quite different approaches but with one
thing in common, the value to sense-making of exploring difference rather than
commonality.

THREE DIALECTICAL APPROACHES
Option One-and-a-Half

It is common that after perspectives have been discussed at length quite entrenched positions develop, preventing any movement forward on an issue
(e.g., in SAST or CSH or Soft Systems). Sometimes at this stage it is important
to know whether the block is one of position and perspective (which can be
reframed or accommodated) or the participants are genuinely stuck and may
need to abandon the task of resolution and move on.

Like many methods developed or adapted by Bob Dick, option one-and-
a-half is group based, disarmingly simple in method, and intricate in what it
is asking people to do (see References and Further Reading).

The description of option one-and-a-half that follows focuses on two opposing proposals, but it can be extended to accommodate more. The main
phases of option one-and-a-half are as follows:

i. Have participants list the two proposals or options. Facilitators can seek
clarification to ensure that all participants understand both viewpoints.

ii. Use processes for information collection and analysis to identify the
important advantages and disadvantages of option one. Do the same
for option two.

iii. Use creative information generation procedures to develop option
one-and-a-half.

a. *List the Solutions*

List the two proposals or options. The facilitator should give participants
a chance to understand the two options by asking questions for clarification
only.

- List the two options at the top of a sheet of newsprint.
- Supporters of one option may ask questions for clarification about the other option. Debating the merits of the options is not permitted. Those asking questions may only request information, while those replying must limit themselves to answering the question.

b.   Analyze the Options

Draw a line down the middle of each piece of newsprint.

- On the left-hand side, list first the advantages of option one. Then on the right-hand side of the line, list all the disadvantages of option one. Select the key advantages and disadvantages. Supporters for option two vote to choose the key disadvantages of option one. Supporters for option one vote to choose its key advantages.
- Repeat for option two.

Participants should try to avoid the advantages and disadvantages being mirror images of each other. So if one proposal is considered by its proponents as having a key advantage of promoting car use, it is not especially helpful for its opponents to suggest that one key advantage of their proposal is that it discourages car use. It is better to say that it promotes walking or the use of public transport. Obviously, this is not always possible and may indeed help participants to seek a complete reframing of the issue.

c.   Devise a Third Option

Now tear each sheet of newsprint down the middle. Place the advantages of options one and two together on one side of a wall. Place all the disadvantages of options one and two on the other side of the wall.

The group collectively now has to develop a new proposal that has all the key advantages listed and as few key disadvantages as possible.

- Use idea generation processes and perhaps creative problem-solving techniques to list ideas for achieving the best of both options. This is done as a joint problem-solving activity by the supporters of both options. Small groups or pairs (equal numbers of the two groups of supporters) are often very appropriate. List ideas as they are contributed.

- Use a voting procedure, cyclic if necessary, to reduce the list of suggestions to a manageable length.

- Have participants combine the key suggestions into one solution, which by definition is an attempt at a best-of-both-worlds approach (that is, option one-and-a-half).

d.   Discuss the Implications of the Result

There are four common results of this exercise. All four in their own way allow the group to become unstuck and move on:

1. Once all the pros and cons have been displayed, everyone agrees on one option as being better. This often demonstrates that the problem has been one of miscommunication, or misunderstandings. It is worth then debriefing what might have been the cause of this and what might be done to avoid this in the future. However, it might also indicate power imbalance issues or one side playing devil's advocate for the sake of it. Again, it is worth discussing why these dynamics emerged and, if undesirable, what might be done in the future to avoid this.

2. An amalgam of both options emerges; a bit of A and a bit of B (generally the most common result). Often this indicates that the differing initial options were also the result of misunderstandings, miscommunications, or lack of information. On the other hand, it might indicate a messy compromise that may have short-term benefits but longer-term disadvantages. Again, a discussion about this is worthwhile.

3. A genuinely new option emerges. Bringing together apparently incompatible ideas that have to be resolved can establish conditions for innovation (see Chapter 13). This process is often called reframing; for example, two proposals that conflict over car use may be resolved when the issue is reframed in terms of what people are using the car to do (e.g., an out-of-town supermarket poorly served by public transport might start up a computer-based delivery service). The systems thinker Russ Ackoff called this "dissolving problems": by reframing the issue, the original problem goes away.

4. No option emerges. This suggests a conflict that is irresolvable. This is common and, perhaps unexpectedly, usually extremely useful. It

demonstrates to a group that is doggedly trying to resolve an issue that it may be irresolvable, at least in its current form. This allows the group to move on from debating the issue toward reframing it, putting it aside, or working out what needs to be done in order to begin resolving the differences within the group. That then provides an opportunity to discuss issues of what people truly value.

Reflections on Use
The main benefit is often not the result but the process to getting the result and the debrief after the result. Therefore it is important that participants feel the four possible kinds of result have equal value. The group does not fail if it cannot produce a novel answer.

The process tends to work better with concrete options and proposals rather than ideas or initial thoughts. Dialectical processes need contradictions and conflicts to give energy and commitment.

Participants should really want to resolve (or dissolve) the differences between them. This can be a tough, challenging process and needs some energy to carry people through.

Contradiction Analysis
Contradiction analysis is a relatively simple yet rigorous means of analyzing data. It is most effective in a group session where stakeholders can jointly engage with the data and collectively make meaning out of them.

The process is focused on analyzing and making sense out of contradictions contained in the data. Procedurally, it moves from relatively minor contradictions (i.e., outliers, exceptions) toward more fundamental and critical contradictions. The focus is to explain how these can occur rather than seeking to explain them away.

The method was developed by Phil Capper and his colleagues at WEB Research in New Zealand and refined by Bob Williams. Its origins are in Cultural Historical Activity Theory (CHAT); see Chapter 13.

The first task is to collect all the relevant data beforehand (or generate the data within a group session) with as little analysis as possible. Once that has been completed, the analysis takes four passes through the data, essentially unearthing and making sense of (rather than explaining away) data at increasingly deeper levels of contradiction. The scaffolding of this journey is carefully managed, starting out with exploring familiar patterns with minor challenges toward deeper puzzling that may have no explanation at all. The journey is posed below as a set of instructions.

Generalizations and Exceptions

What generalizations and exceptions are present in the data (as in "In general . . . but")?

First, ask what generalizations can be made from the data (as in "In general the results display . . ."). For each generalization, identify from the data an exception. In a group session this may also come from a member of the group who effectively adds more data by identifying the exception.

The task now is to explain how that exception and generalization can be present in the data. What insights can be drawn from that?

Contradictions

What contradictions can be seen in the data (as in "On the one hand . . . On the other hand . . .")? How can these contradictions be present in the data? What insights can be drawn from that?

Surprises

Looking at the data, what was expected to be in the data but isn't? Looking at the data, what was not expected to be in the data but is?

How can these differences between what was expected and what happened be explained? What insights can be drawn from that?

Puzzles

Finally, looking at the data, what remains completely puzzling? What does not make any sense? What insights can be drawn from that?

Reflections on Use

This is an extremely powerful method of helping people focus on outliers and data that challenges common sense or beliefs. The important task is to keep people focused on the data. This is especially critical at the beginning when you are identifying "generalizations"; they are generalizations *about* the data (e.g., most people agreed with the option of nuclear power as a means of reducing carbon emissions), not generalized analysis (e.g., nuclear power is a viable option).

In many cases it is not necessary to proceed all the way through from exceptions to puzzles; most deep insights surface relatively quickly. Essentially the process legitimizes opposite viewpoints, and once people understand this, they no longer need the structure.

Convergent Interviewing

Convergent interviewing is a technique associated most closely with Bob Dick and his book *Rigor Without Numbers*. This particular description draws from material used in an online action research course (AREOL) run by Bob Dick.

Convergent interviewing seeks to resolve two age-old interview dilemmas. Broad questioning will probably collect all the data you need to understand an issue, but you may never be able to spot the needle in the haystack. Asking specific questions will be easier to analyze, but you may miss the really important question.

Convergent interviewing is based on several somewhat intriguing premises:

- The best time to design a set of interview questions is once all the interviews have been finished and all the data collected.

- Interview designers and analysts will always introduce their own biases no matter how much they try otherwise.

- When faced with an ambiguous situation, rigor of process (i.e., action informed by general rules) is more important than rigor of content (i.e., ensuring that everyone gets asked the same question).

- Stakeholders know what the key issues are; the interviewer's task is to draw out those key issues.

- The best way to get to a valuable specific answer is to start with a general questioning process.

- Sampling from opposing perspectives is more likely to home in on key issues than is sampling from a continuum of perspectives.

Convergent interviewing achieves its result by leaving much of the content unstructured. You do not ask series of predetermined questions (initially at least). The interview "angle" is therefore determined by the person being interviewed, not by the interviewee or researcher.

The process, however, is tightly structured. You analyze the information systematically. You use only relevant information from earlier stages in subsequent stages—this is part of the process rigor. The systematic approach extends to sampling, data collection, and particularly interpretation. This helps to improve efficiency and reduce bias.

Each Interview

To start each interview, you ask a very open-ended question and then keep your informant talking. The open-ended question should be almost free of content (e.g., "Tell me about this program" or "What is good and bad about working here?"). The content of a convergent interview therefore comes almost entirely from the informant.

Each interview starts this way. All informants are given the chance at first to contribute their perceptions unshaped by more detailed questions. In most interviews, but especially the later ones, you add more specific, precise questions. These specific probe questions occur toward the end of the interview and are developed from analyzing previous interviews (see the following section).

At the end of each interview, you ask each person to summarize the key themes raised during the interview. You also, if possible, get each person to nominate someone else to interview who has a different perspective or different viewpoint than their own.

Probe Questions

The key element in the process is the development of probes. You compare your summaries of an interview looking for themes mentioned by earlier informants.

Suppose, for instance, informants tend to say, "We plan poorly." Your task is to devise a probe question or questions to find exceptions. "What's *good* about the planning you do?" Or "Who is best at planning?" Or "When do you plan well?"

Suppose there is little agreement. Some previous interviewees have said that they plan poorly, and others say they plan well. In that case you start to develop a probe that will help to explain this disagreement. "Some have said planning is done well; some have disagreed. What do you think? Why do you think there are differences of opinion about this?"

These probe questions contribute greatly to the efficiency of the technique. You do not need to carry forward copious amounts of data; you just record the interpretations.

To recap, there are two themes and two corresponding types of probe:

Agreements are tested by seeking *exceptions*

Disagreements for which *explanations* are sought

In other words, in later interviews you *challenge* the interpretations arising from early interviews. You also ask more specific questions, pursuing deeper understanding as you follow up the explanations and disagreements.

By seeking exceptions, you allow disconfirmation of your data and interpretations. The disagreements, and the explanations you seek, are important. They guide you deeper into the pool of potentially available data.

Notice, too, how the process is driven by the informants and the data they provide. Although the probes become more specific, each interview begins with a very open-ended question. Each informant is given a chance to contribute data uncontaminated by your interpretations so far.

The Interview Series

During the interview series, several things converge. First, the general question time gets shorter and the time taken with the probe questions gets longer. Thus the *process* of the interviews converges over time.

Second, the probe questions, by focusing primarily on key differences, start restricting the range of topics covered in the interview series. Thus the *content* of the interviews converge over time.

Reflections on Use

The result is a reasonably efficient form of data collection and interpretation. It allows the quality of data and interpretation to be checked. The process is driven by the informants and the data they provide. If sampling is reasonably good, you can obtain a good understanding from surprisingly few people; complex issues often can be identified in as few as eight to ten interviews. Indeed, one of the most useful applications of convergent interviewing is in the scoping phase of work by identifying issues that can be explored using more traditional means.

REFLECTIONS ON DIALECTICAL PROCESSES
Pros / Advantages

The main benefit of dialectical approaches is that they inevitably challenge mental models, "commonsense" assumptions, and established beliefs. It is, however, vital to do this in ways that do not encourage defensive reactions or encourage trivial use of "straw dolls." All the methods above scaffold their processes carefully to promote acceptance rather than rejection of contrary evidence and debate, as well as avoiding contrariness just for the sake of it. In option one-and-a-half you allow all the opposing views to be expressed first; in contradiction analysis you start off with generalizations (i.e., relatively safe contradictions); in convergent interviewing you start with the interviewees expanding on their own ideas (i.e., an extremely safe place to start a conversation!).

Cons / Challenges

Dialectical methods have their critics. Indeed, it is often claimed that the role of dialectics underpins the difference between the English and American traditions of philosophy and those of continental Europe. Cultural traditions of inquiry aside, clumsily done or poorly scaffolded dialectical methods can encourage defensiveness and trivialization that will undermine the benefits. Richard. A. Cosier (1981) provides evidence to suggest that dialectic methods add little that cannot be achieved by more dialogic approaches. Nevertheless, dialectics is a core element of many systems approaches.

NOTE
Our thanks to Bob Dick for permission to quote from his documentation of convergent interviewing and option one-and-a-half.

REFERENCES AND FURTHER READING
Cosier, Richard A. 1981. "Dialectical inquiry in strategic planning: A case of premature acceptance?" *Academy of Management Review* 6: 643–648.
Dick, Bob. 1997. *Option one-and-a-half.* http://www.scu.edu.au/schools/gcm/ar/arp/options.

Dick, Bob. 2002. *Convergent interviewing.* http://www.uq.net.au/action_research/areol/
areol-session08.html.

Ramage, Magnus, and Karen Shipp. 2009. *Systems thinkers.* London: Open University
and Springer.

Williams, Bob. Web site: http://www.bobwilliams.co.nz.

16

SCENARIO TECHNIQUE

What are the key influence factors that determine the future development of the system in question (e.g., enterprise, community)?

How can the system in question thrive under various possible future conditions, using emerging opportunities but avoiding possible risks at the same time?

What are the core elements of a robust strategy for the system in question?

Which are the early signals indicating that certain contingencies will eventuate?

How can the stakeholders foster the system's resilience by obviating even unexpected disturbances?

WHAT IS THE SCENARIO TECHNIQUE?

The concept of scenarios was drawn from the vocabulary of cinema (as a synonym for *screenplay* or *script*). Scenarios can be devised for companies, organizations, regions, or nation-states or larger entities such as the European Union or the United States. In strategic management, the scenario technique is applied to conceive at least three "alternative futures": the "worst-case scenario," the "best-case scenario," and the most probable course of development. The point here is to obtain models for future risks and opportunities in support of foresight and provident action.

Thinking out various "alternative futures" prepares you to take appropriate measures for the most probable development without getting wrongfooted by unexpected shocks. Scenario thinking and scenario planning help to minimize risks and to configure your resources in an optimal manner. The Athenian statesman Pericles expressed this kind of thinking in this way: "I don't need to know the future, I just have to be prepared for it."

Scenarios have been used in planning, in organizational change projects, and by political organizations for exploring alternative paths to resolve conflicts.

The scenario technique (or scenario planning) is a strategic management tool developed by Pierre Wack and other leading staff members of Royal Dutch / Shell in the early 1970s. According to scenario planning mythology, the scenario technique enabled Shell to imagine the soon-to-ensue oil-price crisis of 1973 and to take precautionary measures. In fact, the scenario process had relatively little impact on Shell's decision making, even though the scenarios themselves were remarkably prescient.

Nevertheless, the perceived achievements of the first generation of scenario planners inspired Wack's successor, Peter Schwartz, and four of his colleagues to found, in 1987, the worldwide alliance Global Business Network (GBN). The GBN currently plays a leading role in the further development and dissemination of scenario thinking and of "strategic conversation" for sustainable global development.

DETAILED DESCRIPTION OF THE METHOD AND ITS FUNCTIONING

The scenario technique can be used in a variety of settings from a narrow circle of key decision makers to broader participative processes. The involved parties identify, select, and assess all the endogenous and exogenous forces that exert an influence on the situation or topic in question.

Although various formats for scenario planning exist, they all follow a common thread by integrating different diagnostic and planning tools, which may vary in accordance to the requirements and the context. In this chapter we just mention a few of them. Once the process is understood in principle, it can be built together in various ways, making use of a broad range of tools. It can also be combined with or be part of other systems methods.

There are two basic types of scenarios:

- *Policy- or objective-related scenarios*: In these scenarios, different strategic options are selected and compared in respect to different possible futures. In this type of scenario, various options of policies or strategies are already on the table and are examined through the scenario method.

- *Development scenarios*: They serve to devise possible alternative futures independently from existing strategic options or objectives. The scenarios span the scope of possible futures; hence the context for different strategic options are then configured and adapted to respond to the assessed potentials and risks in the best possible way.

The following description focuses on development scenarios.

It is an *eight-stage process*:

Step 1: Analysis of the task. This step analyzes the subject of the investigation (e.g., a company or a group of products) in the present situation.

Step 2: Analysis of influence. This step identifies the fields of influence relevant to the subject of investigation. It is advisable to do this step in a participatory setting (e.g., a workshop). These fields of influence may comprise (1) the socioeconomic, geographical, and politico-institutional environment; and (2) particularly important action strategies of various actors (stakeholders).

Within these fields of influence, specific *factors of influence* are identified. These factors (ecological, political, technological, social, and economic) are brought into a coherent framework to derive plausible statements on the dynamics of the relevant environment that influences the subject of investigation. The factors can be rated in terms of their importance for the future and the degree of uncertainty as to their occurrence (see Table 16.1).

Each factor should be rated (in a workshop or conference by each participant) using the following rating system:

- By importance (degree of impact) on the future: 1 = low, 2 = high
- By degree of uncertainty: 1 = low, 2 = high

Table 16.1. Importance/Uncertainty Mix

		Uncertainty	
		Low	**High**
Importance	High	Major known factors that must be taken into account	Volatile trends and key factors (including negative factors)
	Low	Factors that are largely known	Volatile trends that right now have little effect but must be monitored

The points are added up, and the factors placed in the matrix. The selected factors may take on different states (expressions) with more positive or more negative consequences.

Strategic Assumption Surfacing and Testing uses a similar approach (see Chapter 6).

Step 3: Trend projections. The aim of this step is to utilize the influence factors identified in step 2, to combine and recombine them in different ways to outline alternative developments. For example, if energy supply has been selected as a main influence factor, energy supply may come from fossil sources or from renewable sources. Either type of sources may be scarce or abundant due to different conditions.

Step 4: Bundling of alternatives. The aim of this step is to examine and compare the most plausible and instructive alternative developments identified in step 3, according to their consistency, compatibility, and internal logic. Those participating in the scenario process deliberate on consistent trajectories. First, the alternative developments are described in form of a short narrative. These narratives are then juxtaposed and discussed concerning their plausibility and distinction from each other.

Step 5: Scenario interpretations. This is the decisive step for reducing the complexity of possible futures. The emerging alternative developments are packaged into consistent scenarios (future images). There should be at least three scenarios. There should be two extreme scenarios (A and B), as the more you go into the future, the less you can predict what will happen. In addition to the extreme scenarios there should be a hypothetical extrapolation of the most probable combination of factors: a "baseline scenario."

Step 6: Analysis of consequences. The aim of this step is to derive, on the basis of the scenarios, possible opportunities and risks; to assess them; and to define appropriate responses. This eventually leads to the development of a fourth hypothetical trajectory, the "most desirable scenario."

Step 7: Imagination and analysis of possible disruptive shocks ("wild cards"). The aim of this step is to list possible events that might suddenly arise and significantly influence or disturb the development of the desirable scenario (either into a positive or a negative direction). The importance of these events is assessed and adequate responses are designed.

Step 8: Scenario transfer. The aim of this step is to formulate a guiding strategy, on the basis of the opportunity- and risk-related responses derived in step 6 and to break that strategy down into more concrete planning steps, delegating the operational part to the responsible stakeholders (of cooperation systems) or departments (of organizations or enterprises). A monitoring system is established for observing the relevant influence fields and factors, primarily to allow early action in case the situation develops differently than presumed for the scenario (see also Chapter 9, "Assumption-Based Planning").

The scenario technique is usually carried out with the help of various visualization and creativity tools, depending on the intended precision or range. These can range from computer-aided models to simple influence matrices and feedback diagrams.

CASE APPLICATION OF SCENARIO TECHNIQUE

This case application is based on an actual consulting assignment of Leo Baumfeld (ÖAR Regionalberatung). It has been modified in order to make it anonymous.

The part of the assignment that was used for this case application deals with a construction company specializing in the housing sector that wanted to explore the future of these business areas.

Step 1: Analysis of the task. The managing staff of the company wanted to explore the possible and probable future states of the business.

Step 2: Analysis of influence fields and factors. Work group members were asked to place the main influence factors into one of four categories: global environment, specific environment, business branch, and location. After some clustering and regrouping, the number of factors was reduced and a list of questions prepared for each. For instance, in the housing field,

Available land: How available will building lots be? How suitable will they be for public housing projects?

Finance: How accessible will credit be to developers and potential owners?

Housing size: What will be the demand for houses or apartments of particular sizes?

Location: How will local political, social, cultural, and geographic issues affect housing development?

The work groups then put the influence factors into the influence matrix (see Table 16.2). The influence matrix was used to assess the effect of one influence on another, and this for the whole array of influence factors selected in each business field. The cross-effects were assessed using a rating scale between 0 (no effect) and 3 (strong effect). The horizontal axis was for the active interest. For instance, in the example (which is just an extract of the actual table), the effect of housing size on the competition between building promoters was strong (3), whereas the effect of building activity on housing size was small (0).

Each column and row were totaled. Those that scored high on both "active" (i.e., influenced others) and "reactive" (i.e., influenced by others) were picked out for further study. In our example, the participants identified six so-called core factors (out of fifteen). From the six core factors, depicted in Table 16.2, the two highest-scoring items (calculated by multiplying the active/row with the passive/column total) were called key factors:

Key factor 1, "available land": easily available, not easily available

Key factor 2, "housing size": housing size increases, housing size decreases
For each of the six core factors, two opposing descriptors were developed (e.g., rising/falling; expensive/cheap; large/small).

Table 16.2. Influence Matrix

Effect on ⇨	Competition between building promoters	Housing size	Building activity	m² cost per apartment	Income level	Available land	Total
Competition between building promoters		0	3	2	0	2	7
Housing size	3		1	3	0	2	9
Building activity	1	0		2	0	1	4
m² cost per apartment	2	3	0		0	0	5
Income level	0	3	2	2		1	8
Available land	2	3	3	3	0		11
Total	8	9	9	12	0	6	

Key IF 1 / Key IF 2	Buiding lots in region xy are easily available	Buiding lots in region xy are not easily available
The average housing size increases	Building lots are easily available and affordable, and make larger housing projects a promising business	In spite of low availability of building lots, there is a rising demand for larger apartments, and the building promoters act accordingly
The average housing size decreases	In spite of good availability of building lots, the building promoters follow the trend toward small apartments	As building lots are difficult to obtain, apartments are built smaller

Table 16.3. Describe Key Influence Factors

Key influence factors 1+2 / The other 4 core factors	Building lots are easily available and affordable, and make larger housing projects a promising business	In spite of low availability of building lots, there is a rising demand for larger apartments, and the building promoters act accordingly	In spite of good availability of building lots, the building promoters follow the trend toward small apartments	As building lots are difficult to obtain, apartments are built smaller
Building activities	increasing	decreasing	increasing	decreasing
m2 cost per apartment	decreasing	increasing	decreasing	increasing
Competition between building promoters	more	less	more	less
Income level	increasing	decreasing	increasing	decreasing

Table 16.4. Generate Scenario

Step 3: Trend projections. The descriptors of the two key factors were now cross-related with each other; the combined effects are depicted in the four boxes of Table 16.3.

Step 4: Bundling of alternatives. The four states resulting from that exercise were called core scenarios. These core scenarios, based on the two key factors, were now cross-related to the remaining four core factors. The work group estimated the impact of each of the four future states on each of the four remaining core factors (see the scenario in Table 16.4).

Step 5: Scenario interpretations. The work group was asked to sketch a plausible narrative of about half a page for each of the four scenarios in order to make it easier to imagine the possible future states.

Step 6: Analysis of consequences. The four core scenarios were evaluated in respect to strategic choices that the company would be willing to make. The participants identified seven possible strategic choices and rated them as "viable," "unviable," or "uncertain" while discussing their implications.

Step 7: Imagination and analysis of possible disruptive shocks ("wild cards"). This step was not carried out explicitly, but the participants had the opportunity to once more discuss the overall business strategy in respect to possible positive or negative interdependencies and robustness to external (political or economic) shocks.

Step 8: Scenario transfer. In the aftermath of the analysis, a project group under the guidance of the top management staff elaborated on the strategies within the seven business fields and on the overarching components, assuring a maximum of synergies and complementarities between the business fields. Strategic objectives, pathways, and processes were designed as well as the coordination requirements; monitoring parameters were designed in order to establish a strategic observatory within the managing team.

REFLECTIONS ON THE SCENARIO TECHNIQUE
Pros / Advantages

The scenario technique is well suited for assessing the scope for possible developments on the basis of best- and worst-case scenarios, allowing concerned stakeholders to get a feeling for more realistic scenarios and the likelihood of their occurrence. Scenarios are useful for formulating overall or specific strategies.

Another advantage of scenario technique is its emergent capability. You do not have to have any idea of what policy, strategies, or plans are needed. Indeed, scenario technique has been used by governments to locate policy areas, in contrast to deciding those policy areas first and determining the policy implications.

In systems terms, scenario technique is strongly oriented toward pushing multiple perspectives and in some versions (see the following) is highly focused on identifying boundaries.

Cons / Challenges

Scenario technique has many critics as well as adherents. There are several main criticisms.

A comprehensive scenario can be a complex endeavor and may require substantial financial and human resources as well as sufficient time for unfolding, supervising, and accompanying the process. In addition to the work of a core team (information gathering, process organization) there may be multiday large-group events to get all parties involved in the process appropriately. The supervision of the implementation process and the dissemination and transfer of the results into the relevant decision nodes within the enterprise, organization, or region is taken on by a steering group.

Some critics claim the approach is much more arbitrary and subjective than it appears to be. The results depend more on who is involved in the scenario development process than the studied process that it looks like on paper. Factions, fashions, and politics can capture the methodology.

People also confuse scenario development as a reflective tool with forward planning as a predictive tool. Arguments over scenario are often focused on plausibility rather than whether they provide insights useful in developing strategies for uncertain times. Indeed, Michel Godet and Fabrice Roubelat (1996) report the distinction among "possible" scenarios—everything that can be imagined; "realizable" scenarios—all that is possible, taking account of constraints; and "desirable" scenarios, which fall into the possible category, but are not all necessarily realizable. In other words, scenario technique deals with likelihood and not with certainty. The best strategies developed on the basis of scenario planning become obsolete if they are not accompanied by appropriate monitoring and an observation process which recognizes changes in the basic assumptions already in an early stage.

VARIATIONS

There are many variations of scenario technique (e.g., see Chapter 19, "Critical Systems Heuristics"; Chapter 9, "Assumption-Based Planning"; and Chapter 6, "Strategic Assumption Surfacing and Testing"). There are also scenario-like processes in other approaches that seek to anticipate and manage change (e.g., simulation modeling, forecasting, visioning). Selecting which variation to use depends on the complexity of the situation and the availability of information. The scenario technique is best applied in situations where the availability of information is low (which means high uncertainty) and the complexity of issues is high. Forecasting is more suitable with low complexity and high information availability. Simulation modeling often works best in conditions of high complexity and high availability of information.

NOTE

Our thanks to Robert Lukesch and Leo Baumfeld, senior associates of ÖAR Regionalberatung, for permission to draw on their writings and for providing the material used for the case application.

REFERENCES AND FURTHER READING

ESPON Research Project 3.2. 2007. Scenarios on the territorial future of Europe. Luxembourg. http://www.espon.eu/mmp/online/website/content/projects/260/716/index_EN.html.

Flood, Robert L. 1999. *Rethinking the fifth discipline: Learning within the unknowable.* London: Routledge.

Global Business Network (GBN). http://www.gbn.com/about/scenario_planning.php.

Godet, Michel, and Fabrice Roubelat. 1996. "Creating the future: The use and misuse of scenarios: Long range planning." *International Journal of Strategic Management* 29, no. 2: 164–171.

Ringland, Gill. 1998. *Scenario planning: Managing for the future.* New York: John Wiley and Sons.

Schwartz, Peter. 1991. *The art of the long view.* New York: Doubleday.

Van der Heijden, Kees. 1996. *Scenarios.* New York: Wiley.

17

SYSTEMIC QUESTIONING

How can you gain a multidimensional picture of a situation?

How can you identify leverage points in your quest for solution-oriented interventions?

How is it possible to address delicate but relevant content without offending the privacy of those in the dialogue?

WHAT DOES SYSTEMIC QUESTIONING MEAN?

Questioning

An old Jewish proverb says that you should never trade a good question for an answer, and sometimes the best way to answer can be by asking a question. Questions are the quintessence of evaluations and other forms of social inquiry. Through questions we acquire information, and we also generate new information.

A well-thought-out question can liberate, provide more options, expand the horizon of perception, create a new frame in which new solutions emerge. A badly thought-out question can lead you deeper into a problematic state, into a world of restrictions and hopelessness.

So how do you approach this questioning process?

First, be aware of the nature of the question. Any single question occupies a space within three dimensions:

Time: the extent to which the question explores the past, present, or future

Level of abstraction: the extent to which the question deals with functional issues (e.g., shall I reduce the volume of the music?) or questions of meaning (e.g., what does this music convey to you?)

Speculation: the extent to which the subject of the question has already been addressed, an analytical question (e.g., where were you at the time of the crime?), or requires a degree of speculation, a synthetic question (e.g., if you were the murderer, where do you think you might have hidden the gun?).

Each and every question can be located somewhere in this three-dimensional space.

Second, be aware of the assumptions that are embedded in the question itself and about the person expected to answer it, for example, "Did you feel that tense atmosphere during the President's speech?" This sentence can be reasonably answered only if the following presuppositions are accepted:

- The answerer is capable of feeling tensions.
- There is a prominent person who is named by their title.
- This person can exert an impact on the audience.

There can be further presuppositions which are conveyed by the prosodics,[1] clear to a listener but opaque to a reader (this makes e-mail communication so conflict prone, because the reader is left to his or her own mind in "inventing" the prosodics of a written sentence). "President" can, for example, be pronounced reverently or mockingly. This difference might change the overall meaning of the question.

Finally, there are questions that, although not questions in a grammatical sense, nevertheless imply questions. For instance:

- Pleas: "I would like you to call me back in the afternoon." The distinction between a plea and an order can be made only *ex post factum*: by how the refusal to the request will be handled by the pleading person.

- Invitations: The distinction between an invitation and summons is made likewise.

- Hidden orders or pleas: "There is a strong air draft hitting my neck." If the boss says such a thing in the presence of an office clerk, it most probably means "Could you close the window?"

Systemic Questioning

Systemic questioning developed from systemic family therapy. However, it has spread far beyond the therapeutic context, into organizational development, pedagogy and social work. Having evolved into many forms of questioning techniques, it is today broadly applied in systemic coaching, consulting, and management.

Systemic questioning uses the linguistic and semantic richness and ambiguity our languages offer us. Techniques of systemic questioning are applicable and useful in situations where the aim is to broaden the perspective, to mark differences, to bring forth rapid solutions for organizational, social, and psychological problems, or to identify hitherto untapped resources that can be mobilized for solutions. They can be used in any context: in a one-on-one setting or in larger groups or in a personal conversation but also in standardized surveys.

Systemic questioning can be used

- when you want to solve a problem and seek support from a professional consultant or coach;

- when you assume that problems are hidden, but have to be solved in order to achieve the mutually agreed upon aims of a consultancy contract;

- when your managerial task is to be supportive but you are aware of problems that those directly involved would be ready to solve if ever they got an idea how.

DETAILED DESCRIPTION OF THE TECHNIQUE AND ITS FUNCTIONING

The family therapist Karl Tomm (1994) defined four basic types of systemic questions: linear, strategic, reflective, and circular (see Figure 17.1).

Linear Questions

Linear questions assume relatively simple relationships between cause and effect. Questions are posed in the manner of a detective: "Who did what, when,

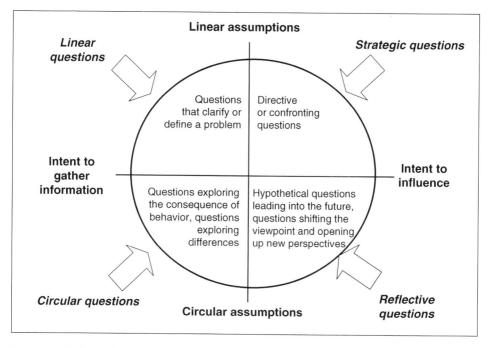

Figure 17.1. Four Types of Questions
SOURCE: Adapted from K. Tomm, *Die fragen des beobachters* (Heidelberg: Carl-Auer-Systeme, 1994).

and why?" This manner of posing questions secures a lot of information. However, even with seemingly "innocent" linear questions, there are always embedded value judgments. "Why are you so late, my darling?"

Strategic Questions

Strategic questions are also based on relatively simple assumptions about cause and effect, but in this case the interviewer intends to instigate change in the mind of the person being questioned. The person who poses the question acts like a teacher or a judge. A typical question would be, "Have you noticed how other people are suffering from your behavior?" While this risks moving a conversation toward "blaming," in certain situations it may trigger rapid shifts toward a solution.

Reflective Questions

In reflective questions the interviewer wants to facilitate the emergence of new perspectives in the mind of the interviewee. Reflective questions are based on circular assumptions about causes and effects. The person posing the questions acts like a coach or trainer. A typical reflective question is, "If there were some unsettled differences between you and your colleague, who would make the first move and apologize to the other?" These questions have the potential to trigger new thoughts by adopting new viewpoints, inviting the client to step into another one's shoes.

Circular Questions

Circular questions are posed in order to

- obtain information on the communication context;
- "disrupt" patterns of deadlocked communication and behavior patterns;
- offer alternative communication patterns that seem attractive for all those involved;
- get ideas for new patterns of interpretation (reframing) and for new options to act.

The interviewer has the intention to explore a situation on the basis of circular assumptions. A typical question is, "Ms. B, what is Mr. X usually doing while having an argument with Mr. Y?" (This question can also be posed when Mr. X is present; he will be all ears).

Circular questioning provides better insights into a communication system (e.g., a family, a team, an organization) and at the same time has a liberating and mind-opening effect. It is therefore of specific importance in the field of systemic family therapy, which dates back to the 1970s, the "Milano School" (e.g., Mara Selvini-Palazzoli). Several specific forms of questioning were developed in this field, for example:

- Questions aimed at "liquefying" entrenched behaviors and self-limiting worldviews: "How would your sister react in this situation?"
- Questions aimed at contextualizing hypothetical threats in order to downsize corresponding bad feelings: "In which situations exactly do you feel that anxiety?"
- Questions aimed at uncovering a person's contribution to unpleasant experiences (e.g., the relationship between perpetrator and victim).

SYSTEMIC QUESTIONING IN PRACTICE

As systemic questioning is a technique rather than a methodology, it can be used for a range of explorative purposes. As exploring and coaching functions are intertwined, it is a key technique in systemic change consultancy and management. Systemic questioning has been successfully applied in the following circumstances:

- Facilitated self-evaluations and formative evaluations: A facilitator in focus groups aims at enhancing the dialogue by posing appropriate questions.

- In-depth interviews: In the phase of information gathering, be it for planning or for evaluation purposes, in-depth interviews are often carried out with key stakeholders. In these interviews the questionnaires are just semistructured, if at all, so this requires adequate questioning skills on the interviewer's side.

- Coaching: Individual or team coaching in many contexts (e.g., leadership coaching, social work, learning assistance) requires systemic questioning techniques as a *conditio sine qua non*.

REFLECTIONS ON SYSTEMIC QUESTIONING

Often, people feel pressured or even ashamed when they are confronted with questions. Consequently, it is important to

- be aware that the coach or consultant should never show more eagerness to solve a client's problem than the client himself or herself;

- stay confident that the capacity and responsibility for finding solutions is on the client's side and that the interview just aims at strengthening his or her creativity and sense of responsibility.

Each and every question can be located somewhere in the three-dimensional space (time, abstraction, speculation) described at the beginning of this chapter. Having in mind this coordinate system makes it easier to avoid misguiding questions. We all know that, for explorative purposes, it is advisable to avoid "closed questions" and to pose *wh . . .* questions. However, no interrogative word has ever been used more awkwardly than *why*. *Why* covers a very wide comprehension space. If you use *why* for getting an answer relating to the future purpose ("Why did you leave your workplace so early?"), you might get an answer relating to the past, either the formal reason ("Because my work was done") or the material reason[2] ("Because I was ready to go")— neither being what you really wanted to know. If you asked the question more precisely ("For which purpose did you leave work so early?") or even more elegantly ("What hindered you to stay on your workplace until the usual time?"), you might get the answer you needed. But there is also a second quagmire you could step into: when we want to know the functional reasons, let's say, of a car crash and ask, "Why did it happen?" (instead of "How did it happen?"), we might uncover the value system of the answerer ("Because the driver of the other car was a woman"), but again, that is not what we wanted. Referring to the coordinate system, we climb up into the meaning heights instead of descending into the functional downs.

VARIATIONS

Systemic questioning is an integral part of many change methodologies, such as Solution Focus, constellation work (both in Chapter 11). Circular dialogue (Chapter 18) and Appreciative Inquiry (see Chapter 11) are also strongly related to systemic questioning.

Neurolinguistic Programming (NLP)

Neurolinguistic programming is based on two questioning techniques:

- The *Meta-Model*, the intention of which is to degeneralize, undelete, and undistort the "surface structure" of language, with the aim to reconnect the speaker with the largely unconscious "deep structure"[3] in which his or her subjective experience is encoded. According to the basic assumptions of NLP this reconnection should open up more options to think, to act, to communicate. The Meta-Model questioning techniques have been modeled by Richard Bandler and John Grinder, who studied the communication patterns of the gestalt therapist Fritz Perls and of the family therapist Virginia Satir in the 1970s. Meta-Model questioning is mainly related to linear and strategic questions according to Tomm's typology.

- The *Milton Model*, which in linguistic terms can be seen as the inverse Meta-Model. Bandler and Grinder modeled these language patterns from the hypnotherapist Milton Erickson (1901–1980). Milton patterns lead you away from everyday awareness into focusing on your inner self. The "hypno-talk" may serve as a slipway to "install" embedded suggestions which guide you from self-limiting, recurring behavioral patterns. Milton patterns are not necessarily formulated as questions, but they can be, or at least be accompanied by them, be it just for seeking consensus from you during the course of the interview.

NOTES

Our thanks to Robert Lukesch and Leo Baumfeld, senior associates of ÖAR Regionalberatung, for permission to draw on their writings and to extract from their papers and training materials.

1. *Prosodics* of oral languages involve variation in syllable length, loudness, pitch, and the formant frequencies of speech sounds.

2. Aristotle distinguished between "four reasons": the material, the formal, the efficient, and the final reason. Only the last type is always "located" in the future, the third one sometimes.

3. The terms *surface structure* and *deep structure* are derived from Noam Chomsky's linguistics theory.

REFERENCES AND FURTHER READING

Brown, J. *Circular questioning: An introductory guide.* http://www.anzjft.com/pages/articles/940.pdf.

Chartered Institute of Personnel and Development (CIPD). *Factsheet about interview techniques.* http://www.cipd.co.uk/subjects/recruitmen/selectn/selnintvg.htm?IsSrchRes=1.

Deissler, K. 1987. *Recursive creation of information: Circular questioning as information generation. Part I: Proposals for the development of solution-oriented questions in the co-creative process of systemic therapy.* Marburg: InFaM.

Goldberg, M. C. 1998. *The art of the question: A guide to short-term question-centered therapy..* Wiley.

Milton Model. http://en.wikipedia.org/wiki/Milton_model.

Neurolinguistic Programming. http://en.wikipedia.org/wiki/Meta-model_(NLP).

Tomm, K. 1994. *Die fragen des beobachters.* Heidelberg: Carl-Auer-Systeme.

Watzlawick, P., J. H. Weakland, and R. Fisch. 1974. *Change: Principles of problem formation and resolution.* New York: W. W. Norton.

18

CIRCULAR DIALOGUES

How can a situation be seen from different angles or perspectives?

How do other points of view challenge our way of seeing things?

What can we learn from opposing viewpoints, and how can they be overcome?

How can different perspectives lead to a new understanding of the situation?

WHAT IS A CIRCULAR DIALOGUE?

Dialogue techniques are based on three key assumptions:

- Different perspectives are valued positively: Exposing oneself to different views helps to overcome mental barriers or unilateral thinking and increases the chances for finding solutions or answers that are acceptable for all.

- A system can be changed only from within: A dialogue never aims at direct influence or persuasion, but is seen as a means to experience different perspectives which in turn should help the participants to change their "mental maps."

- Language makes a difference: Attention is placed on the specific language patterns used by the participants (e.g., terms and connotations). This helps participants understand their mental maps "from within" and at the same time to overcome their limitations or to identify possible connections.

The word *dialogue* comes from the ancient Greek word διαλογος (diálogos), which means the flow of words through (= δια) a group. A dialogue is a means to foster collective intelligence, by transcending individual insights. The intelligence of the group is used to arrive at new insights, which individual members have not yet reached—and perhaps would not reach without such a process. To communicate in a dialogue is a creative act, bringing forth something that was not there before. And it is futile to aim at "winning" a dialogue, because everyone who participates "wins" in the sense of gaining by participating in the collaborative effort.

In circular dialogues, participants have the opportunity to perceive a given situation from at least three perspectives. Guided by facilitators, participants are asked to communicate in a strictly structured manner, mutually interviewing and observing each other without direct discussions. The participants represent different roles and are invited to contribute from various perspectives.

The different perspectives or roles are used as a resource. They can be identified from the particular situation, represent the view of participants, or be deliberately "constructed" or assigned because they are considered useful for dealing with the situation at hand. The aim of the dialogue is to look at a situation from various angles and to use these different perspectives for critical appreciation, for generating and validating experience, or for revealing solutions. In this way, a situation is considered several times and observed from various perspectives until it ends up where it started. That is why the dialogue is called circular.

Circular dialogues are rooted in the tradition of role-play and are based on the method of systemic questioning (see Chapter 17). The dialogues presented in this chapter were either conceived for consulting organizational development (Königswieser and Exner 1998) or were applied in regional development (Baumfeld 1999). But they are used in a range of other fields, for example, management, social work, and conflict prevention.

DETAILED DESCRIPTION OF THE METHOD AND ITS FUNCTIONING

The basic features of a circular dialogue are the following (see Figure 18.1):

- Perspectives are defined by those who have taken the initiative or instigated the dialogue session. They should be meaningful for the topic or the purpose of the session (see below).

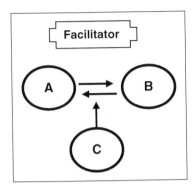

Figure 18.1. Perspectives in
Circular Dialogue

- Perspectives are assigned to the participants (individuals or small groups). At least three different perspectives (a triad) must be involved (A, B, C in Figure 18.1).

- Communication takes place in a strict order and setting. Representatives of each perspective express their points of view consecutively (first A, then B, then C).

- While these representatives are talking, the others observe these expressions (verbal and nonverbal), and reflect on them; one perspective can have the specific role of observing or synthesizing the communication of others (e.g., C).

- There is no interruption during each deliberation or questions afterward.

- Participants keep in role and avoid referring to previous presentations (as in "I agree with X" or "I disagree with Z"). This is a dialogue, not a discussion.

- Connecting individual perceptions (feelings, ideas, etc.) leads to an "enlarged" perception that is used as a collective resource.

- Someone who is not involved in the dialogue acts as a facilitator and assure the discipline required, that is, keep time and stop discussions between participants.

The length of the circular dialogue sessions varies between thirty and ninety minutes. This depends on the number of participants and the number of perspectives involved. As a rule of thumb, each of the perspectives involved speaks at least twice. Usually the dialogues are not documented, as the attention of participants should be focused on the session itself. But if considered useful and if the participants agree, the entire session can be recorded or someone can be assigned to take notes (but the notes should be visible for all, e.g., by using a flip chart).

There are many variations to this basic sequence, and the setting can be applied to different situations and purposes and varied to suit specific needs. For instance, perspectives can be assigned according to specific functions, or they are meant to represent stakeholders' views.

Some examples of circular dialogues follow, with a brief outline of their key purpose and essential features.

Presentation of Ideas or Proposals

First, someone presents the ideas or proposals, and then participants are invited to dialogue by taking on roles that can also be found frequently in "normal" discussions: enthusiast, critic, and pragmatist. In this way, a diversity of opinions is created purposefully, which can provide the presenters with suggestions for further developing their ideas (see the case study later in this chapter).

Circular Inquiry

The setting is suitable for a heterogeneous audience that has a varying degree of familiarity on the subject. Three perspectives are assigned: the "Experienced," who have some experience or knowledge on the subject, are willing to share this knowledge, and act as resource persons; the "Curious," who have little experience but want to find out more and are invited to put forth questions; and the "Observers," who observe this exchange and comment on it based on a role description defined beforehand (e.g., acting as skeptics, highlighting strengths and weaknesses, summarizing the dialogue).

In this way also, those considered "ignorant" can be used as a resource, different types of experience can be shared, and up-front lecturing by those who "know" is avoided. This approach is particularly suited for achieving a balanced communication in situations where knowledge about an issue is distributed unevenly, or in "asymmetric" situations where some participants have much more experience than the others (e.g., in cross-cultural contexts).

Role Play

In role plays, people take up assigned roles, consciously act them out, and behave in a way that is fitting with their role. This enables them to experience what it is like to see things from another perspective, brings forth new insights, and can modify previous perceptions about others. With this approach, the roles and functions of participants can also be deliberately redistributed to others. Then a facilitated dialogue can be carried out with these newly assigned roles. Such a combination of dialogue and role play is particularly helpful when it takes place on a "hot topic" for the people present in the session.

Since participants are forced to present from a position different than their own, a stimulating discussion is generated, an effect that can even be reinforced if people are deliberately assigned roles that are opposite to the ones they assume in real life. It is essential for learning that afterwards the original bearers of roles or functions reflect on their experience in the dialogue (jointly or individually).

Info-Board

Rumors often have considerable influence on an intervention but are hard to deal with. With this setting, informal information is deliberately addressed and brought out into the open. Participants are asked at the beginning of a meeting or presentation what they have already heard about the issue and which presumptions they have.

The Info-Board is particularly suited to accompany presentations of interim reports (or preliminary findings) of controversial projects that take place in a highly dynamic context. Acknowledging informal information can also increase the willingness of an audience to take up formal information or presentations.

The principle of circularity is also used in other settings, which are not explicitly dialogue oriented, for instance:

The Present "Absentees"

This setting brings the viewpoints of important external actors into a discussion. First the participants draw up a list of relevant external stakeholders who are not present, and the most important ones are selected. Then some participants are asked to represent these absent actors. The group carries out the discussion, and periodically the representatives can bring forth their ideas, observations, or feelings.

This very efficiently brings forth views from others who are not present but are considered relevant to the topic, and it is a suitable way for encouraging a group to look beyond its current boundary.

Taboo Circle

This setting enables a group to speak about the "unspeakable." Participants are first asked to write specific taboos ("what cannot be talked about") on small cards in a "neutral" form (e.g., capital letters). These cards are then reshuffled and passed around to be read by all the participants, who are invited to read them without talking. In this way the taboos become known to everybody and are thus available as a resource for further discussion.

Problem-Solving "Onion"

In this setting, participants act according to the three steps for solving a problem in a systemic manner: (1) diagnosing the problem situation, (2) formulating a hypothesis, (3) elaborating solutions. Three subgroups are formed that correspond to these perspectives. While the first subgroup presents the problem, the second formulates hypotheses about the problem's origin, and the third thinks about possible solutions. These subgroups present their findings one after the other, peeling layer after layer from the originally presented problem, like in an onion. Then the sequence is repeated again, taking into account the findings of the previous round. At the end of the session, participants jointly assess the usefulness and feasibility of the solution found.

CASE APPLICATION

The case described here deals with a situation that is appropriate for applying a Circular Inquiry. In a meeting a new subject came up on which the other participants had a varying degree of familiarity. The participants were divided into three subgroups, with roles being assigned to them:

- Curious: They had little experience on the subject but wanted to find out more.

- Experienced: They had some experience on the subject and were willing to share this knowledge.

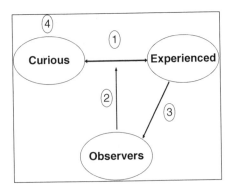

Figure 18.2. Circular Inquiry: Roles and Sequence

– Observers: They were asked to observe and comment (this role could have been split up further—skeptics, convinced).

The dialogue session took place in the following sequence (see Figure 18.2):

1. It started with a question-and-answer session between the Curious and the Experienced.

2. Then the Observers commented on this sequence from their respective perspective(s).

3. Next the Experienced responded to the comments of the Observers.

4. At the end the Curious concluded what they had learned from the entire dialogue session.

Thirty to forty-five minutes was sufficient for the group to achieve a more thorough understanding. If more time had been available or if the participants (the "Curious" in particular) felt that an additional exchange was needed, the Curious could have been invited to start another round of dialogue by raising a new set of questions, followed by a similar sequence as above.

REFLECTIONS ON THE USE OF CIRCULAR DIALOGUE

Circular dialogues are a specific form of communication for dealing with presentations, results, or experiences of participants who come from different backgrounds. They can be used in small gatherings or with large groups; the number of participants can vary from six to forty participants. Circular dialogues are usually part of a larger process or an event (meeting, workshop) with participants who have some degree of familiarity with the topic (e.g., project teams, working groups). However, they can also be used as a stand-alone intervention and with complete strangers.

A dialogue is different from discussion or a debate, which aims at adjusting different points of view to render them compatible. Whereas in discussions or debates standpoints are confronted and if possible harmonized with each other, a dialogue is a means to foster collective intelligence. A well-structured, meaningful dialogue is a gain for all individual participants and for the group mind. In contrast to a debate, it does not make sense to try to "win" a dialogue.

Circular dialogues share some similarities with dialectical methods of inquiry (see Chapter 15), for example, the use of opposing viewpoints to gain meaning and challenging mental models. But the focus is on the "triad" principle, that is, using at least three significantly different perspectives for the emergence of new or collective understanding.

In evaluations, circular dialogues can be used to gather evidence on an issue or evaluation question from different stakeholder groups or for the validation of findings. And they can be used to generate new insights and solutions by working constructively with differences in stakeholder views or perspectives.

Pros / Advantages

Circular dialogues are a simple yet powerful tool for dealing constructively with different perspectives. They require relatively little time, because the strict procedures focus attention and allow working in an intense way. By organizing participants as a joint learning system, different viewpoints and roles ensure that new understandings can emerge.

Circular dialogues use the creative and appreciative resources of the participants in a focused, yet relaxed atmosphere. They are particularly useful when participants perceive their differences as a threat and potential source of conflict. By assigning the very behavior that is threatening as a role-task (e.g., the Skeptic, the Critic), it is rendered legitimate and the respective fears can be enacted in a constructive way without putting relationships between participants under strain (indeed, the contrary is often the case).

In situations where participants know each other fairly well or have rather fixed opinions about each other, circular dialogues can have an "un-freezing" effect. Accustomed attributes of roles or behavior can be challenged, interrupted, or even dissolved. In social systems all members are mutually observing each other and are "co-constructing" attributes about their respective roles and behavior. In a circular dialogue, observation is turned from an implicit, casual activity to an explicit task, and this focused attention can lead to the "deconstruction" of assigned attributes, as a joint act of observer and observed.

Cons / Challenges

It is essential that the facilitator is *not* involved in the dialogue session. The facilitator can either be passive (watching the time, cutting off discussions) or have a more active role, for example, intervening to clarify questions or answers or refocusing the dialogue if participants go astray.

The facilitator has to manage carefully two aspects of role playing. One is safety. People often take on the roles a little too enthusiastically and can say things that may cause harm or bad feelings, even if they do not really believe those statements. The other challenge moves in the opposite direction; statements are made that are either trivial or incorrect; the conversation dives into stereotypes (often humorous ones) that undermine the strength of the method. The facilitator should intervene in such circumstances.

Dialogue works best if the room has a flexible layout. Chairs should be light so they can be moved easily, to allow participants to group and regroup according to their roles or perspectives. There should be enough open space to allow subgroups to sit in a semicircle, with the facilitator located in the center. Any formal presentation should to be in the center as well.

VARIATIONS

In many ways the group-based dialogue merely models what goes on in an individual's brain when trying to take a decision. There are various versions of these "internalized" or "personal" circular dialogues, but they all suggest that it is valuable for any person or group to go through a formal process of considering an issue from several different perspectives.

Walt Disney Strategy

This method goes back to Walt Disney, who was a person with great dreams and visions. He proceeded by separating three different phases of developing goals and distinguishing them by space and time: the Dreamer, the Planner, and the Critic. For every position, Walt Disney customized a special room equipped to put him in the right frame of mind and to create the right ambience for the task in hand. This helped him to remain focused and avoid mixing up these positions; thinking about the feasibility while dreaming, fear the critics while planning, and so on.

Later on, Robert Dilts developed a corresponding creativity technique that is, for instance, widely used in Neurolinguistic Programming (NLP—see Chapter 17). The target is to bring the Dreamer, the Planner, and the Critic into balance, that is, to prevent the Critic from dominating and the Dreamer from being underrepresented.

The sequence of the Walt Disney strategy begins with the Dreamer writing down feelings, ideas, and wishes. Next, the Planner contemplates how the dream can be realized and notes down the required activities, tools, or resources. Finally it is the turn of the Critic, searching for mistakes and weak points in the concept. Then the whole sequence is repeated by redreaming and replanning, noting down all the modifications, until the Critic finds no more objections and becomes silent.

This method is useful for working out targets and improving your creativity without forgetting the feasibility. It is normally applied individually, by consecutively slipping into the different roles. But it can also be implemented in group settings (similar to circular dialogues), where the roles are enacted by different individuals or subgroups.

De Bono's Six Thinking Hats®

Edward de Bono suggests that it is worth exploring issues from six different perspectives. As in the Walt Disney approach, he encourages you to associate the physical (in this case, different-colored hats) with the cognitive. The yellow and black hats are similar to the enthusiast and skeptic roles in circular dialogue.

The six hats and their functions are as follows:

White hat: facts and information

Red hat: feelings and emotions

Black hat: critical judgment

Yellow hat: positive

Green hat: new ideas

Blue hat: the big picture

Some action researchers add a silver hat—for reflection.

NOTE

Our thanks to Leo Baumfeld, senior associate of ÖAR Regionalberatung, for permission to draw on his writings and to extract extensively from his papers and training materials.

REFERENCES AND FURTHER READING

Baumfeld, Leo. 1999. *Projektorientiertes arbeiten in komplexen situationen.* Vienna: ÖAR-Regionalberatung.

De Bono, Edward. 1985. *Six thinking hats.* London: Penguin Books.

Dilts, Robert. B. 1994. *Strategies of genius.* Vol. 1, *Aristotle, Sherlock Holmes, Walt Disney, Wolfgang Amadeus Mozart.* Capitalo, CA: Meta Publications.

Königswieser, Roswitha, and Alexander Exner. 1998. *Systemische interventionen.* Stuttgart: Klett-Cotta.

19

CRITICAL SYSTEMS HEURISTICS

What and who are being excluded, marginalized, or made a victim by the way in which a situation is bounded (i.e., is being viewed, framed, and/ or operated)?

How might different and often conflicting boundary judgments on a situation be reconciled?

What are the implications of not questioning and/or not debating boundary judgments?

WHAT IS CRITICAL SYSTEMS HEURISTICS?

Critical Systems Heuristics (CSH) was developed by Werner Ulrich and modified in various ways by Martin Reynolds and Gerald Midgley. It draws from two intellectual traditions.

The first is the work of the systems theorist and sociologist C. West Churchman, whose concerns centered on the decisions taken when constructing systems viewpoints. He argued that our choice of what lies inside a system is essentially an ethical decision. By choosing what lies inside a system, you implicitly or even explicitly marginalize what lies outside the system. Thus Critical Systems is essentially about boundaries. Churchman argued that your choice of what lies inside a system's boundaries depends on your perspective or more deeply your values. If these choices are not reflected upon, they may well result in exacerbating the very problem you are seeking to address. Indeed, it may well cause you to frame the problem in unhelpful ways. Churchman developed methods of identifying these boundaries so that further viewpoints could be identified, addressed, and brought into the analysis. He called this process "sweeping in."

The second tradition is that of the American and European practical philosophers who emphasized the importance of dialectic and discourse around different perceptions of reality. While Churchman's ideas brought in the systems idea of boundary *identification*, this tradition added the philosophical notion of boundary *critique*.

In many ways the Critical Systems tradition challenges the popular systems idea of "holism." As we stated in the Introduction, it is physically and intellectually impossible to take everything into consideration. We have to draw a boundary somewhere. The Critical Systems tradition argues that because we have to draw a boundary, we have to be acutely aware of, and highly critical of, why and where we draw that boundary.

There are two reasons for being self-aware and critical of boundary decisions, one pragmatic and one ethical. The pragmatic reason is that unless we understand and address the consequences of boundary decisions, we will never fully understand the consequences of our own intervention in a particular situation, nor can we anticipate the responses of others to that intervention. The ethical reason is that without that critical assessment of the boundaries we (and others) draw around a situation, we may inadvertently increase social and environmental inequities.

This orientation became known as *Critical Systems*. Using these notions, Werner Ulrich developed a *heuristic* (i.e., a tool for learning) that provides a means to apply the Critical Systems ideas in a systematic and even more critical way.

The heuristic identifies twelve key boundary decisions (influenced by Churchman). Each of these boundary decisions is explored in two orientations: a normative mode (what *ought* to be the boundary choices) and an "objective" mode (what *are* or *were* the boundary choices). The dialectic generated by comparing the "ought" and the "is" provides the source material for the boundary critiques. There are also dialectics within each mode, for instance, in the normative mode whose "ought" is being privileged and whose "ought" is being marginalized.

DETAILED DESCRIPTION OF THE METHOD

The heuristic organizes the components of a system and its environment into four main categories (Midgley 2000).

1. Motivation: the system is achieving what to whom?
2. Control: the system has decision-making power over what?
3. Expertise: what are the necessary and sufficient knowledge and understanding to inform the system?
4. Legitimacy: what makes this the right thing to do?

Each category has three components enabling boundary critique. The first is a "what," the second is a "who," and the last one poses critical questions of these two boundary decisions.

Briefly, then, CSH has twelve components (Reynolds 2008):

Motivation (Value Basis)

- *Purpose*: the purpose of the system
- *Beneficiary*: the client or beneficiary of the system's purpose
- *Indicators of success*: how the values that underpin the purpose are made explicit

Control (Power Basis)

- *Resources*: the resources (money, time, and physical, natural, human, and social elements) necessary to achieve the system's purpose
- *Decision maker*: who controls those resources to enable the system to achieve its purpose
- *Decision environment*: important factors likely to affect the system but outside the decision makers' boundary of control in order to place boundaries on the decision makers' use of resources and to ensure accountability for that use

Expertise or Knowledge (Knowledge Basis)

- *Expertise* (guarantor attributes): the formal and informal expert skill sets or relevant knowledge that ensures, or implies a "guarantee" that the purpose is achieved. This could be formal technical and disciplinary skills, facilitation skills, and other relevant experiential, nonformal, and professional skill sets.

- *Expert* (or designer): those who possess the necessary skills
- *Guarantee*: factors that will assure or prevent these experts' providing the necessary expertise

Legitimacy

- *Emancipation*: the means by which those negatively affected by the system, or have an alternative worldview, can challenge the system. This could be marginalized stakeholders, future generations, non–human nature, or ideas associated with beliefs, values, morals, and ideologies.
- *Witnesses*: those who represent the interests of the system potential or actual victims, particularly those interests that cannot speak for themselves.
- *Worldview*: the source of the tension between the system and the negative effects of the system, or alternative worldviews. A key factor in identifying how to reconcile those tensions.

A NARRATIVE DESCRIPTION OF CSH

What does this mean in practice? The following narrative, largely developed by Ulrich and Reynolds (2010), provides a way of understanding the overall logic and arc of a CSH-based inquiry.

Motivation

The development of a system starts with some notion of "purpose." Since a purpose reflects embedded values associated with some person or persons, it is valid to ask, "Whose purpose?" Identifying first what the *purpose* of the system should be helps identify who the intended *beneficiaries* ought to be. This in turn suggests what should be appropriate *measures of success* in securing some improvement to those beneficiaries. These measures of success are not selected without critique because they express how the underpinning values ought to be given formal expression (quantifiably or qualitatively) to gauge improvement. Together these three boundary critiques make transparent the *value basis* of the system.

Control

The exploration of motivation leads to questions regarding the *necessary resources* or *components needed for success*. Financial capital and other forms of tangible assets like natural, physical, and human capital might be complemented with less tangible factors such as social capital (access to networks of influence). But who ought to be in control of such resources and thus be best placed to provide them? This in turn prompts questions as to what should be left outside the control of such decision makers in order to ensure some level of accountability. There is a risk of having all the necessary resources under the control of the system. If the system has all the resources, then the system cannot be controlled or held accountable in any way by those outside the system. In other words, what should be part of the system's decision environment in order to keep it in check and accountable? For example, if a system initiated with good intention becomes malignant, corrupt, or disabling because of changing circumstances, are there factors in the environment that might ensure that this system (which may have outlived or been diverted from its purpose) is prevented from continuing indefinitely? Such questions help make transparent the *power basis* of the system.

Expertise

One such set of factors requiring independence from the decision maker is knowledge or expertise. In an ideal setting, human capital (embodying expertise) ought not to be under the sole control of the decision maker but should have some degree of independence. So what ought to be the necessary types and levels of competent knowledge and experiential know-how to ensure that the system actually has practical applicability and works toward its purpose? Who ought to provide such expertise? The whole point of having experts is to provide some degree of success. So the question is, how might such expert support prove to be an effective guarantor, a provider of some assurance of success? This invites the need to look out for false guarantors, that our reliance on these experts or that expertise is unwise or misleading. For example, hiring qualified medical practitioners from Brooklyn for a relief effort in Haiti does not necessarily guarantee that Haitians get the necessary medical treatment. Their medical qualification may constitute a *false guarantee*. Such questions help to make transparent the *knowledge basis* of the system.

Legitimacy

Any assessment of the values, motivation, power, control, knowledge, and expertise associated with any system is bound to be biased in some way. So what gives this system the legitimacy to carry out its tasks? How does it fit within wider spheres of human interests? In other words, if the system is looked at from a different, opposing viewpoint, in what ways might the system's activities be considered coercive or malignant rather than emancipatory or benign? Who or what holds such concerns, that is, who are likely to be the "victims" of the system, and, importantly, what type of representation ought to be made on their behalf? That is, who is capable of making representations on the victims' behalf, and on what basis would they make this claim? Finally, how might the underlying worldview associated with the system be reconciled with these opposing worldviews? Where might representation of opposing views be expressed, and what action ought to happen as a result? Such questions help to make transparent the worldview or moral meaning underpinning the system, providing in turn a sense of social and legal approval to the system at any one time.

Ought and Is

The above narrative was in the "normative" or "ought" mode. As mentioned earlier, CSH requires you to repeat the exercise in an "objective" or "is" (or "was") mode: a description of what is or was actually observed. This distinction is fundamental, not trivial, nor is it a simple distinction between what was planned and what actually happened. The purpose is to challenge those within the system to consider the extent to which their "objective" stance is essentially normative and, if so, what the consequences of this are or were. In other words, comparisons between the results of the "ought" analysis and the "is" analysis provide further opportunities to critique the boundary decisions in both modes.

For instance, "indicators of success" are often delusions of measures of value or worth; student test scores do not necessarily indicate the worth of their education. The comparison between "is" and "ought" can highlight these assumptions. Some examples of indicators comparisons are the following:

- Indicators of learning experience (ought) versus exam results (is)
- Indicators of employment satisfaction (ought) versus performance-related pay (is)

- Indicators of quality of care (ought) versus waiting times for seeing a doctor (is)
- Indicators of relationship with non–human nature (ought) versus carbon footprint (is)

In this case it is clear that even in the selection of common performance indicators there are assumptions about how the world works and who judges how it works.

The heuristic can be displayed as in Table 19.1.

Table 19.1. CSH Framework

		What (Stakes)	Who (Stakeholders)	Key "issues" (Stakeholdings)
Sources of motivation		Purpose	Beneficiary/client	Indicators of success
	"is"			
	"ought"			
	critique "is" v. "ought"			
Sources of control		Resources	Decision maker	Decision environment
	"is"			
	"ought"			
	critique "is" v. "ought"			
Sources of knowledge		Expertise	Expert	Guarantee
	"is"			
	"ought"			
	critique "is" v. "ought"			
Sources of legitimacy		Emancipation	Witness	Worldviews
	"is"			
	"ought"			
	critique "is" v. "ought"			

SOURCE: Based on Martin Reynolds, "Evaluation Based on Critical Systems Heuristics," in *Systems Concepts in Evaluation: An Expert Anthology*, ed. Bob Williams and Iraj Imam (Point Reyes, CA: EdgePress / American Evaluation Association, 2007).

As you can see from the narrative, there is no set of fixed questions or order of addressing the system. Much will depend on the purpose of using the heuristic (see the following case application) and the nature of the situation being explored. However, experienced users generally recommend starting with the "ought" mode and following the sequence in Table 19.1, starting from the top and moving from left to right.

As discussed later, CSH can be used in different ways at different stages of an inquiry for different purposes. It can be used to shape the questions asked within an inquiry, it can create discussion around an inquiry, or it can be used to analyze the results of an inquiry (Reynolds 2007).

CASE APPLICATION OF CRITICAL SYSTEMS HEURISTICS

A European aid agency supported a project to reduce the incidence of HIV/AIDS and other sexually transmitted infections (STIs) in an African mining area, where several thousand sex workers operated from different bases (e.g., hotel based, home based, street based).

The formal purposes of the project were to ensure that commercial sex workers and single women (who engage in occasional sex work)

- are knowledgeable about STIs, HIV/AIDS, and reproductive health, via a peer-educator program;
- have alternative sources of income to protect themselves against HIV, STIs, and other reproductive health conditions, via a micro-credit business loan scheme;
- have access to suitable reproductive health services and have appropriate attitudes and life skills, via improved STD health services.

What actually happened was the following:

A peer-to-peer education program for commercial sex workers. Commercial sex workers were recruited to organize educational sessions with their colleagues; these peer-educators contacted thousand workers over a five-year period, even though the bicycles promised them never arrived (which limited the physical distance the peer-educators could travel). Free condoms and preprinted educational material were initially provided to the sex workers via the peer-educators. However, the supply of free condoms was discontinued after a couple of years, forcing the peer-educator to purchase and sell them. The pre-printed material contained little information that was new to the sex workers, and the peer-educators had to develop their own out of their own pocket.

Alternative income via micro-credit. A micro-credit scheme was established as a means of allowing sex workers to develop alternatives to sex work. In most cases, the credit was used by them to establish hairdressing businesses as a further economic thread to their lives. Unfortunately, the scheme was badly mismanaged by the agency responsible for running the scheme. This resulted in a troublesome brew of delayed loans (anything up to two years), incomplete loans, unpaid loans, and nonexistent loans. Because of the hassles, it also tended to discourage rather than encourage the recruitment and retention of peer-educators.

Improvement of local STI services within the health system. Primarily this was focused on training local health providers and (given the degree of self-medication practiced in the community) with chemical drug sellers. The training focused on HIV/AIDS testing, symptom recognition, health education, counseling, partner notification, and addressing employment issues. Overall this seemed to go well. However, local doctors tended to give medicine away rather than sell it (primarily as a means of avoiding medicines going out of date), infuriating the funding agency, who ended up having to pay for the medicines.

Was this a project nice in theory, but a pity about the practice? Or was it fundamentally misconceived from the beginning? CSH provides some clues.

Motivation and Values

Clearly, the purposes imply educational and economic benefits to commercial and occasional sex workers. The formal indicators of performance were

- commercial sex workers (and some single women) relying less on commercial sex for income and some leaving the business altogether;
- prompt target group access to quality health services;
- correct and consistent use of condoms by commercial sex workers;
- an increasing proportion of commercial sex workers and single women knowledgeable of modes of transmission of HIV.

While the indicators clearly value the health and well-being of the sex worker, the first indicator raises an interesting question about sex work per se. Why is it important that sex workers rely less on sex work, and why is a measure of success that they leave the business entirely? What might that say about the way in which sex work is judged or valued by project organizers or funders? If sex work is an activity to be discouraged rather than made safer, then is this project the best way to do it? Ironically, the micro-finance scheme was such a disaster that these issues were never discussed. It was easier to heap blame on the operation of the scheme than to look at the fundamental values underpinning the project. You could speculate (and investigate), for instance, about whether the fact that the micro-credit scheme was aimed at sex workers (rather than workers engaged in more acceptable economic activities) was one reason for its poor organization and management. If so, then the interests of the peer-educators and the sex workers were marginalized right from the beginning, resulting in a significant decline in support for the program.

There are also embedded assumptions that sex workers were not accessing health services correctly at the start of the project, that condoms were not being used consistently, and that women were ignorant about HIV transmission. As it happened (see under Expertise), some of these assumptions were very wrong.

Put together, this suggests that the value base of the funders might have been somewhat patronizing toward sex workers and at least in part opposed to sex work. Maybe something about the project's fundamental value base can help us understand why the project had such limited effect.

Control: Power Base

The central concern here is, what control should be located within the project and over what should it be accountable to keep it honest? The peer-educators were key decision makers, yet they had relatively little control over the resources they needed to do their jobs. They had no control over their budgets (which meant they could not pay their bills on time), the supply of free condoms was erratic and eventually dried up (which meant they had to buy them from drug stores and then sell them to other sex workers), and they had no control over their transportation (i.e., no bicycles), and thus certain key sites were excluded from the project. Moving control of these items into the hands of the peer-educators would not have significantly altered the need for the system to be accountable to the local community or to the project's funders. In that sense, in the name of "accountability" the system had too *little* control over resources rather than too much. Peer-educators also had no control over the micro-loan scheme—a major resource, although you could argue that in this case the narrow boundary was appropriate, because of the risk of corruption. However, those running the micro-credit scheme seemed accountable to nobody—which suggests that the boundary was drawn too broadly. Clearly here the decision-making boundary (i.e., resource control) was very poorly selected.

The health providers were supposed to sell the drugs, not give them away. Here two boundary judgments clashed. The project funders were operating under the view that medicines were more wisely and fairly used when people have to pay for them. It is a view common in medical circles and based on plausible evidence. However, the local health service staff were motivated by the need to see life-saving and expensive drugs with short shelf lives used rather than thrown away. The medical imperative is to save lives, and the accountability of the health workers *to their profession* (as opposed to their accountability to the funders) is strongly focused toward that end. Neither of these boundary judgments is inherently right or wrong, but there seemed to be no means by which these boundary judgments were discussed or debated (i.e., which "ought" was appropriate). In the end, the health workers' accountability to their profession outweighed their accountability to international donor standards of behavior. They gave the drugs away. This indicates the power basis of the health profession relative to that of the donors. The assumed, formal boundary of accountability for medical resources was wrong, largely because there was no discussion over which "ought" was likely to benefit the system's purpose most appropriately.

Expertise

In terms of expertise, the project managed to bungle some important boundary decisions. The project was littered with false guarantees. Three important ones were the following:

HIV/AIDS knowledge. It was assumed sex workers had little knowledge or expertise about HIV/AIDS. In fact, most of them had considerable knowledge and expertise. Thus the extensive and expensive literature prepared for the peer-educators to distribute provided a false guarantee of success of the project. In the end, the knowledge and expertise of the peer-educators about the industry and how to handle difficult clients were the most valuable part of the project. Using the sex workers to help design the program from scratch may have helped focus the project toward the key areas of knowledge that sex workers needed.

Condom access and use. It was assumed that sex workers were the best way of distributing condoms around the community and encouraging men to use them. In fact, subsequent research showed conclusively that men were the best way of distributing condoms (especially to sexually active adolescent boys) and may well have been the best to encourage use. Sex workers' possessing condoms was a false guarantee; the involvement of men in the project may have been a stronger guarantee.

Micro-credit scheme. It was assumed by the funder that a local agency would possess the necessary expertise to manage the micro-credit scheme. That was a significant false guarantee, the consequence of a chain of poor boundary decisions.

All this suggests that the project was developed initially with little investigation of the local circumstances and boundaries were set according to a somewhat technocratic approach to a complex sociotechnical situation.

Legitimacy

At face value, the legitimacy of the project is self-evident. HIV is a preventable infection that kills people. Sex workers are at risk and pass on that risk to others. Thus helping sex workers manage that risk more successfully must be a good thing.

But certain interests were marginalized by boundary decisions taken uncritically. The project, in practice, focused strongly on female street-workers. Hotel-based workers and single women who used sex work as a casual source of money were largely excluded from the project for access reasons. In the former case, access was restricted by hotel owners and in the latter case access was restricted because of nonexistent networks. In the micro-credit scheme, the interests of traditional money lenders were excluded. The worldviews assumed by project organizers (perhaps incorrectly) of money lenders (profit instead of social good) and hotel owners (control of sex workers instead of the well-being of sex workers) may run counter to the goals of the project's promoters, but these stakeholders may have been substantial players in the relative lack of success of those parts of the project. Could those interests have been incorporated by the project designers while still focusing on the formal purpose and beneficiaries of the system (i.e., sex workers)?

The project can also be seen to have strong coercive elements. We have already highlighted the possible motive of removing women from sex work. There is no formal recognition of that or any investigation into what the consequences of that might be. Who might be the victims of removing sex workers from the industry? What could be the consequences of experienced sex workers' moving out of the industry to be replaced by new women without experience? What does that say about the project designers' view of sex work? Another, perhaps more powerful coercive force is toward men and their sexuality. Male clients had no input into the design of this project, so how did the project designers know how men would react when faced with the choice between sex with a condom or no sex at all? Will they be coerced into using a condom or resist coercion—by going somewhere else, by upping the price offered (where coercion mutates into bargaining), or with physical violence? Will the result of client coercion rather than client involvement be sustainable? What about the next time the client approaches a sex worker? So the question then is whether the interests and motivations of sex workers' clients should be articulated in the design and implementation of the project. If so, then what is the most effective way of canvassing and including the interests of clients while still retaining the formal purpose and beneficiaries of the project? Or does the purpose now have to expand, maybe to include both sex workers and their clients as beneficiaries? In that case, what would be the boundary decisions and their related critiques on control, expertise, and legitimacy?

So while the implementation of the project had its problems, a CSH analysis suggests they sprang from deeper, more systemic problems of uncritiqued boundary choices.

REFLECTIONS ON CRITICAL SYSTEMS HEURISTICS
General Reflections

There are many methods that traverse parts of CSH territory. The "is"/"ought" distinction is common in many strategy and community development processes as well as in the evaluation field. The tensions within and between motivation and control are common in many applied social science approaches and evaluation. CSH, however, adds three important features.

One is the critique of expertise and especially the notions of "guarantee" and "false guarantee." What are we risking by assuming that those with the expertise are the right people for the job? Have we judged the correct expertise? Have we excluded or do we intend to exclude expertise that might prevent the purpose from being achieved?

The second is the addition of "legitimacy." A major tenet of Critical Systems thinking is that a system cannot legitimize itself; legitimacy can be awarded to a system only by those who reside outside the system's boundaries. CSH provides a mechanism by which those issues can be exposed and explored.

Finally, Critical Systems highlights that every endeavor, both intellectual and practical, has to draw boundaries. The notion of holism is flawed; we can never look at everything from every perspective. Therefore, boundaries have to be drawn. CSH demands that these boundary decisions are critiqued. CSH especially challenges boundary decisions that are wrapped in terms such as "technocratic," "realistic," or "inevitable." These are all based on values and worldviews that are subject to challenge.

Pros / Advantages

We make boundary decisions and critique them all the time. All that CSH does is provide a means of making those decisions explicit. However, Werner Ulrich and Martin Reynolds (2010) identify three core areas where CSH can provide special benefits:

Making sense of situations: understanding assumptions and appreciating the bigger picture. The boundary questions try to make sense of a situation by making explicit the *boundaries* that circumscribe our understanding. Such boundaries inform all our thinking about situations and systems including *values and motivations* built into our views of situations and efforts to "improve" them; *power structures* influencing what is considered a "problem" and what may be done about it, *the knowledge basis* defining what counts as relevant "information", including experience and skills; and *the moral basis* on which we expect "third parties" (i.e., stakeholders not involved yet in some way concerned) to bear with the consequences of what we do, or fail to do, about the situation in question.

Unfolding multiple perspectives: promoting mutual understanding. The boundary questions (i.e., the questions contained in each of the 12 steps in the heuristic) reveal *contrasting* judgments as to what aspects of a situation ought to be/are part of the picture we make ourselves of it and what other aspects ought to be/are left out. They offer a way to examine how we frame situations. When people talk about situations, it often happens that their views differ simply because they frame the situations differently; more often than not, people are unaware of this source of misunderstanding and conflict, and even if they are vaguely aware of it they do not know how to examine its influence systematically. Thus seen, CSH offers a tool for understanding the *multiple perspectives* people bring into situations. By examining the different underlying boundary judgments, we can better understand people's differences and handle them more constructively.

Promoting reflective practice: analyzing situations—and changing them. The boundary questions support first of all an *analytical focus* on understanding situations, by revealing to ourselves and to others the boundary judgments at work and allowing everyone to understand their implications. Such understanding then also enables a *practical focus* on ways to improve a situation, by engaging with people having different perspectives. The aim in both cases is to enable *reflective practice*.

Cons / Challenges

Reflective practice and identifying assumptions and values sound like good ideas, and most people will support the idea in principle. However, like many other processes that promote deep reflective practice, the results of using CSH can be rather more revealing than intended. Safety can be a major concern if issues are revealed that challenge important power bases or the many "nonnegotiables" that lie around any endeavor. Those involved need to understand the journey and the likely consequences.

CSH is what it says. It is a heuristic, a learning tool for exploring situations, not a questionnaire framework. Unfortunately it is tempting to treat the heuristic as a questionnaire framework and apply it mechanically without understanding fully the principles that underpin CSH. Practitioners need to know some of the theory behind the heuristic more than with most systems tools; otherwise, in practice they may find themselves getting lost somewhere in the process.

VARIATIONS ON CSH
The Questions

The entire heuristic is challenging and revealing. However, often the three basic questions at the beginning of this chapter are enough to sensitize people to the idea of boundaries and their critique.

Modes of CSH

Ulrich and Reynolds (2010) suggest two modes in which CSH can be used. One is essentially a post-hoc mode. What did happen, and what ought to have happened? It implies no collective deliberation on an ongoing situation. The other is a more participatory, ongoing, and deliberative mode where key stakeholders continually assess and reassess a situation using CSH as a framework.

Scenario Development

Bob Flood (1999) identifies three key areas of scenario development (see Chapter 16) and explores how CSH can add insights to the process.

Area One: Explore the current action area: Where might we be heading?

Undertake boundary judgments to explore the current action area. In particular, identify the four different stakeholders highlighted by CSH: beneficiary, decision maker, experts, and witnesses.

Area Two: Draw forth shared vision: What ideal would we really like to work?

Undertake boundary judgments to explore alternative action areas and what ideal shared vision we would like to work toward. Also, encourage people to influence shared vision with their personal vision.

- Who ought to be the stakeholders? Reflect on the four categories.

Area Three: Projects to achieve shared vision: How might we change direction toward what we would ideally like?

Undertake boundary judgments to explore and enhance each (proposed) project.

- Who would be the stakeholders? Reflect on the four categories.

Soft Systems

Gerald Midgley and Martin Reynolds suggest a variation on soft systems (Chapter 14) that borrows key elements of CSH. Essentially they suggest two changes to the CATWOE modeling stage.

The first is to expand the "Customer" element into two categories, "Beneficiaries" and "Victims," turning CATWOE into BATWOVE. The second is to further expand this notion to cover things as well as people.

The modification to soft systems may seem trivial, but in practice it throws the soft systems deliberation between the "model" and "reality" into a significantly different framing.

NOTE
Our thanks to Martin Reynolds for allowing us to draw on his work. Our thanks also to the American Evaluation Association and EdgePress for permission to use material from *Systems Concepts in Evaluation: An Expert Anthology* and to Springer for their permission to draw from *Systems Approaches to Managing Change: A Practical Guide*.

REFERENCES AND FURTHER READING
Flood, Robert L. 1999. *Rethinking the fifth discipline: Learning within the unknowable.* London and New York: Routledge
Jackson, Michael C. 2000. *Systems approaches to management.* London: Springer.
Midgley, Gerald. 2000. *Systemic intervention: Philosophy, methodology, and practice.* New York: Kluwer Academic/Plenum.
Midgley, Gerald, A. Winstanley, W. Gregory, and F. Foote. 2005. *Scoping the potential uses of systems thinking in developing policy on illicit drugs.* Drug Policy Modeling Project Monograph 13. http://www.turningpoint.org.au/research/dpmp_mono-graphs/res_dm_monographs.htm.
Reynolds, Martin. 2007. Evaluation based on Critical Systems Heuristics. In *Systems concepts in evaluation: An expert anthology*, ed. Bob Williams and Iraj Imam. Point Reyes, CA: EdgePress/American Evaluation Association.
Ulrich, Werner. Home page. http://www.wulrich.com/.
Werner, Ulrich, and M. Reynolds. 2010. Critical Systems Heuristics. In *Systems approaches to managing change: A practical guide*, ed. Martin Reynolds and Sue Holwell. London: Springer, The Open University.

INDEX

Motivation: behavior and, 20–21; in Critical Systems Heuristics, 305, 306–307; factors influencing, 223; perspectives and, 20–21
Motives, 219
Multiple perspectives, 316–317

Negative causal links, 34
Negative feedback, 32–33
Networked problem analysis, 43
Networks: information flows, 69; structural measures of, 65–66
Network theory, 73, 164, 179
Neurolinguistic programming (NLP), 290–291
Normative steering, 210–211

Objective-related scenarios, 275
Observers, 27
1234-model, 209–212
Ontology, Cynefin and, 164, 173–175, 182
Operational steering, 211
Option one-and-a-half, 263–266
Organizational development, 2, 39, 162, 182, 185, 209, 293
"Ought" and "is" analysis, 308–310
Outcome and performance monitoring, in outcome mapping, 78–79
Outcome hierarchy, 90, 96, 98, 105
Outcome journal, 79
Outcome Mapping (OM), 8, 75–91, 93, 94
Outcomes systems, 106
Outcomes theory, 106

Paper computer, 42
Patton, Michael Q., 180
People-Centered Evaluation (PCE), 89–90
Performance journal, in Outcome Mapping , 80
Perls, Fritz, 290
Perspectives, 3; appreciation of different, 246, 248; choices and, 303–304; in

circular dialogues, 293–294; Cynefin and, 173–175, 178–179; different, 99; multiple, 316–317; in Soft Systems Methodology, 241–243; thinking systematically and, 19–22
Planning, 3, 57, 111–112; business, 222; forward, 282; outcome hierarchies for, 105; in Outcome Mapping, 75–76, 77, 80–81, 85–86, 89; probing questions about, 269–270; in SAST, 117–118; scenario, 274, 277, 282; in SNA, 73; strategic, 10, 81, 105, 153. See also Assumption-Based Planning (ABP)
Planning, Learning, and Accountability systems (PLAs), 81, 83
Policy-related scenarios, 275
Positive causal links, 34
Positive deviance, 197
Positive feedback, 32–33
Power: 26, 41, 66, 77, 144, 207, 221, 253, 265, 305, 308, 312, 313, 317; boundaries and, 22; in critical systems heuristics, 307, 316; issue of, 4
Probe questions, 269–270
Problem analysis, 184–185
Problem situation, 187, 194, 244, 245, 297
Problem-solving onion, 297
Process Monitoring of Impacts, 8, 92–106
Program logic models. See Logic models
ProLL (Program Logic and Linkage) model, 98

Questioning, 284–286
Questions: circular, 288; linear, 286–287; reflective, 287–288; strategic, 287

RAPID Outcome Assessment (ROA), 89
RAPID Outcome Mapping Approach (ROMa), 88–89
Rasappan, Aru, 98
Reactive elements, 42
Realistic Evaluation approach, 90, 97–98,

Stock-flow diagrams, 46–48, 50–51
Stock variables, 47, 48
Strategic Area Assessment (SAA), 9, 123–135
Strategic Assumption Surfacing and Testing (SAST), 8–9, 108–119, 154, 156, 254, 276, 282
Strategic planning, 10, 81, 105, 153
Strategic questions, 287
Strategic steering, 211
Strategy journal, 80
Structural analysis, 68–69, 223
Structural Fund programs, 92–95, 97, 100–104
Suchman, Edward, 105
Supervision function, in 1234-model, 212
Sweeping in process, 304
SWOT analysis, 124, 129
Synthesis stage, of SAST, 113
System Dynamics (SD), 7, 19, 45–58, 253
Systemic: definition of, 3–4; orientations of being, 23–28; vs. thinking systemically, 17
Systemic family therapy, 27
Systemic questioning, 13–14, 284–291, 293
Systemic Structural Constellations, 196–197
Systemic thinking, 17, 18–23
Systems: definition of, 16; evolution of, 25; as human construct, 18; overview, 16–17
Systems archetypes, 43–44
Systems field, development of, 3–4, 16
Systems methods: classification of, 6; selection of, 4–5

Systems thinking, 3, 186, 217, 244–245, 258, 316. See also Systemic thinking

Taboo circle, 297
Temporal sequencing, 96
Thinking systemically, 17, 18–23; about boundaries, 22–23; about interrelationships, 18–19; about perspectives, 19–22
Tomm, Karl, 286
Tools, for obtaining information, 221–223
Transforming exchanges, 139–140, 140–141
Trend analysis, 157
Trend projections, 276

Ulrich, Werner, 303, 304, 316
Undiscussible contradictions, 228
U.S. Army, use of ABP by, 157–159

Value basis, 306
Variables: auxiliary, 47; flow, 47; stock, 47, 48
Variety, in VSM, 203
Vester, Frederic, 42
Viable System Model (VSM), 11, 199–213
Vygotsky, Lev, 217, 218

Wack, Pierre, 274
Walt Disney strategy, 300–301
Weiss, Carol, 105
Wild cards, 277
Williams, Bob, 162, 266
Worst-case scenario, 273

Zone of promixal development, 239–240

Made in the USA
San Bernardino, CA
19 August 2015